STRATEGY &
MARKETING

STRATEGY & MARKETING

A CASE APPROACH

Kenneth Simmonds

London Business School

SECOND EDITION

Philip Allan

NEW YORK   LONDON   TORONTO   SYDNEY   TOKYO   SINGAPORE

First published 1982 by

Philip Allan

66 Wood Lane End, Hemel Hempstead,
Hertfordshire, HP2 4RG
A division of
Simon & Schuster International Group

Printed and bound in Great Britain by
Dotesios Ltd, Trowbridge, Wiltshire.

British Library Cataloguing in Publication Data

Strategy and marketing: a case approach. —
  2nd ed.
  1. Marketing — Case studies
  I. Simmonds, Kenneth
  658.8′00722   HF5415

  ISBN 0-86003-543-3
  ISBN 0-86003-645-6 Pbk

4 5   93 92

Contents

Managing Competitive Strategy

Organising and Implementing the Marketing Effort

Preface

Strategy and marketing go hand in hand. Although strategy has been given more attention recently than in the past, marketing was never intended to be studied as a tactical field divorced from its strategic implications. As a wise man once said, 'If you do not know where you are going, any direction will get you there'. And it is the strategy component of marketing that is concerned with direction. It is concerned with those core actions for any business which determine the direction it takes within its marketplace and which are the essential cause of improvement or reversal in performance.

In choosing these core actions the strategically-aware marketer must decide not only the particular grouping of customers that are the target of his actions, but also allow for the actions of competitors. He must evaluate the opponents' competitive positions and likely moves and even the probable effects of his own moves on those positions.

Design of the Casebook

This casebook is a second edition of the text on Strategy and Marketing published in 1982. One-third of the cases are new additions and others have been updated.

The cases have been selected to provide a basic course in strategic marketing for British students. They have also been chosen to give a balanced treatment of consumer products, services, industrial products and capital goods industries.

The text is divided into five sections which follow a common pattern for teaching strategic marketing. Instructors, however, may consider that a quite different sequence of problems is appropriate. Each case has numerous facets and most could be readily classified in other ways.

Case Discussion

Case discussion plays a role in extending marketing skill that is difficult to fill with direct lecturing or worked examples. Marketing skill is essentially one of diagnosis. It is not an ability to apply a standard set of theories, nor deploy a collection of 'modern business techniques'. It is a skill in reasoning from the market situation back to a strategy for success, bearing in mind opposing forces of direct and indirect competition. Case discussion forces students to develop this skill by making their diagnoses explicit and defending their reasoning to each other and the instructor.

Just any set of marketing cases will not do. Cases should contain enough data for students to carry through a reasonable diagnosis and argue their proposals on the basis of the facts of the situation and reasonable projections of buyer and competitor reactions to change. Examples that follow a situation chronologically right through to its final outcome, or 'success' stories that include no basis for evaluation of alternatives, generally miss the point of case learning.

All the cases in this text have been chosen carefully to meet the demands of business school teaching. They have been included only if they are of a level that challenges keen business minds and provides some excitement in group discussion. This does not mean, however, that all the intricacies of a case are immediately evident. What may on the surface appear quite simple and straightforward will, with some thought, disclose problems requiring considerable marketing competence in their full diagnosis and solution.

Acknowledgements

I should like to express my personal thanks to all those who have contributed cases.* Good case writing is a demanding and time-consuming task quite definitely under-recognised for the work involved. A good case can require as much effort as a publication in an academic journal. Furthermore, good case writing is the mark of a good teacher. Authors of the individual cases are acknowledged on the front page of each case; for those who would like to know a little more than the names of case-writers, however, a brief biography of each contributor is included after the next section.

In particular, I wish to thank my present and past colleagues at the London Business School who have since 1969 provided so much support in establishing marketing teaching with a strategic approach. I also want to thank Sally Mitchell for her sustained effort in shaping most of the cases included in the text.

KENNETH SIMMONDS
September 1986

TO THE STUDENT:
Learning Through Case Analysis

The purpose of this book is to provide a comprehensive set of case problems against which you will sharpen your marketing skill through individual preparation and group discussion. The cases are designed to cover a range of marketing situations that it would take many years to encounter in actual business practice.

In each case, you are placed in the role of the decision maker and expected to reason through to a preferred set of actions. The greater the amount of preparation you put into the case and the more you are prepared to participate in class discussion, the more you are likely to develop your own skills. Other class participants and the instructor will fill the role of critics and competitors showing up any flaws in your reasoning or interpretation of case facts and offering alternative prescriptions to fit the situation.

You will miss much of the opportunity for developing your own skills if you rely on other people for your ideas and reasoning. Force yourself to read a case thoroughly, specify the problems, identify alternative ways of handling the problems, and reason through as to which seems most appropriate. Keep on asking yourself, "Why?" until you are persuaded by your own answers. Also think about how your conclusions would be implemented. Suggestions are frequently ruled out because there is no reasonable way of achieving them. Rather detailed description of how you would implement your conclusions is often needed. It makes little sense to advance generalities such as "increase marketing emphasis", "more sales effort", or "lower prices".

At the end of the day, many business decisions hinge on their incremental costs and revenues. Not only may these be difficult to identify, but the difference between profit and loss may be a very small percentage. Do not avoid quantifying actions. Wherever possible have a clear idea of how much you would spend and to what effect.

In many of the cases the obvious problems and decision alternatives are not the most important. The diagnosis of the decision maker in the case, for example, may focus on the symptoms and not the disease. In studying each case you should be prepared to dig deeply and uncover facts that are not spelt out directly. Question opinions, analysis and decisions presented by those in the case and even evaluate hard data against its source and any other data presented in the case.

Some of the cases require you to assess results produced using a particular quantitative technique, some require you to build a model, and many require you to read financial figures. If you do not understand the technique or figures involved, it is up to you to go to an appropriate text to cover the gap in your knowledge. Just because the casebook focuses on marketing does not provide an excuse for inadequate understanding of some other aspect basic to the case.

Finally, use your imagination and creativity. Business is not a discipline achieved through the application of basic principles or fundamental laws. Like any form of strategy, it requires flair in a very complex situation.

In the class discussion sessions be prepared both to participate and listen. Other participants will almost always have strong and well-argued suggestions that differ from yours. Attempts to make reasoned comparisons will build your own skills. Unwillingness to do so will hinder everybody's learning.

Practice in presenting your recommendations can provide valuable experience for later management situations. Be prepared to state your recommendations simply and clearly and support them with the most important elements of your reasoning. Remember, too, that a large proportion of your audience will be strongly committed to other courses of action, so endeavour to indicate the relative undesirability of these in support of your own conclusions. Avoid wasting time and interest by repeating facts from the case that the others have all read.

Do not expect the instructor to carry the class discussion or necessarily provide his own best solution. Of course, he will push the class to consider important aspects that may have been overlooked or make calculations that have been omitted or made incorrectly, but he is not there to do your learning for you. He may tell you at the end of the case discussion what actually happened in the real-world situation, but do not place too much emphasis on this. Marketing skill is not a question of guessing what actually happened, but of reasoning through a "best" solution at a given point in time.

Contributors

Patrick Barwise is Lecturer in Marketing at London Business School and Director of the London Executive Programme. His M.A. from Oxford was taken in engineering science with economics and he also holds an M.Sc. and Ph.D from London Business School. Prior to joining London Business School in 1976, he worked for IBM as a systems engineer, for Pentos, and for Graphic Systems Ltd as Marketing Manager. Paddy's main research interests are in television viewing behaviour and in making written information more usable.

Jules Goddard is Mercer's School Memorial Professor of Commerce at Gresham College and Managing Director of Planners Collaborative Ltd. He received his M.A. in geography at Oxford, an M.B.A. from Wharton School, University of Pennsylvania and his Ph.D from London Business School. Specialising in advertising, Jules has worked with Ogilvy and Mather in New York and London and with J. Walter Thompson Co. Ltd. Prior to his present appointment, Jules was founder and managing director of a building firm in the Dordogne, Reader in Marketing at Thames Polytechnic and Lecturer in Marketing at London Business School.

David Jobber is Lecturer in Marketing at the University of Bradford Management Centre. Educated in economics at Manchester University and management and business studies at Warwick University, he worked as a marketing executive with T.I. Raleigh. He is co-author of a book on selling and sales management and his special academic interests are in the use of mail surveys for data collection and marketing information systems.

Kamran Kashani is Professor of Business Administration at IMEDE where he is Director of the Managing Marketing and Managing the Sales Force Programmes. He received his D.B.A. from Harvard University and the B.A. and M.B.A. from University of California, Los Angeles. Before joining IMEDE, Kamran was a member of the Faculty and the Chairman of the Faculty Council of the Iran Centre for Management Studies. He has also held an appointment as Visiting Professor at INSEAD, France. He is the author of more than thirty case studies in Europe and the Middle East. Kamran's current research interest is in the area of strategy formulation and implementation among multinational firms.

Philip Law is Senior Lecturer in Marketing at London Business School and Director of the Continuous Executive Programme. Educated in chemical engineering at Cambridge University and in business administration at Manchester Business School, he spent many years as an executive with Shell. He is a chartered engineer and a member of the Institution of Chemical Engineers. Since joining London Business School in 1969 he has lectured widely around the world on university and company executive programmes particularly in Hong Kong, China and Malaysia. Philip has a special interest in the teaching of business administration and has also been director of the London Executive Programme and the International Teachers Programme.

Shiv Mathur is Midland Bank Research Fellow at City University Business School, London, and Director of the Centre for the Study of Financial Institutions. He received a B.Tech. degree from the Indian Institute of Technology and M.Sc. and Ph.D. degrees from London Business School. Shiv held appointments with Pilkingtons India in marketing and corporate planning before joining London Business School as a Research Officer in 1974. He has taken a special interest in the management of multinational corporations and marketing for capital goods and financial services firms.

Hugh Murray is Midland Bank Professor of Export Management and International Business, City University, London. He received his B.A., M.A. and Ph.D. from the University of Liverpool. He has held appointments as Lecturer in Marketing at the Chinese University of Hong Kong and London Business School, where he directed the London Executive Programme, and taught on a regular basis for business schools in Germany, Portugal and Japan. Prior to his academic career, Hugh worked as an Assistant Manager with Attwoods Marketing, Assistant General Manager for Newcastle Chronicle & Journal Ltd, Marketing Manager for Liverpool Daily Post & Echo Ltd, Marketing Director for Letraset Ltd, and as Managing Director for Transprint Ltd and Graphic Systems Ltd.

Adrian Ryans is a Professor of Business Administration at the School of Business Administration, University of Western Ontario. In 1985–86, he was Visiting Professor of Marketing at INSEAD in Fontainebleau, France. Until 1981, Professor Ryans was Associate Professor of Marketing at the Graduate School of Business, Stanford University. He has served as a consultant on marketing strategy and marketing research to many US organisations and taught widely on executive programmes in North America, Europe and Australia. His major research interests centre around marketing strategy and sales force management. He is co-author of *Canadian Marketing: Cases & Concepts* and has published many papers in professional journals. Professor Ryans received his B.A.Sc. in mechanical engineering from the University of Waterloo in Canada, and his M.B.A. and Ph.D degrees from Stanford University.

John Saunders is Lecturer in Marketing and Strategic Management at the University of Warwick. He studied engineering at Loughborough and management studies at Cranfield Institute of Technology, and obtained his Ph.D from the University of Bradford. He worked for Hawker-Siddeley for a number of years and was subsequently Lecturer at the Bradford University Management Centre. His current academic interests are the use of analytical techniques and model building in solving marketing problems and the development of computerised business games.

Kenneth Simmonds is Professor of Marketing and International Business at London Business School. He received B.Com. and M.Com. degrees from the University of New Zealand, a Ph.D from the London School of Economics and a D.B.A. from Harvard Business School. Ken joined the London faculty in 1969 after holding the first chair in marketing at Manchester Business School, and establishing marketing as Senior Lecturer at Cranfield in 1962. He has also taught international business at Indiana University and the University of Chicago. He has run advanced management programmes for some 60 multinational corporations, and advised as a strategy consultant internationally. Ken is a chartered accountant, a management accountant and a chartered company secretary, and worked in various commercial positions in New Zealand from 1950. He has been a consultant with Arthur D. Little Inc., Harbridge House Inc. and MAC Inc. and an external director of several corporations in Britain, including Redpath Dorman Long and EMAP PLC. His special research interests lie in industrial and international marketing strategies.

Ralph Sorenson is President and Chief Executive Officer, Barry Wright Corporation. Prior to this he was President of Babson College after a period as Associate Professor at Harvard Business School where he headed the first-year marketing programme and also led the advisory group that set up the Asian Institute of Management in the Philippines. Earlier, he was a research associate at IMEDE and a marketing executive at Nestle Alimentana in Switzerland. Bud received his Bachelor's degree from Amherst College, and M.B.A. and D.B.A. degrees from Harvard Business School.

Charles Weinberg is Alumni Professor of Marketing at the University of British Columbia. He received his Sc.B. from Brown University in applied mathematics, an M.B.A. degree from Harvard Business School, and his Ph.D. from Columbia University. Prior to his appointment in Vancouver, he was Associate Professor at Stanford, Lecturer at London Business School and Assistant Professor at New York University. Professor Weinberg has taken a special interest in the use of analytical techniques and model building in solving marketing problems, and has also published two books on marketing in public and non-profit organisations.

Robin Wensley is Professor of Marketing and Strategic Management at the University of Warwick. He was previously Senior Lecturer in marketing at London Business School and prior to that worked with Rank Hovis McDougall as a brand manager, with Tube Investments Ltd as an internal consultant, and with Ashridge Management College as Deputy Director of Studies in Marketing. He spent 1980—81 at the University of California, Los Angeles. His special academic interest is in market share strategy. Robin holds the B.A. (natural sciences) from Cambridge, and M.Sc. (business studies) and Ph.D. from London.

The Mareketyng Mans Tayl
(apologies to Prof. J.R.C. Chaucer)

A marektyng man was wyth us ther
Untydy dresst wyth shaggy her
Brown baggy sweater, unpressed trews
For any taylor he was bad news.
From eek student, he asked each tyme
1 page, 10 page, yt was a crime.
Yn mareketyng lectures he bygan
With wycked subtyltee to scan
Our weaknesses, and flaws, and quyrks
Destroyed our faith, and damned our wyrkes.
He made fact, out of rumour
Marektyng fools ye consumer
Tho hys technyches have many a name
Hys vyew of the world remayns the same
Eech man is a vayne and greedy snob
And yf t'were false, he would be out of a job
How trew, methinks, but what kind of man
Wyll choos hys job wher he kan
Exployt folkes common faults? In hys soule
A hoste of gymmycks fills the hole.
Hys holy writ was participation
Hys class has cerbal constipation
A wel-payed hacke I wolde assess
A B-school rebel ruined by success

Deciding the Business Strategy

This case was prepared by Kenneth Simmonds of the London Business School. © Kenneth Simmonds revised 1981

CASE 1

Spanline Engineering

George Kent was introduced to Michael Burton, the majority owner and managing director of Spanline Engineering Ltd of Manchester, at a neighbourhood party and their conversation drifted into a discussion of the design and layout of advertising campaigns. On learning that George was a marketing consultant and adviser to some well-known national corporations, Mr Burton asked him if he would visit his works the following week and give him an opinion on his new advertising proposals.

Michael Burton had started Spanline Engineering on a shoestring some seven years earlier when the light engineering firm for which he was Works Manager was taken over by a foreign producer who closed the works and replaced the manufacture with imports. Michael had been able to purchase some of the machinery at throw-out prices and hand-pick a team from the 600 men who were being laid-off. Initially he had concentrated on precision machining of light mechanical parts for machinery manufacturers on a jobbing basis, but later added a range of chain hoists of his own design. These had been very successful, with their sales growing until they now represented nearly 50% of Spanline's output.

Spanline hoists were made in three lifting capacities of 5 cwt, 10 cwt, and 1 ton, and consisted basically of a lifting block with an electrically driven sprocket that engaged the links of the lifting chain. Chain hoists of this type were officially designated as Class I cranes and appropriate for light use of up to 6 hours per day with continual lifts of up to 20 minutes. Heavier use would be likely to damage the hoist. Chain hoists were used widely in garages and workshops for loading machinery and on loading docks. Mr Burton claimed that the Spanline models had no particularly outstanding features, but they worked efficiently and there had been very few complaints. Although Spanline hoist blocks were larger and heavier than other makes and might last longer than the average hoist life of about 5 years, competitors emphasised lighter weights as a prime sales feature. Despite this, Burton felt that the larger block looked more significant and professional when installed.

The first large order for Spanline hoists came from Century Steel, a firm specialising in supplies for smaller steel fabricators and constructors. In addition to its main line of steel stocks and erection equipment, Century supplied tanks, boilers, cranes and other equipment to its customers from a network of depots throughout Britain. Century's initial order was for 500 hoists marked with their Century brand, and this had been followed with orders that grew each year, then settled down to about 2,700 a year.

From time to time over the years, Michael Burton and Eric Davis, his Sales Director, had also called on most of the large engineering plants and engineering supply houses in the North. Orders were sporadic from these sources, but totalled around 600 annually. Several large orders for Spanline hoists had also come from tenders to the Ministry of Public Works and to

3

large industrial developments, but open invitations to bid were limited. Representatives for the various makes of cranes frequently visited purchasers before invitations to bid were issued and influenced them to limit the subsequent invitations to a few suppliers.

Two years ago Spanline had moved into a new factory built to accommodate up to 110 men, and was currently operating at about 75% of this capacity. Over the past year growth had been minimal, however, and Michael Burton and Eric Davis had finally taken a careful look at their work opportunities and decided to place more emphasis on hoist production. According to their calculations, hoists were their most profitable activity. The retail prices for the 5 cwt, 10 cwt and 1 ton sizes were £180, £255 and £330 plus VAT respectively. A 17½% discount was allowed to Century Steel and most other customers and this left Spanline with an average net revenue of just over £210 per hoist, of which 55% represented materials, 20% direct labour and 25% contribution to overheads and profit. Spanline purchased castings, bearings, gears, motors, chains and electrical control gear, and then carried out the machining assembling and finishing.

Michael Burton thought there were around a dozen crane producers in the country and knew that the Spanline production could not be enough to cover more than a small share of the national market. Compared with what he knew of the prices of competitors, moreover, Spanline's prices were among the lowest. There was thus plenty of scope for expansion, and after several long discussions Burton and Davis decided to mount an aggressive advertising campaign to extend Spanline's share of the market. Together they visited a London advertising agency, recommended to them by one of their friends, which undertook to draw up a proposal for them, and Eric Davis also undertook to recruit a representative to help him on the sales side.

Most of the prospects for this sales representative post came through leads from Davis' wide contacts in local engineering circles. He finally chose Albert Wisdom, aged 45, who had come up from the shop floor of one of the largest manufacturers of heavy cranes and then spent ten years in their design office with responsibility for adapting basic crane designs to individual customer requirements. As Davis told Michael Burton, Wisdom knew all there was to be known about cranes. Wisdom was appointed on a good fixed salary of £9,000 with a company car, and Mr Davis indicated that he would be allocated a grouping of industries for which he would be solely responsible. In this way he could build up expertise in the particular requirements of different industries.

Eric Davis planned to retain some customer industries himself and also to cover the customers for whom jobbing work would continue. Eric had joined Michael Burton from the same firm when Spanline was founded and held 10% of the shares. In his previous post he had been customer service engineer, responsible for liaison between manufacturers and the works and had provided many of the initial contacts for Spanline jobbing work.

When the draft proposal for the advertising scheme arrived from the agency, Burton and Davis were impressed with the professional way in which it was drawn up. In brief, it proposed a campaign focusing on the Spanline brand name built into a new symbol of similar shape to the hoist block. The supporting copy emphasised the reliability and general all-purpose value of Spanline hoists. The agency recommended that the annual appropriation be set at £30,000 in order to make a significant impression on the market, and that it be allocated to handling and equipment journals. They proposed the schedule of journals set out in Exhibit 1.

Exhibit 1   *Proposed Advertising Schedule*

Journal	Circulation	Frequency	Proposed Annual Insertions	Page Size of Insertions	Additional Colour	Rate £	Annual Appropriation £
Materials Handling News	20,000	Monthly	12	Full	1	492	5,904
Mechanical Handling	6,918	Monthly	6	½	—	156	936
Freight Management	20,367	Monthly	12	½	—	216	2,592
Storage & Handling Equipment News	24,972	Monthly	12	½	—	252	3,024
Industrial Equipment News	33,807	Twice Monthly	12	Full	1	744	8,928
Factory Equipment News	26,000	Twice Monthly	12	Full	—	606	7,272
							28,656

Average Monthly Readership 128,000
Cost Efficiency = £18.9 per 1,000 readers per month

This advertising appropriation was a large sum for Spanline and Michael Burton found himself postponing a formal letter to the agency. It was not that Spanline lacked funds, as can be seen from the previous year's annual accounts in Exhibit 2, but rather it was due to Burton's unfamiliarity with advertising. Consequently, during his conversation with George Kent about this time, he decided to place the proposal in front of George for a second expert opinion.

Exhibit 2   *Spanline Engineering Ltd: Previous Year's Annual Accounts*

Profit and Loss Account (all entries net of VAT)	£000s	£000s
Sales		1,422,000
Labour	288,000	
Materials	660,000	
Work in Progress Variation	114,000	
Direct Cost		1,062,000
Gross Margin		360,000
Variable Factory Expense	171,000	
Fixed Factory Expense	57,000	
Selling, Administrative and Interest Expense	48,000	
Directors' Remuneration	33,000	
Total Expense		309,000
		51,000
Taxation		21,000
Net Profit		30,000

Balance Sheet end of year

Sundry Debtors	159,000	
Materials	75,000	
Work in Progress	153,000	
Current Assets		387,000
Bank Overdraft	72,000	
Sundry Creditors	138,000	
Provision for Taxation	21,000	
Current Liabilities		231,000
Net Working Capital		156,000
Buildings	195,000	
Plant and Machinery	69,000	
Fixed Assets		264,000
		420,000
Long-Term Loan (secured)		135,000
Shareholders' Funds		285,000

This case was prepared by Kenneth Simmonds of the London Business School. © Kenneth Simmonds, 1986.

CASE 2

Metropolitan National Bank Ltd

As Chief Properties Manager for the Metropolitan, Brent Elliott held overall responsibility for negotiating purchase of new sites, construction of new premises and disposal of properties no longer required by the bank. Metropolitan operated over one thousand branches in the United Kingdom; consequently Brent was concerned with numerous building and renovation projects at any one time.

Brent was annoyed: his professional competence had been indirectly criticised during a recent regional management meeting when the Properties Division was blamed for failing to provide adequate teller windows and floor area for waiting customers in a branch opened only six months previously. Design and construction of this particular branch had extended over four years and there had been more new office buildings in the immediate vicinity than expected when the designs were drawn up. Moreover, no competitor banks had moved in to take up the additional growth. Anyway, Brent was sure the design would have been adequate had it not been for the large number of customers using the branch facilities whose accounts were with other Metropolitan branches, or other banks entirely.

Customers of any Metropolitan branch could use their cash cards to obtain cash from the new branch's cash dispensing machines — two inside and one outside. Alternatively they, along with anyone else, could withdraw up to £50 in cash from the four tellers' windows by presenting their cheque card with their cheque. These facilities had encouraged customers to leave their accounts with their original branches and to use the new branch as a convenient cash point. At peak times, the lines at the tellers' windows were becoming entangled with the lines for the cash dispensers on the opposite wall. There was no reserve floor space in the branch, however, and it would be difficult to add even one more dispenser.

It seemed to Brent that heavy traffic through the new branch was an indication of success in choosing a good site, not a cause for criticism. Still, he planned to avoid criticism in future by asking a consulting firm to develop a standard procedure for forecasting customer traffic for any potential branch location. Before he did so, however, Brent thought he should make a preliminary list of the considerations that the consultants should allow for in their procedure.

This case was prepared by
Hugh Murray of the
London Business School,
1973.

CASE 3

Josiah Doncaster Ltd

On the 4th of March, the board of Josiah Doncaster met for the second time in three weeks. The main item on the agenda, as before, was what decision to take on the proposed New Product Strategy, which arose out of the Consultant's Report commissioned by the Marketing Director.

Established in 1740, the company had built up a world-wide reputation for fine household china. Its management was paternalistic, very conservative financially, and committed to preserving company traditions. Yet over the last 10 years the company had extended its product range into industrial porcelains for high-voltage insulation, and it had been very successful.

Bill Hawkins, the newly appointed Marketing Director, opened the meeting with an aggressive presentation. At 35, he was a good 20 years younger than anyone else on the board; and with a Harvard M.B.A., he was the only member of the board with formal management training.

"I hope that certain members of the board have reconsidered their positions since our last meeting. As far as I am concerned, my recommendations of three weeks ago still stand. Let's go through them once again, shall we? What are the main facts from the Consultant's report? Let's take them one by one, shall we?

(a) At a £4.50 selling price per filter unit, and a market size of 1 million units, the present market size is £4.5 million.

(b) One company, Western Ltd, has an estimated 85% market share.

(c) The market does not like working under a monopoly, and especially as Western Ltd do not give volume discounts.

(d) The number of buying points is estimated at 20,000, of which 220 in Birmingham, 150 in London, and 70 in Manchester, take 55% of the total.

(e) There are 35 manufacturers of equipment powered by compressed air, who dominate the market; and 15 major suppliers of air compressors.

(f) Western's don't make a thing themselves — they assemble bought-in parts. So could we. There is no technical barrier to our entry into this market.

(g) Their estimated fixed costs are thought to be £100,000; with variable costs estimated at £2.7 per unit. Total cost/unit on sales of 850,000 is thought to be £2.82.

(h) Our fixed costs are estimated at £180,000; but our variable costs are clearly lower than theirs. We estimate them at £2.12 per unit. On any kind of volume the total cost of our ceramic core is down to ½p each; their sintered bronze core costs them 60p to buy in.

(i) We have a patented technological edge over Western in the ceramic core. They can only filter down to 64 microns with the sintered bronze; whereas we can tailor ours down to any desired filtration level.

(j) Finally, we have a name which is known and respected. Everyone has heard of Doncaster. We have a 200-year reputation for quality.

... So I say let's make our move. Look here ..." He went over to the new flip chart, which was mounted on an easel, by the Adam fireplace. Pointing, he said,

"Page 1. Strategy: Exploit the anti-monopoly feeling of the market, our cost advantage, and our product superiority, by launching our Filter Unit against Western.

Page 2. Tactics: Price 10% below Western. Give 25% bulk discount. Personal selling to the key buying points, and the equipment manufacturers. Sell to the rest by direct mail and trade journal advertising.

Page 3. Targets:
10% of the market in Year 1.
15% of the market in Year 2.
25% of the market in Year 3.

Page 4. Costs:

Sales in units	100,000	150,000	250,000
Fixed cost/unit	£1.80	£1.20	£0.72
Variable cost/unit	£2.12	£2.12	£2.12
Total cost	£3.92	£3.32	£2.84

Page 5. Profit/Loss:
The average price per unit is £3.48; our estimated position is

a £0.44 loss/unit year 1 i.e. £44,000 loss
a £0.16 profit/unit year 2 i.e. £ 24,000 profit
a £0.64 profit/unit year 3 i.e. £160,000 profit.

Page 6. Conclusion: The downside risks are small. Breakeven is at 13% of the market. With all we have going for us, there should be no problem in reaching breakeven, and soon!

... If we are to do our duty to the shareholders of this company, our action is clearly indicated. Our duty is clear. No further hesitation. Let's approve the project. Let's go!"

"Bill, your last remarks are totally uncalled for. This Board does not need reminding of its duty to its shareholders," said Paul Doncaster, almost before Hawkins had sat down.

"Sorry Paul. I apologise. I guess my enthusiasm ran away with me."

"It's my job to see that it doesn't run away with all of us. Your proposition, as you have outlined it, is too one-sided, too easy. No real account has been taken of the risks involved. And risks there are. When you have had as much experience as I have, you will realise that taking on a market leader is no easy task — especially when they are as strongly entrenched in the market as Western is in this one. 85% market share — that's market domination with a vengeance!

Filtration is their business, and they do it well. There is no complaint anywhere in the report of their product performance, nor of their service, nor of their price. Only what amounts to a general comment that it would be nice if they were not quite so dominant! What good is that to go on? There are another 11 filter manufacturers in the market. And what have they done? Very little. They have tiny, specialised sections of the market. And their total market share adds up to what? 15% — amongst the 11 of them!

No account has been taken of Western's competitive reaction. React they will. Quickly. And hard. This isn't marginal to them as it is to us — it is their bread and butter! Market-share loss to us would hit their profits hard. The 25% market share targeted for the third year would reduce their gross profits by 25%. No company would take that quietly. We wouldn't. Why should we expect them to do so?

They have all the original equipment manufacturers sewn up; and as a result, automatically get all the replacement re-orders from the users in the factories. On average these filters last 6 years. Moreover, I doubt if any buyer regards them as a significant cost item. Take the 440 chief buyers . . . in total they spend per annum about £2,475 million, i.e. £5,600 each. Since the replacement parts are bought throughout the year, this amounts to about £470 per month. This is hardly major expenditure, for the buyer of a large company.

Finally, remember that these filters are safeguards to extremely expensive machinery, and they are often specified under the terms of the guarantee. The incentives to save pennies, at the potential risk to thousands of pounds' worth of machinery is small."

"What you say about the buyers may be right, Paul; but the Engineer is certainly aware of these filters." Bob McGregor, a dour Scot, in his mid-sixties, and Works Director, went on, "There is a point barely made in the Report. The life of these units averages 6 years. We find, like everyone else, that we have to clean the sintered bronze every three months. We use a caustic soda solution, then neutralise it with a weak acid. It is a costly operation, both in materials, labour, and sometimes in machine down-time. Why don't we say with our new filters, you throw away the core, and put in a new one?"

"If we did that, we'd really have to lower the price of the filter cores, and that would give the game away. The only difference between our Filter Unit and that of Western is the filter core. They even look alike, except for the difference in colour. And just because we have a price advantage, I don't see why we should charge a superior filter at a lower price in the market place. Incidentally, the Report says that the market likes the clear plastic bowl, because they can see the residue left by the filter. But I remember, and my staff have looked it up, that there was a court case in 1962, when one of these plastic bowls exploded, after an air pressure surge down the pipe line. There was a lot of publicity at the time. Very unfavourable. Don't let me lose sight of the fact that 80% of this company's profits, almost £1.74 million, come from the household china division. Anything that might put that at risk needs to be looked at very closely. If we go into this field at all, then we can't risk the use of a plastic bowl. We must use something stronger, a metal, or a metal alloy." John Davies, the longest serving member of the Board, and the

Financial Director, finished speaking abruptly, when he saw that Hawkins had risen to his feet to make a reply.

"But to do that, John, would be to go against what the market demands. You must give the market what it wants."

"No Bill, we don't have to in this particular case," said Paul Doncaster. "I'm not altogether happy with the proposal as it stands, and I think that other members of the Board feel the same. Perhaps we would be well advised to commission a more general survey into potential new products, which don't involve a risk to our main product line, and don't involve taking on a dominant market leader.

I propose, notwithstanding your enthusiasm, Bill, that we take no further action on this Report, and commission a more general survey into the possibility of product diversification. I formally propose this to the Board. May I have your votes please?"

This case was written by Professor Kenneth Simmonds and Simon Slater of the London Business School. The case was prepared as a basis for class discussion only and is not designed to present an illustration of either effective or ineffective handling of an administrative situation. Certain facts have been omitted or disguised.
© *Kenneth Simmonds, 1984.*

CASE 4

Ansafone Corporation

In March 1982, Frank Rogers, the non-executive chairman of Ansafone Corporation, was particularly concerned about the product strategy and marketing philosophy of Ansafone. He had been chairman since the management buy-out nearly a year previously and had some months ago set up a Product Planning Group reporting to a new non-executive director with product planning expertise. An outline strategy from this group was now available and so, too, was a survey assessment of Ansafone's marketing and sales functions prepared by an outside consultant.

Ansafone leased a range of Telephone Answering Machines (TAMs), with features ranging from simple dual tape machines without remote control to sophisticated remote control devices. The company also produced TAMs with extended recording capacity and specialised 'multi-announcers' for use by airlines etc. Call logging devices (TELCOST) and viewdata terminals, which were either leased or sold outright, completed the product range, as listed in Exhibit 1. Ansafone manufactured all TAM equipment from basic components, buying in tape transport mechanisms from a large UK manufacturer, and built TELCOST 1 itself. The advanced logging equipment, TNA 25, and the viewdata range were bought in.

The Buy-out and Liberalisation

Under the leadership of Mr John Evans, the managing director, Ansafone had been bought from Lord Grade's Associated Communications Corporation (ACC) in March 1981 by nine senior executives. Investment support came from City institutions organised by 'takeover consultants'. This was the UK's largest management buy-out up to that time. The executives held all the ordinary 'A' shares representing 9% of the voting capital and 1.2% of the entire financing as shown in Exhibit 2. Of the nine, the managing director and finance director served on the board along with the chairman and the two non-executive directors appointed during 1981.

During the buy-out negotiations, a fundamental change came about in Ansafone's principal market which was to have considerable consequences. The Thatcher government adopted a policy of privatisation of public sector commercial activities. The General Post Office was split into separate postal and telecommunications units, and liberalisation of the monopoly was commenced. On 1 April 1980 Sir Keith Joseph (Secretary of State for Industry) made an announcement which permitted direct sale of telephone answering equipment and various other phone peripherals, provided that Post Office and British Standards Institute requirements were met in the form of certification for use on the public network. The British Telecom Act that followed on 1 October 1981 provided for the licensing of a whole range of equipment from handsets to answer-phones and data transmission units.

Exhibit 1   *Ansafone Product Range, March 1982*

Model	Features	Annual Rent £	Purchase Price £	Total Sales (Units) 1981—82 (actual)	Total Sales (Units) 1982—83 (budgeted)
TELEPHONE ANSWERING MACHINES (TAMs)					
6	Answering and recording, dual tape.	180	—	1,800	—
6A	As 6, plus choice of only answering.	230	—	1,050	4,700
600	As 6A, *plus* will not answer if cassette full; two-way recording; remote playback to voice or bleeper coding; dictation facility.	290	—	1,400	1,160
7	Voice-controlled recording; 2 hour capacity. Two-way recording, dictation, dual tape.	300	—	90	100
7P	As 7, plus voice-coded playback.	240	—	1,000	1,400
S100	Simple play and answer; dual tape.	110	—	570	1,400
ANNOUNCERS					
Mini Multi	Up to 10 lines and 3 mins message, twin tape; records message.	728	—	100	100
Multi	Up to 100 lines, in 10-line modules; plays message only, call counting.	366	—	30	15
CALL LOGGING					
Telcost 1	Single-line monitor; 24-hour clock, no display; integral printer, reprogrammable.	—	249	200	1,500
TNA 25	Monitors 50—700 lines giving various usage and cost summaries by lines. Separate hard copy printer.	4,220	11,275	6	2,000
VIEWDATA TERMINALS					
VDUs	Various models (UTT, PYE, SONY)	276	695	1,000	2,800
Keyboard	Alphanumeric	—	?	500	1,500
CODE-A-PHONE TAMs					
Non-remote ⎱ Withdrawn		—	139		
Remote control ⎰ 1982		—	199		

Exhibit 2   *Ansafone Capital Structure as at 1 April 1981 (£000s)*

'A' Shares	65
'B' Shares	675
Preference Shares (10%)	2,700
Loan Stock	1,000
	4,440
Bank Loan (National Westminster)	1,000
	5,440

This Act effectively broke the equipment supply and services monopoly of British Telecom, although the full extent of the Act was delayed by three years to permit adjustment by UK suppliers while temporarily protecting them from foreign competition.

Ansafone had been aware of lobbying moves leading up to the Secretary of State's announcement, and was seen as a potentially glamorous company because of the opportunities to be gained from liberalisation. On the day of the announcement, Mr Evans was reported thus:

> We are lean and hungry; deregulation of telecommunications will provide a super opportunity to develop new products ... and the company could achieve growth by adding thrusting new companies in the telecommunications field.

Within six months, Ansafone had set up Viewdata Business Systems, a wholly-owned subsidiary, to supply interactive viewdata terminals to business users on a rental or purchase basis. Based on British Telecom's predictions of Prestel use — 50,000 subscribers by October 1982 — Ansafone considered that the best segments would be direct Prestel information users such as stockbrokers and travel agents and private user networks such as that planned by British Leyland for its dealers. These dealers could use it to call up details of vehicles and parts available around the country.

Management Strategy for an Independent Ansafone

Towards the end of 1980, and before the details of the buy-out were finalised, Mr Evans produced a document entitled *Ansafone as an Independent Company*, setting out the general policy and strategy to be pursued after the buy-out.

Mr Evans had taken over as managing director in 1978, and he first pointed out that his policy had turned around an adverse profit trend by means of:

— strict financial and cash control
— strict control of manning levels
— introduction of marketing skills
— personnel development and training
— product rationalisation
— elimination of export losses
— closure of unprofitable subsidiaries
— review of component pricing policies
— design of products for defined markets

Exhibit 3 sets out the profit record.

Mr Evans then went on to state that the foremost strength in the company was "the capacity of senior management to meet the defined commercial objectives of the business" and "flexible management capable of spearheading advances into new market areas". He depicted the company's attributes as follows:

1. *Nationwide Sales*
   "More than a hundred people engaged in a single task ... highly rewarded for a specialist sales approach ... the operation is nationwide and provides an excellent infrastructure for expansion".

Exhibit 3 *Ansafone Profit Record,*
Years Ending 31 March (£000s)

1975	350
1976	(150)
1977	360
1978	1,200
1979	1,500
1980	820

2. *Nationwide Service*
    "A major area of strength ... skills in the installation and maintenance of electro-mechanical and electronic equipment as well as a comprehensive knowledge of the telephone industry ... capable of absorbing and integrating new products and additional skills". The service operation was based in Cricklewood, North London. Total service staff numbered 157.

3. *Rentals, Finance and Administration*
    'One of the best organised and managed operations in the UK and, with the installation of a computerised system at Camberley, capable of absorbing new products, more contracts, and possibly new conditions of business, such as hire purchase'. Staff, including management, clerks and others totalled 70.

4. *Manufacturing*
    'The results of a programme of rationalisation, modernisation and heavy investment can be seen in the efficiency of the semi-automated production line at Camberley'. Manufacturing personnel numbered about 100, having been reduced from 200 the previous year as the plant at Camberley in Surrey was redesigned and modernised.

Looking ahead, Mr Evans budgeted £2 million net profit after interest for the year to March 1982 and commented:

> ... basic successes will be achieved to ensure a platform for growth. The emphasis is in building on strengths and to take advantage of new opportunities as they arise. There are five elements to our plans, and the suggested approach illustrates the adaptability of the management team to new circumstances:
>
> 1. Appointment of a new advertising agency to increase the level of enquiries through creative promotion; to increase effectiveness of yellow pages' advertising, the largest source of enquiries; and to move from propagation of the Ansafone name in conjunction with a telephone receiver as visual impact to feature selling.
> 2. The Sales Department to negotiate favourable terms for customers wishing to terminate contracts.
> 3. Extension of the large account sales function, emphasising the total service capabilities of the company.
> 4. Reorganising sales by promoting younger branch managers to regional manager level.
> 5. Announcement, on 2 March 1981, of a distribution agency for two models of TAMs imported from Hong Kong under the Code-a-Phone

brand and for sale only, but to be used also as a "switch—sell" device to promote rental contacts.

In addition, Model 800 will be relaunched in April 1981 as a top-of-the-range machine.

Mr Evans had further aspirations for diversification. These included merchandising of telephone peripherals to multiple retailers, established wholesalers, and large commercial accounts. He planned to build up merchandising as the British Telecom monopoly was gradually liberalised. As he stated in *Ansafone as an Independent Company*:

> This type of activity calls for a small marketing team backed by a merchandising group with a tightly controlled distribution centre having a skilled buyer and stock system.

He also planned further acquisition

— of another rental company — concerned with TAMs;
— of an existing manufacturer of telephone logging equipment;
— of a suitable trading company which could be integrated into the Ansafone Group to handle low cost telephone peripherals.

He would pursue this method of growth by acquisition actively as it would be the fastest way to expand the Ansafone operation. It would require significant front-end investment, but the management skills within the organisation could bring a very fast and high return.

Call Logging Equipment

After the buy-out, Ansafone moved quickly into the call logging field. The UK rights were acquired for a Canadian call logger that could monitor the calls of between 50 and 700 lines on a Private Branch Exchange (PBX). This equipment, called a TNA 25, operated in conjunction with a hard copy printer and could print out tabulations of call frequency, call costs and call timing, by department or extension. It was bought in from outside and sold or leased, with a gross margin of 40%. The launch took place in October 1981. Subsequently, half the customers ended up buying outright.

Ansafone had also acquired the rights to manufacture and sell a single-line monitor branded 'Telcost 1'. After considerable development and testing, this was launched in February 1982. It was for direct sale by the Telephone Answering Machines (TAM) sales force and for indirect sale by another 'executive sales' group, via distributors and wholesalers. The product was not much larger than a standard telephone and depended on 'meter pulses' to generate call cost information. Although meter pulse was not universally available in the UK in 1982, the company was developing a version (Telcost 2) which could, with its own algorithm, calculate costs without outside assistance from meter pulses. This version was expected to come on the market towards the end of 1982. Also under development was 'Telcost 10', an intermediate machine for 10 to 50 lines.

The call logging market was likely to be large. Logging equipment has a variety of uses, including cost control, activity measurement (e.g. of telephone sales forces) and charging calls to individual accounts (e.g. by a solicitor). Potential customers could be gauged from the numbers exceeding a certain telephone bill size and the numbers of certain user types, as well as from the actual number and size distribution of private exchanges in the UK.

Ansafone executives believed the size of the market could be over 100,000 units.

Performance after the Buy-out

Despite the various strategies and subsequent actions, it was apparent by the end of 1981 that Ansafone would not meet its profit targets for the financial year. Exhibit 4 shows the actual result achieved by March 1982 as against the budget for the year, and Exhibit 5 shows the balance sheet as at that date.

The recently relaunched TAM 800 at the top of the range had done well for a short time but then ran into problems as it proved both unreliable in the field and difficult to sell, even at a rental cost of £80 per quarter. Production costs were around £1,200 per set. The 800 machine had been invented in the early 1970s and first launched in 1976. It was intended as an ideal machine, but it had 13 circuit boards, versus the one or two in the normal TAMs, a tape transport mechanism developed in-house, and a frame model designed before the contents. The product was dropped in October and stocks had to be written off to the extent of £1 million.

Further problems in matching product features to market needs were associated with 'Graphmate", an *ad hoc* product bought in from Japan for use as a stand-alone graph-plotter. In this case, two sales personnel had done a rapid piece of field research (with little positive response), and the marketing manager had conducted a brief survey of companies likely to need such a service. The product was launched in April with optimism and a 40% gross margin, but it was rapidly discovered that few companies could afford the machine, and fewer still required a stand-alone facility costing £1,850. Compared with initial estimates of 620 units for the year, under 50 were sold. The machine was withdrawn in March 1982.

Viewdata had not yet taken off. Although no profit had been budgeted, the immediate future for the unit was looking less rosy. Prestel's 1980 target of 50,000 users by the end of 1982 now looked decidedly optimistic. As of March 1980, there had been 2,500 Prestel subscribers. In the following nine months, British Telecom spent £0.75 million on promotion with only 5,000 additional sales resulting. In March 1981, a new £1.5 million advertising

Exhibit 4 *Ansafone Performance (£ millions)*

Years Ending 31 March	1981 Actual	1982 Budget	1982 Actual	1983 Budget
Turnover	12.2	n.a.	11.2	n.a.
Group Trading Profit	1.9	3.5	0.8	1.8
Less:				
Overdraft Interest	(1.2)	(1.2)	(1.1)	(1.3)
£1m. Term Loan Interest		(0.1)	(0.2)	(0.2)
Loan Stock Interest		(0.2)	(0.2)	(0.2)
Preference Dividend		(0.2)	(0.2)	
Tax on Dividend		(0.1)	(—)	
Group Net Profit	0.7	1.7	(0.9)	0.1

Exhibit 5 *Ansafone Consolidated Balance Sheet as at 31 March 1982 (£ millions)*

Funds Employed		
Share Capital	3.4	
Reserves	3.1	
	6.5	
Loans	2.2	
	8.7	
Represented by		
Fixed Assets*	13.5	
Associate Companies	(0.2)	
	13.3	
Current Assets		
Stock and Work in Progress	3.1	
Debtors	2.1	
	5.2	
Less Current Liabilities		
Creditors	2.0	
Bank Overdraft (Limit £9m.)	7.8	
	9.8	
Deficit on Working Capital	(4.6)	
Net Assets	8.7	

	Balance Sheet £m.	Estimated Current Value £m.
*Land & Buildings	0.9	2.1
Plant, Fixtures & Fittings	1.0	0.4
Vehicles	0.6	0.4
Equipment on Hire	11.0	8.0
	13.5	10.9

budget was set against a target of 2.5 million user sets. But by August, there were only 10,700 sets in use — 9,200 business, 1,500 private. An article in *The Financial Times* put it this way:

> So far, the story of Viewdata in Britain has been a saga of ambitious targets followed by abysmal sales, followed by lower targets, followed by lower sales, coupled with exhortations and admonitions to do better.

In December 1981, aware of the mounting problems, the chairman asked Mr Fearnside, a newly-appointed non-executive director, to chair a Product Planning Group to review Ansafone's new product strategy. Technological change and market developments were proceeding at such a rate that Ansafone needed to formulate afresh its product strategy. The company had never systematically developed new products, and had experienced cannibalisation and obsolescence problems with its range of TAM machines. The introduction of microprocessors in the "600" machine had outmoded a large part of the existing range which was nevertheless being retained to meet rental obligations. In fact, the 6, 6A, 7 and 7P models were now all technically obsolete.

The chairman also arranged for Mr Evans and his senior staff to meet senior officials at the Department of Industry to discuss the impact of the liberalisation of telecommunications. During the discussion, the idea of acting as a local assembly, sales, rental and service organisation for a large Japanese firm was examined, but was not picked up by the Ansafone executive team. An alternative of ordering a large quantity of cheaper TAMs from the Orient with Ansafone branding and using these for both rental and a new wholesaling activity also presented difficulties, given the established "park" of Ansafone users. How could it maintain high rentals, yet sell an identical machine at a very much lower price in the general market?

Also, in December, the chairman invited an outside consultant to report on Ansafone's market position. The consultant interviewed the functional heads in marketing and sales in some depth.

The Marketing Function

Mr Denis Judd, who joined the company in January 1981, described his responsibilities as including:

1. *Provision of Marketing Services to Divisions*
   Public relations and publicity liaison; promotion of existing and new products; development of the new corporate image and communications problem solving. As an example, he cited the recent launch of Telcost 1 for which he felt that there had been good editorial coverage in magazines read by "decision makers", mentioning *Business Equipment Digest* in particular.

2. *Advertising*
   Using a new company agency to stimulate enquiries from potential TAM and other product users.

The advertising policy had recently gone through 3 phases:

(a) A humourous conveyance of the Ansafone "proposition" of service quality in cartoons in the national press, plus regional and trade support. This lasted four months, until July 1981, before being scrapped.

(b) A move from an "umbrella image" sell to one stressing the individual products. (This was considered a somewhat bold step by some of his fellow managers.) He increased coverage in the Yellow Pages, and also in trade and technical magazines. Costs per enquiry remained high and the campaign was stopped in October 1981.

(c) Since neither of these approaches had worked, Mr Judd spent some weeks "having a think" about how to raise awareness of the company and the vital enquiry level. He now felt that "name" advertising was basic and "title corners" (small ads on the top corners of newspaper front pages) were an important part of this in conjunction with national press name advertising.

Currently, Ansafone was spending £50,000 annually on Yellow Pages and £30,000 on local classified. Mr Judd's total marketing budget for next year was £300,000 of which half was earmarked for advertising, £100,000 for promotion and the rest for miscellaneous costs.

Mr Judd produced a monthly analysis of enquiries, a sample of which is shown in Exhibit 6. The "historical" conversion of enquiries to sales was said by the Sales Manager to have been of the order of 2.5 : 1 for TAM equipment, but had been dropping. To look further into the causes of an apparent recent drop in enquiries, Mr Judd had just commissioned a "user attitude and awareness" study — looking into the needs of 200 current or potential TAM customers and 200 lapsed contracts. He felt this would be potentially useful in the future drafting of policy. In describing the 48,000 customer base for TAMs, Mr Judd said that there was very little pattern to customers. He saw a "huge variety", with self-employed and small proprietorships being typical.

Exhibit 6 *Sales Enquiry Analysis, March 1982*

	Enquiries	Contracts
TAM Equipment		
Local Classified Ads	75	30
Users	60	40
Post Office	20	5
Yellow Pages	300	75
Reputation	250	50
Recommendation	30	15
TNA 25	65	1
TELCOST 1	300	10
Total	1,100	226

There had been a recent "holocaust" of cancellations among small businesses, although medium and large concerns were not so affected. Mr Judd felt that there was a "natural base" of 25,000 customers for TAMs, towards which figure the current base might erode. Mr Evans' view differed. He argued that only the "bottom end" of the customer base, the smallest and most financially insecure, was being lost, either by substitution to purchased machines or by insolvency because of the recession. But any impact on rental company business was still only marginal.

The Sales Function   Mr Clarke, previously a Regional Sales Manager, had been promoted to National Sales Manager by Mr Evans in August 1981. Mr Evans, himself, performed the function of Sales Director. Mr Clarke outlined the two company selling approaches.

1.   *The Direct Approach*
     This was a "tried, tested and liked" system involving a clear-cut sequence of events: "Cold" telephone call to arrange an appointment with the "key personnel" in the organisation; "follow

lefthand curb", covering every business in the area; during appointment, demonstrate the top-of-the-range machine whilst probing for TAM needs, concentrating on product benefits to seek *closure* or price presentation (covering objections by stressing service benefits etc.) and full completion of contract plus down payment.

2. *Enquiry-led Sales*

This gets most of the business, but also exposes the salesman to competitive pressure from purchased TAM options. Here one policy had been to use Code-a-Phone machines as a 'switch—sell' device to gain a foot in the door, and then to demonstrate against a superior rented machine.

Mr Clarke expressed concern about the recent reduction in enquiries together with very high salesperson turnover resulting from "loss of confidence". The 1981 turnover level was around 75%, against the normal level of around 50% per year. The difficulty of selling Ansafone TAMs was increasing and Mr Clarke had recently instituted a "quota club" with an annual prize for those who reached 100%. Quotas were set on the basis of £31,000 annual rental per salesperson to cover costs and give a reasonable profit. In 1981, only nine reached this target. As a minimum standard, £1,500 per month was recently raised to £2,000 with a target of £2,600. Statistics on sales operations are shown in Exhibit 7. The TAM sales force was also responsible for Telcost 1 sales, although Mr Clarke mentioned that sales results had been disappointing because of the difficulty of using sale arguments on the same customer whom they had been persuading to lease.

Mr Clarke was also concerned about the level of cancellations of contracts which had only recently become very significant. In 1981, the company gained 6,000 contracts and lost 8,000. A feature of the rental contract

---

Exhibit 7 *Sales Statistics*

Average TAM Salesperson Weekly Performance

Direct Approach Calls	60.0
Demonstrations	6.6
Contracts	1.1
Enquiries	3.4
Demonstrations	2.0
Contracts	1.0

Forms of Commission

(1) No salary, £4,500 advance on commission
　　37% commission on first year's rental
(2) Basic £4,000, £2,000 advance on commission
　　19% commission on first year's rental

Sales Cost per Contract 1982
　Budget — £220
　Actual — £270

was that it was renewed automatically and six months' advance written notice was required for cancellation even at the *end* of the typical three-year contract. An analysis had shown that cancellations fell into the following categories:

	1981
Bad debts/gone out of business	2,000
Closing down	1,000
No further need	2,000
Going for purchase substitute	3,000

The 'rental base' of contract commitments with their varying completion dates was valued in December 1981 at £17.3 million, or roughly £360 average per contract, and in taking steps to halt the erosion, Mr Clarke had arranged for Rentals Administration to inform Sales of impending cancellations by forwarding the written notices received. Discounts of up to 35% on rental renewals were now authorised to be proffered, in stages, by the sales force. Commission would be paid to sales staff as if the full annual rental had been obtained.

The New Competition

Even prior to deregulation, small trading entrepreneurs had been selling telephone handsets and peripherals in the UK. Under current legislation, *sale* of equipment was now legal, but *use* on the public network was illegal unless connected by British Telecom. Initially machines came to the UK via the US from Hong Kong and Japan, and were cheap goods "dumped" on the market. When deregulation became a public issue, several other companies entered in earnest — mostly now with Post Office certification.

Answercall, which entered the market in 1979 as an "illegal pirate" selling unlicensed machines from the Far East, was the most successful. It had sold around 90,000 machines and expected to continue at an equivalent annual rate of 30,000. Its advertising claimed: "A large number of companies automatically renew their rental contracts because they have a trouble-free machine without realising that they could drastically reduce costs by buying instead". Commenting on this aggressive approach, Mr Judd said:

> The small operators are spending a lot of money up front on glossy ads, and I daresay if you gave me a quarter of a million pounds I could make stale bread look like a desirable commodity but that doesn't bear any relation to the real quality.

Another entry just prior to deregulation was GMTC, which also relied on heavy promotion to push through sales. Margins were low, however, and shared with the distribution chain. The company went into liquidation in 1981 — largely because the sales volume did not generate enough margin to cover promotional expenses.

The heavy advertising and the low purchase prices, compared with Ansafone's rental-only rates and prices of the limited number of other manufacturers operating under licence from British Telecom, had, nevertheless, stimulated the market to an annual value of approximately £50 million. Current retail prices are shown in Exhibit 8. New methods of distribution had also fuelled the growth. Mail order solicitation now appeared in *Exchange and Mart* and there was a growing number of small local retail outlets, many set up by ex-rental TAM sales staff. The "telephone shop"

Exhibit 8   *Retail Prices of Competing TAMs*

	Light Usage	*Heavy Usage*
Non-Remote Control	£65—£100	£100—£160
Remote Control	£100—£150	£170 upwards

seemed to have sprung up on every High Street. These developments appeared to have stimulated the hitherto dormant domestic sector. Small traders and the self-employed, being more price conscious, had also taken readily to the option of a cheap answering machine.

The rationale of the new competitors was to operate as traders, with low overheads. A typical company might have 50 or 60 distributors, together with some large retail chains such as W.H. Smith, Boots, Currys or Harrods. Extreme reliance was placed on their distributors' selling efforts and associated minor repair, or "first aid", work. The sales were covered by a one-year warranty, then an annual maintenance contract at around £30. Repairs were conducted centrally and machines returned by Securicor express. Reliability of machines was said to be high, with roughly 1.5 to 2% of machines expected to give trouble once in a useful life of five to six years. Costs were thus lower than Ansafone's 1982 maintenance costs per installed machine of £29, although customers of purchased machines would be without machines during service.

A Strategy from the Product Planning Group

By March 1982, the Product Planning Group had drawn up a new outline strategy with the following major elements:

Company Strengths
— The Ansafone name, synonymous with TAMs.
— Forward secured rental of about £16.5 million and consequent cash flow.
— Nationwide sales and service organisation.
— Research and development skills.
— Manufacturing capacity (overheads estimated at £0.8m.).

Product Areas (existing and feasible)
— Call answering (TAM, radio paging, call diversion).
— Call monitoring (TNA 25, Telcost 1, 2, 10).
— Information systems (extension from viewdata).
— Factored sales.
— Service subcontracting (e.g. on behalf of a microcomputer company).

Telecommunications Market
— It is large and growing fast.
— It is reasonable to expect Ansafone to gain a 1% market penetration with a Telecom related product — e.g. Telcost, call diversion, etc.
— The market potential based on 1% of business lines is, therefore:
    UK   95,330
    Europe   458,040
    Total world   1,228,518

— In 1977 there were seven million unanswered calls per day in the UK! These calls could become answered calls if they were handled by TAMs, answering services, paging or call diversion equipment.

The report ended with a table of additional contributions amounting to over £500,000 that might be expected from new products by 1983/84. This table is reproduced in Exhibit 9.

Presenting the report, Mr Fearnside stated that the strategy of the company should be to plan the new product field thoroughly and also to consider the direct sale using a separate brand, different distribution channel and sales force for, firstly, a "combined" TAM, autodialler and hands-free telephone and, secondly, a low-cost TAM range, both imported from the Far East. He believed, however, that the basis of Ansafone's existing reputation for reliability and service, which was expensive but cost effective, enforced a top-of-the-market strategy for rentals. This implied a direct sales and service network with countrywide coverage and consequent minimum sustainable numbers. He also believed that internal overheads were cut to the limit without withdrawing major functions. Manufacturing staff had now been reduced to forty and Ansafone was left with a large, modern and greatly under-used factory in which output could be increased four or five times without difficulty. Nevertheless, it would not be difficult to dispose of the unit, subcontract production and refurbishment, and retain only a testing unit to ensure quality.

Exhibit 9 *Contribution from New Product Strategy (£000s)*

		1982–1983	*1983–1984*
(1)	*Radio Paging* Rent 2,250 units in 1983–84, 3,000 p.a. thereafter	(2)	60
(2)	*Call Logging Telcost 10* Launch January 1983. Sell 1,000 p.a. from December 1983. Gross margin 20%.	(6)	301
(3)	*Information Systems* Supply complete systems as a development from Viewdata	?	?
(4)	*Factored Items* One every six months from October 1982. Average selling price £2,000, 40% gross margin, 100 p.a.	15	75
(5)	*Service Department* Service another company's TAMs at £22.50 per service per year, £19.50 per installation or recovery.	65	130
		72	573

This case was prepared by Kenneth Simmonds and Robin Wensley of the London Business School, with the co-operation of Vogue management, as a basis for class discussion rather than to illustrate either effective or ineffective handling of a business situation.
© *Kenneth Simmonds, 1976*

CASE 5

Vogue Bathrooms

The management of Glynwed Bathroom and Kitchen Products Ltd, trading as Vogue Bathrooms, was concerned in late 1975 with deciding whether to commit the firm to sizeable investment in modernising its plant. Vogue was the dominant producer of cast-iron baths in the United Kingdom and management believed that a failure to improve the enamel finish of Vogue baths would lead to a loss of the premium image for cast-iron over plastic and a more rapid decline in market share and sales. Moreover, with new plant it would be possible to reduce the gauge, and hence the weight, of the cast-iron baths and make some improvement in the plant working conditions. The production process for cast-iron baths was basically the same as it had been 100 years earlier with a little automation added. The bath was cast in a mould, then spray enamelled and baked. Dust from the foundry sand and a great deal of noise and heat combined to make an unpleasant work environment.

Vogue could continue to produce for another ten years without modernising its two existing casting and enamelling plants which had been built in the late 1950s. Nevertheless, management considered that it should make the investment decision urgently because sales of plastic baths seemed to be gaining at the expense of cast-iron ones at an increasing rate. As a precaution against building too much capacity, however, the Managing Director proposed to ask professional consultants to prepare a report on the rate at which buyers could be expected to switch across to plastic baths. The cost of new plant would involve a net investment of around £2 million after allowing for Government investment grants and depreciation allowances.

Vogue's Facilities and Profitability

Glynwed Bathroom and Kitchen Products Ltd, (Vogue), was a fully-owned subsidiary of Glynwed Ltd, a manufacturing group principally concerned with components for the building industry. Vogue had been acquired by the Glynwed group in 1969, and its headquarters were located in Bilston in the West Midlands.

Until 1974 Vogue operated three plants with a total capacity of about 370,000 cast-iron baths per annum:

Plant	Capacity
Bilston, West Midlands	130,000
Falkirk, Scotland	110,000
Greenford, London	130,000

At the end of 1974, however, the Greenford plant had been closed. The major United Kingdom recession had led to a steady decrease in demand for cast-iron baths from an annual rate of around 500,000 per year reached in mid-1973, to 350,000 in mid-1974. Vogue's inventory had risen to 45,000 units with no further storage possible at the plants. Moreover, there were

Exhibit 1 *Vogue's Expected Performance for 1975*

		£m.
Sales		6.30
Cost of Sales		
Materials — Direct	2.30	
Indirect	1.00	
Labour — Direct	0.60	
Indirect	0.70	
Wage Ancillary	0.25	
Factory Overheads (Rent, rates, depreciation, insurance etc.)	0.25	
Scrappage Sales	(0.10)	
		5.00
Gross Margin		1.30
Expenses		
Administrative Expenses — Vogue	0.40	
Glynwed	0.15	
Selling Expenses	0.15	
Distribution Expenses	0.33	
Rebates and Cash Discounts	0.27	
		1.30
Net Profit before Tax		...

strong indications that the decline would continue for some time and no sources predicted growth in the house building sector until late 1976. Vogue management reacted by closing the Greenford plant and putting the others on short-time working. Greenford was the plant with the highest wage and overhead costs and its closure, though costing £600,000, saved an estimated £150,000 in annual fixed costs and avoided losses from under-capacity operation in the short term.

With the difficult market conditions Vogue had recorded losses for 1973 and 1974. Directly variable costs represented 84% of total costs and only when volume was maintained at a constantly high level were the fixed costs covered. For 1975, however, Vogue expected to break-even at a sales level of £6.3 million as shown in Exhibit 1. This represented production of 190,000 baths as detailed in Exhibit 2. The order book was much healthier and delivery had risen to seven weeks on the average, although much shorter for the standard white models.

Both the Bilston and Falkirk plants had been designed to produce large quantities of standard white baths, which were acceptable to the market in the 1950s and 1960s, but by 1975 were bought by only 25% of the market. Fashion shapes requiring grip handles and a wider range of colours slowed down the production rate in both of Vogue's plants and increased the average cost of the baths produced. In 1975, standard factory costs varied

Exhibit 2 *Vogue Estimated Unit Sales 1975* ('000s of baths)

	White	Colour	
Standard Range			
Vogue 54	2.0	—	
Vogue 60	13.1	0.7	
Vogue 66	65.2	25.0	
Atlanta 1700	11.0	—	
Vogue 72	1.6	0.6	
Atlanta 60S	7.6	—	
Vogue 60 Twingrip	1.4	0.4	
Vogue 66 Twingrip	10.9	11.7	
Vogue 72 Twingrip	0.6	0.7	
Luxury Range			
Harmony 66	1.7	6.9	
Caribbean 1700	2.0	15.6	
Caribbean 1800	0.1	0.4	
Mayfair 1700	0.7	5.9	
Mayfair 1800	0.3	1.4	
Super-Luxury Range			
Elysian 1840	—	0.3	
Florida 1700	0.2	1.9	
Bahama Corner Bath		0.1	
Total	118.4	71.6	190.0

from £21 for Vogue's basic white "Vogue 60" model at the bottom of its line, through to £29 for its middle-of-the-line "Caribbean 1700" model (either white or coloured), and up to £39 for its extra-wide, super-luxury "Florida 1700". Four years earlier, however, the basic white "Vogue 60" had cost only £8 to produce.

Competing Bath Materials

Bath production in the United Kingdom was divided between steel, plastic and cast-iron as shown in Exhibit 3.

(i) Steel baths represented about 30% of the UK market by number in mid-1975, although slightly lower in share when measured by value. Baths were pressed from mild steel mainly of thin gauge (about 2 millimetre) and then enamelled. With these thin pressings the enamel chipped easily, leading to high losses in transit. Moreover, the baths were not as rigid as for cast-iron

Exhibit 3 *United Kingdom Bath Production by Material of Manufacture* ('000s of baths)

	1973	1974	1975
Cast-iron	454	340	226
Plastic	320	306	291
Steel	274	198	213
	1,048	844	730

and sounded "tinny". Over the previous two years, thicker steel baths had begun to appear on the UK market — first 2.5 mm and subsequently 3.5 mm. The enamel chipped less readily and the difference in mass and rigidity between steel and cast-iron was greatly reduced. Vogue management expected that heavy gauge baths would provide very severe competition for standard cast-iron baths, particularly in the contract field. In European countries, steel already took a much larger market share — 40% in France, 50% in Italy and 65% in Germany. One drawback to steel was the limitation to its shaping. Only rectangular shapes were possible and there were limitations to other styling features imposed by the pressing process and the cost of dies. In variable cost, however, steel baths undercut even plastic baths.

(ii) Plastic baths were taking 40% of the market in mid-1975, a percentage that had grown from under 15% in 1970. Plastic baths were mainly vacuum formed from "Perspex", an acrylic sheet produced and promoted by Imperial Chemical Industries Ltd. A small proportion of "plastic baths", however, were made entirely from fibreglass (Glass Reinforced Polyester). These were usually very large baths of unusual shapes — such as sunken round baths and corner baths. Perspex could be moulded in different thicknesses, but standardisation had taken place around two thicknesses of 3 mm and 8 mm. The bulk of the sales were at the low end of the market in 3 mm Perspex, with Glass Reinforced Polyester sprayed on underneath. Perspex was relatively easily shaped by a vacuum forming process with few limits to the range of shapes. Though not as solid and stable as cast-iron, the frames attached as plastic baths were installed had been improved to give a reasonable stability. Handling costs were low due to the light weight. A plastic bath weighed about 30 lbs against the normal 250 lbs of a cast-iron bath.

ICI had readily made Perspex available in a wide range of colour matches. Apparently there was no difficulty in adjusting the tint to get the required match, nor in producing a wider range of colours. While plastic did not chip readily like enamel, it could scratch and lose its sheen and the thinner mouldings had been known to bend out of shape with very hot water. On the other hand, scratches could be rubbed out with a mild abrasive because the colour went right through the material. The Plastics Bath Information Bureau claimed that the surface could be repolished with any liquid metal polish and that even major accidents like allowing a cigarette to burn out on the edge of a bath and produce a yellowish scar could be easily remedied. They claimed that wire wool would eliminate the blister and the yellow stain and that the liquid metal polish would put back the sparkle. Plastic was resistant to acids and alkalis, but could be attacked by acetone (nail polish remover) and would also burn in the event of a fire. However, plastic would not rust or corrode.

(iii) Cast-iron baths represented the remaining 30% of the market in mid-1975. This estimate showed a substantial fall from cast-iron's 60% share of the market in 1970. The glazed porcelain finish of a cast-iron bath was extremely durable and reglazing was possible. Around a general rectangular shape there was considerably more flexibility in developing luxury shapes in cast-iron than in steel. Sides, edges and corners could be rounded, bevelled and indented in a great many ways. But the sides had to slope away from the base to facilitate the bath's removal from the mould, and it was difficult and expensive to match in enamel some of the deeper shades of pottery, especially deep red.

Vogue's castings had a gauge of about 6 mm and with new plant it was considered likely that this gauge could be reduced by up to 30%. Size was limited to castings 1800 mm by 850 mm due to casting box limits. Anything larger in cast-iron, however, would have been very costly to handle because of the weight.

Market Segments and Competing Materials

Demand for baths was traditionally forecast separately for three segments — public new housing; private new housing; and modernisation, replacement and community. This last segment was really made up of three quite separate elements, but figures were not available separately. Past sales and the most recent forecasts for these segments are shown in Exhibit 4.

Periodically, Vogue's marketing staff estimated the number of baths of each material purchased in each of the three segments. The last attempt had been made in July 1974 and the figures are shown in Exhibit 5. In support of their projection of the material allocation by segments for 1978, the marketing unit made these comments:

1) "Plastic baths, mainly of the cheap composite type, are believed to have increased their share of new public building. By 1978, their lead is expected to be overtaken by steel baths through severe price competition, and cast-iron is expected to have virtually disappeared from this segment."

2) "The greatest growth in new private building is expected to be in plastic bath models which offer a colour range and shapes at lower prices than cast-iron. Steel is expected to increase its share of this segment, possibly to the same level as cast-iron, because heavy gauge steel baths in colours will be available for installation by the private builder at lower prices than cast-iron."

3) "The great majority of the private replacement and modernisation markets are expected to be retained by cast-iron through 1978. However, the share of plastic baths will grow for replacement markets as more expensive models are introduced. The steel share in this sector will be concentrated mainly in community building, renovations of hospitals, hotels and council housing."

Exhibit 4 *United Kingdom Bath Market Forecast by Market Segment* ('000s of baths)

	Actual		*Forecast*		
	1973	*1974*	*1975*	*1976*	*1977*
New Housing — Public	114	135	151	161	170
— Private	190	143	149	154	160
Modernisation, Replacement and Community	744	566	430	410	470
	1,048	844	730	725	800

Exhibit 5   *Estimated Bath Material Shares by Market Segment*   ('000s of baths)

		1970	1974	1978
New Housing — Public	Cast-iron	108	35	5
	Plastic	30	40	25
	Steel	50	35	100
		188	110	130
New Housing — Private	Cast-iron	124	35	60
	Plastic	30	60	100
	Steel	20	25	60
		174	120	220
Modernisation, Replacement and Community	Cast-iron	245	270	250
	Plastic	56	180	260
	Steel	116	180	190
		417	630	700
Total	Cast-iron	477	340	315
	Plastic	116	280	385
	Steel	186	240	350
		779	860	1,050

Customer Attitudes Towards Different Bath Materials

In 1973 Vogue had commissioned a qualitative study of consumer attitudes towards baths by a commercial research firm. The research was carried out from June to October 1973 and involved firstly a series of twelve in-depth interviews with men, women and couples in London and Cheshire who had acquired a new bath within the previous three years. These were followed by six group discussions. Each group discussion included a mixture of couples who had and had not chosen baths within the previous three years, including at least one couple who had bought a plastic bath. All interviewees were drawn equally from age groups 20 to 39 and 40 to 55, and two discussions were held in each of Chorley (North of England), Edinburgh (Scotland) and Colchester (South of England). The ratio of cast-iron to plastic purchasers among the interviewees was two to one. Extracts from the report describing attitudes towards different bath materials are set out below and details concerning bath purchasing generally are included in Appendix A:

> As far as materials were concerned, most of the sample considered they were traditionalists and preferred cast-iron. This material for baths was proven, lasted 30—70 years, was strong, sturdy, did not break, even if it chipped, was easy to clean, was more sensible with children and could be re-enamelled.

> On the other hand, cast-iron was very heavy to transport and a 'do-it-yourself' man had to think twice about installing one upstairs unless he had help with the labouring. Cast-iron was considered to be more expensive than other bath materials, because of the raw materials involved.

> Not everyone was aware of the manufacture of baths in plastics, although the majority had heard of them even if they thought they had not seen one. Few were sure exactly what materials plastic baths were made from and called them variously and most frequently plastic, fibre glass and perspex and less frequently acrylic and nylon.

A number of the sample had actually considered plastic baths before making up their minds and not bought them; others had tried to find out from unbiased sources about plastic baths, been unsuccessful and decided to stick to cast-iron. Showrooms were accused of either trying to sell one kind or the other, but not supplying the potential purchasers with all the pros and cons of each type. For example, in one group in Chorley, a couple in the group said they had been really put off buying a plastic bath by showroom staff, while another couple had been told, by the same showroom, they only had plastic baths. In London one lady had been told the shop did not sell cast-iron any more, that they were too difficult to fix, were not being manufactured and were not safe with children.

To say the least, there was an amount of confusion and lack of correct information about plastic baths. The general criticisms were as follows:

(a) Plastic baths had not been manufactured long enough to be as well-proven as cast-iron. They were not as strong, tough or durable as iron.

(b) They were too light to be used as baths. The plastic moved when a person plus water were in it as the weight of the person and the water was greater than that of the bath:

> "It's easier to fix a fibre glass one yourself, but you need a deal more fixing points. There's flexibility with fibre glass and movement is the drawback ... they have to be strengthened underneath. The feeling in a plastic one is that you are going to topple over because of the movement. So it's no good for elderly people who are unsteady."

> "That *does* worry me — being rather heavy — they seem to be too light to hold my weight."

(c) They were not safe for children because of the movement, particularly if the children were rather boisterous when in the bath:

> "Children are not good with plastic baths ... not the same durability as cast-iron, swings when you get in — not the same rigidity, it's supposed to be fixed to the wall in a certain way, but it never happens with a cast-iron bath."

> "My husband felt, especially with two young children, that perspex gives a bit and we thought, if they were jumping up and down, we'd be better off with a cast-iron one — especially as everyone will be standing in the one spot when we are having showers."

(d) When they came away from the walls where they were fixed because of movement, they had to be replugged and screwed back. Some of those who had purchased plastic baths were not happy with their baths because either the baths themselves or the walls they were fixed to had cracked:

> "We tiled up to the bath and it's splitting and slipping from them. It wouldn't happen to cast-iron — it's strong and solid. Perhaps the perspex ones are prone to poor installations — I don't know."

(e) Plastic baths were thought to burn into holes with cigarette ash and were cracked or pierced by sharp objects accidentally dropped in them (e.g. by a shattered glass bottle). Women were worried that their hair lacquer, nail varnish remover, hair colourant, or some medicines might harm the surface if accidentally splashed on such a bath.

(f) Plastic baths were thought to lose their "sheen" and "lustre" after 6 months, "with the hot water — as plastic reacts to temperature changes". Purchasers stated that they scratched easily and were not easy to clean, so the surface lost its shine very soon (even with detergents and liquid abrasives). One explained:

> "The family did not wipe it round enough at the shower end and a deposit seems to have accumulated. One end will be stained and I don't know what to use to clean it any more."

(g) With the plastic bath one sometimes had a plumbing problem in connecting the waste to the existing piping. A couple of men had experienced or had heard that the plastic baths were prone to cracking at the waste.

On the positive side, there were fewer perceived advantages. These were that plastic baths were cheaper in cost, lighter in weight and lighter, therefore, for a DIY man to install; and they were of bright colours, with a smoother, shinier and more even surface finish than cast-iron baths. In the Colchester hard water area, the women thought plastic baths were easier to clean and this, apparently, had been one of the showrooms' "selling points". Some plastic bath purchasers felt the plastic bath was maligned by narrow thinking and rumour and that, at any event, in 10—15 years time raw materials would have become so scarce that no cast-iron baths would be available any more.

Those who had bought plastic baths did so for economy, colour and design, "without even thinking", for their brightness and finish and apparent ease of fixture, on the advice of plumber or showroom assistant. Some had been swayed by the argument (even where price was not of importance) that plastic baths were safer where children were concerned, as it did not hurt them so much if by any chance they fell in the bath. The main selling points were that they were warmer, both initially to touch and when in the bath; that they retained the heat in the water longer than cast-iron, and consequently, that they were cheaper to run in terms of hot water than cast-iron.

Those with friends who had plastic baths were impressed and could not find fault with them on the whole in reality. The cast-iron die-hards still stated that they would not expect the plastic models to last the "lifetime" that the cast-iron units would, but that they would probably last 10—12 years.

Hardly anyone was aware of the manufacture of *steel baths*. Those who were tended to be connected with the building/plumbing trade in some way. Steel baths were thought to be cold, shiny, "stainless steel" by most of the women, but some of the men pointed out that they were more noisy and tinny sounding than cast-iron, and that the enamel was more likely to chip than on cast-iron. A few hazarded guesses that they were cheaper to buy than cast-iron, although one could only tell the difference by tapping them in the showroom for their sound.

However, two male interviewees had bought steel baths as they were cheaper than cast-iron and easier to carry up the stairs for installing themselves, but they had found that, like plastic, they also "moved" when one got in and out and while actually bathing.

Vogue's Associates   Glynwed management was well aware of the threats to Vogue's cast-iron production from competing materials. They had therefore taken steps to set up production of both steel and plastic baths. Under the "Leisure" brand name, a separate Glynwed subsidiary manufactured pressed steel baths, shower cubicles, vanity basins and units, and sinks of various descriptions. Production was approximately 20,000 baths per annum in two styles. The

Vega 66 in 2mm steel was priced for quantities over 45 at £18.50 in white and £21.00 in colours. The Vega 1700 in 2.5 mm steel was priced at £23.90 in white with surcharges of £2.15 and £4.25 for different colour groups. Vogue's sales force in certain areas had for several years represented this line to the outlets they called on.

The Glynwed move into plastic bath production was more recent. Production had just started in mid-1975. Spurred on by the high growth rate for plastic baths in 1973 and 1974 and the major emphasis placed on plastic baths by the Carron Company, who had always been the major cast-iron competitor, Glynwed drew on Vogue's expertise to draw up plans for a significant plastics operation with an eventual annual capacity of 75,000 baths.

The new unit was set up as Jupiter Plastics operating under Glynwed Plastics Ltd — a Glynwed division quite distinct from Glynwed Bathroom and Kitchen Products Ltd. Distribution was confined to builders' merchants, but a separate salesforce was hired to give plastic baths undivided attention. By mid-1975 six styles had been launched. At the bottom of the range was the Palermo with a list price of £22.50, followed by the California at £28.75. The remaining models went up in price steps until the Seychelles was reached at the top of the range with a list price of £150.00. The Seychelles had a modernistic design almost twice the width of the lowest priced styles.

Vogue's Competition   The only significant United Kingdom competition to Vogue remaining in cast-iron production was the Carron Company with a capacity of about 60,000 units per annum. Carron themselves were the leading UK producers of plastic baths in 1974 and had placed increased emphasis on plastics. Vogue saw no likelihood of any other firm entering cast-iron production on any scale, even should they themselves decide not to modernise.

In addition to Glynwed's "Leisure" line there were only two United Kingdom manufacturers of steel baths. Carron also had a steel bath unit and so did Curran, part of the Reed International Group. Combined output of these two competitors was about 150,000 per annum. There were several European manufacturers with much higher volume production in steel than any of the United Kingdom manufacturers and competition on a cut-price base was currently being felt from them. Material and labour cost advantages, however, probably contributed more to this competition than economies from high volume. High volume production was achieved by the German firms where steel baths were the rule, yet Spain seemed to be the most competitive source of imports. In the first six months of 1975 imports fell slightly compared with 1974, but rose from 14% to 28% of the steel bath demand which was recording at an annual rate of 200,000 units. United Kingdom production for export also dropped from 64,000 in the first six months of 1974 to 28,000 in the first six months of 1975. Curran had introduced heavier gauge 3.5 mm steel in early 1975 aiming at the cast-iron market. To match this move Vogue had entered into negotiations with a West German supplier for heavier gauge baths, and supplies would commence in 1976.

As opposed to cast-iron and steel, the number of competitive manufacturers of plastic baths was large. There were about 30 firms involved and the range of a dozen included ten or more styles. Vacuum forming equipment was easily acquired, so investment in production facilities was not a barrier to entry. At the end of 1975, plastic bath manufacturers were suffering from a drastic surplus of capacity as evidenced by the ease with which an offer of delivery within a week could be obtained — even when stocks of the manufactured baths were not held.

Bathroom Pottery Suppliers

While some firms had recently begun merchandising plastic basins and plastic cisterns for toilets, almost all washbasins, toilets and bidets were of pottery. The pottery firms held the lead in introduction of new colours. At the impending 1975 Building Exhibition, for example, Vogue management expected there would be three new hard colours in pottery introduced by each of the three main manufacturers — possibly nine colours in all. It would be over to Vogue to react by introducing matching bath shades if it thought the sales would justify the cost.

Vogue had not been able to arrange for supply of an exclusive Vogue range of pottery from any manufacturer. However, in an implied threat to UK pottery suppliers as to where Vogue could turn if forced to by attempts to design Vogue out of bath markets via pottery colour changes, Vogue had just imported several sets of French pottery for the impending exhibition.

There were seven pottery manufacturing firms in the United Kingdom. By 1975 all had their own plastic bath manufacture and five were associated with major groups producing components for the building industry. In order of size of output these firms were as follows:

Armitage Shanks Glynwed made an attempt to take this independent firm over in 1973, but the bid was dropped when a reference was made to the Monopolies Commission.

Ideal Standard This was the UK subsidiary of the large US corporation. Glynwed had purchased Ideal's cast-iron capacity some years previously and had continued to supply them with their bath range in custom colours which they merchandised.

Twyfords Twyfords was the object of a bid by Glynwed in August 1971, but the firm went instead to Reed International who were also strong in building materials though not in bathroom furnishings. Twyfords' management claimed that a merger with Glynwed would hamper Twyfords in winning a larger share of the sanitaryware market. Twyfords had since acquired Curran Engineering, manufacturing both steel and plastic baths.

Royal Doulton The Doulton group was extensive and had taken over Peerless Plastics, a major plastic bath manufacturer. Although to date this firm had not come up with any major innovations, Vogue viewed Doulton as a slumbering giant who could awaken at any moment.

The remaining pottery manufacturers were Outram, a member of the 'Ladyship' group, Shires, a member of the Chloride group and Balterley of Stoke. This last firm was a private venture started about two years previously on a green field site by an experienced small producer who after merging his firm with a larger group did not agree with subsequent policies. Vogue executives estimated that manufacture of pottery could be made profitable at 250,000 pieces per annum, the equivalent of say 60,000 bathroom suites, but with the declining Vogue output they were not prepared to initiate a proposal for investment to the Glynwed group board.

Cost Movements for Competing Materials

Vogue's management did not think it possible to make sensible projections of cost increases for cast-iron, steel or plastic materials over any length of time. They were inclined to believe that the margin between the cost of acrylic and cast-iron materials would not change much for a while, but that labour content in the casting and enamelling would ultimately mean greater overall cost increases.

Imperial Chemical Industries had had the United Kingdom market for acrylic to itself up until about five years previously when Rohm entered from Germany. More recently, Swedlow International had also entered from America. Their quality was slightly lower than that of ICI, but so were their prices. There was one other very small UK manufacturer.

It was believed that for a number of years ICI did not increase the price of acrylic sheet for baths in line with cost increases. ICI had apparently decided to keep prices down in order to establish a greater usage. Prices of acrylic for other uses had increased faster. Over the previous 12 months, however, prices for bath acrylic had been raised substantially (62% for white and 40% for colours). Unless competition from continental manufacturers forced ICI to keep prices down, it was thought that increases in the future would be of the order of 15—20% annually, although little was known of the economics of ICI production.

From Jupiter management Vogue had established that production cost for plastic baths varied mainly with the quantity and quality of the acrylic used. Although Jupiter's output was so far quite small, the unit received the maximum discount from ICI for large quantity purchasers, so the bulk of the competitors were supplied at similar prices. Costs for Jupiter's standard shaped baths were as follows:

	£
Acrylic sheet, resin, glass fibre	10—15
Frame, hand grips etc.	4—8
Reject allowance	1
Direct labour	1
Overhead 500% on labour	5

Vogue's Outlets

The traditional outlets for baths were builders' merchants. Vogue supplied its baths through members of the British Federation of Builders' Merchants of which there were 3,000, the majority of whom handled cast-iron baths. Many were extremely small and of the 2,400 supplied by Vogue, fewer than 700 had reasonable showrooms. Only forty or fifty of the largest dealt in steel baths.

The merchant usually added 65% to 75% to his works purchase price for showroom sales to individuals, but out of this he would pass 10% to 20% of his selling price on to the plumber. Builders installing a number of baths received a larger discount, but would not be supplied from the merchant's stock. The merchant would quote a price for delivery ex-works with his own margin depending on the size of the contract. His margin could vary from $1\frac{1}{4}$% for a large contract to 10% for a few baths.

Vogue estimated that builders' merchants had carried about one month's supply of cast-iron baths in early 1974, but had subsequently begun to destock, thus multiplying the market fall-off at the factory level.

The largest chains of builders' merchants were the Tilling Group, United Builders' Merchants and the Sankey Group. Of the three, the most creative in bath merchandising had been UBM. In 1973 they developed a concept of 'Home Plan' presentation of a full bathroom suite in a limited range of styles and colours. Purchasers of Home Plan were promised 6 weeks' delivery instead of the more usual 6 months at that time. A lot of sales resulted, but only 30 of the planned 100 showrooms were running by mid-1975. UBM had recently discussed with Vogue the possibility of obtaining its own brand, but had not pursued the idea. As opposed to UBM, the Tilling Group with a larger unit sales volume had consistently emphasised the low end of the market, selling 70% in standard white baths.

Home improvement centres, bathroom centres, and even bathroom boutiques were beginning to find a place in bath purchasing. Unlike builders' merchants, these outlets were found alongside other retail stores and sometimes in a prime site in the centre of the High Street. They tended to stock a wider range of plastic baths. Firms supplying these outlets usually also supplied builders' merchants, but Vogue was reluctant to make any major steps into new outlets for fear of upsetting the Federation of Builders' Merchants who were responsible for much of Glynwed's other sales. Among the builders' merchants, the fifth in size had moved into the High Street with Do-It-Yourself centres and also into cash-and-carry. Most innovation, however, had come from other types of outlet.

Vogue's marketing director believed that bathroom display centres would expand in numbers and that department stores would devote more attention to bathroom displays. Higher class stores such as Harrods, Heals and Debenhams were particularly moving in this direction and there were already about 50 specialist bathroom display centres. In Manchester, Elegant Bathroom had established a 4-floor bathroom display store near Piccadilly Gardens selling direct to the public. This was the only outlet buying directly from Vogue. But, like the other centres, it also bought from builders' merchants who acted as factors.

Vogue's Range, Colour and Pricing Policies

The Vogue range was divided into three groupings of standard, luxury and super-luxury baths. There were nine models in the standard group, five in the luxury group, and three in the super-luxury group as listed in Exhibit 6. Prices were quoted for quantities of any models in any one order of 50 units or above, 25 to 49 units or below 25 units. For models in the standard range price per unit rose approximately 10% below 50 units and below 25 units a further 20%. For the luxury range the steps were smaller and uneven, but averaged around $7\frac{1}{2}$% for each step. Price did not change at all for quantity in the super-luxury range.

All prices were subject to a $2\frac{1}{2}$% cash discount if payment was received by the end of the following month. Discounts were also given on standard baths according to the annual volume of the builders' merchant. These discounts had been matched by Carron Company. Numbers of merchants receiving these volume discounts were as follows:

| | | 1974 Unit Sales | | |
Discount on List Price	Number of Merchants	Standard	Luxury	Total
7½%	3	60000	13000	73000
5%	1			
2½%	14	60000	13000	73000
1¼%	18			
		120000	26000	146000

Exhibit 6 *Prices of the Vogue Range August 1975*

	Prices for 50 or more units or any quantity for super-luxury		
Standard Range	White £	Group 1 £	Group 2 £
Vogue 54	38.50	—	—
Vogue 60	30.55	33.65	—
Vogue 66	30.55	33.65	38.75
Atlanta 1700	30.55	—	—
Vogue 72	38.20	42.20	48.45
Atlanta 60S	36.70	—	—
Vogue 60 Twingrip	38.50	42.25	46.45
Vogue 66 Twingrip	38.50	42.80	46.45
Vogue 72 Twingrip	45.45	50.00	55.00

Luxury Range	White and Group 1 Colours £	Groups 2 and 3 £
Harmony 66	50.10	54.50
Caribbean 1700	45.45	48.25
Caribbean 1800	60.85	65.35
Mayfair 1700	59.15	63.85
Mayfair 1800	75.65	81.80

Super Luxury Range	White and Groups 1–3 £	Penthouse £
Elysian 1840	271.60	361.10
Florida 1700	69.75	110.00
Bahama Corner Bath (Plastic)	166.95	—

The cheapest bath had a basic list price excluding VAT of £30.55 for 50 or more units of the standard white Vogue 60, 66 or Atlanta 1700 styles as shown in Exhibit 6. The style numbers referred to lengths in inches or millimetres. Prices then rose for size, style or colour variations. For pricing purposes colours were classed as Groups 1, 2 and 3, and Penthouse, as follows:

Group 1	Primrose	*Group 3*	Wychelm
	Pink		Autumn
	Turquoise		Flamingo
	Sky Blue		
Group 2	Pampas	*Penthouse*	Beige
	Sun King		Night Blue
	Avocado		Tan
	Honeysuckle		Deep Turquoise Green
			Dark Plum

Over the previous three years Carron had led Vogue in price increases, because unlike Vogue they were below the size of company required to gain prior approval from the government for price increases. Nevertheless, Vogue marketing staff felt a continual pressure from the financial side to increase prices to cover the escalating labour, material and overhead costs, hence increases had been instituted approximately every three months, roughly doubling prices over three years. The most recent price increase in August 1975 raised the level 13% above that ruling at the beginning of the year.

Vogue's Sales and Promotion Activity

Vogue operated a regional sales organisation calling principally on builders' merchants. There were fourteen area representatives with northern and southern regional sales managers reporting to one sales administrator. The area representative endeavoured to influence the display policy of the merchants and in doing so called on the services of Vogue's two merchandisers who designed and set up display bathrooms. Each of these merchandisers set up between 20 and 30 outlet displays a year, as well as playing a major role in Vogue's displays at shows and exhibitions. Work done for an outlet in setting up displays was charged at cost and sales representatives had generally used the argument of higher turnover to justify better display. Reply coupons requesting further information received from the public as the result of advertising campaigns had also been used in the past by the sales force as levers for expanding the display of cast-iron baths in an outlet. A substantial amount of time of the salesforce was concerned with complaints and replacements, despite the development of a separate complaints department. Vogue's spending on its salesforce was running at an annual rate of £100,000 and the complaints section cost around £30,000. The sales representatives were mainly in their mid-50s and generally well-known in their areas. There had been no recent sales training as most were experienced salesmen inherited with the takeover, but one particularly good salesman operating in the West Country was being used extensively for arranging and managing exhibitions. Salesmen were paid fixed salaries and a proposed move to a commission basis had been generally opposed by the salesmen in late 1973.

Expansion of cast-iron display had been the principal objective of the sales staff over the preceding eighteen months and by August 1975 there were some 400 outlets with 2 to 3 cast-iron baths on display. In 1973, with shortage of cast-iron capacity during the building boom, delivery rose to three months or more and many outlets sold their display models. It was found during 1974, when the position reversed, that showrooms had either replaced their displays or else had installed plastic baths.

During 1973 Vogue had been the top spender on advertising baths in the United Kingdom, with budget around £40,000. A similar budget for 1974 was curtailed as demand dropped off. At that point Carron came in with a massive £40,000 campaign, but dropped out again in 1975. Vogue had spent only £6,500 up to August 1975, representing a one-third share of a joint promotion with Ideal Standard and Pilkington on Ideal's Penthouse suite. This appeared in April and May with one insertion in each of *Daily Telegraph, Observer Magazine, Good Housekeeping* and *House and Garden.*

Vogue's promotional literature was limited to one brochure of 6 pages illustrating the Vogue range ("How to Get Into Vogue") and to single sheets for each model setting out measurements and specifications for builders and installers. Approximately 200,000 of the brochures were distributed in a year at a cost of under £10,000 and the single sheets were available widely throughout the building and associated industries. At one time a prestige handout entitled the "Good Bath Book" was made available to selected outlets, but this had been discontinued.

APPENDIX A
Customer Attitudes
Towards Bath
Purchases
(Extracted from 1973
Consumer Attitude
Report)

In most cases the decision to purchase was a joint one, and in some it was really a wearing away process by the wife, until the husband agreed. In some cases, the wife chose the colour, in most it was a joint decision, but the wife collected the information in brochure form and made the first visit to the showroom. The husband meanwhile dealt with the plumber, obtained estimates, and enquired about materials and about fitting a bathroom oneself.

The *reasons for purchase* were many, but fell into three main types:

necessity
replacement after time or breakage
the need for change or modernisation

Within these main types, the following reasons occurred:

(a)   Some younger respondents had bought an old house without a bathroom and were converting it bit by bit.

(b)   Some older informants had not had a bathroom and were encouraged by local Council grants to make the decision to complete a bathroom, irrespective of whether, in the end, they made use of such a grant.

(c)   When people moved into a brand new house they had to purchase a new suite. In many cases, however, the purchase was made without reference to the house buyer. One couple in Cheshire, for example, bought a new house from plans and didn't even think of asking what kind of bathroom it would be, the colour of the suite or style. They were a little disappointed when they moved in to find it was a standard and uninteresting suite, in white.

(d)   A few people had to buy a new bath or bathroom item because of breakage and either decided on one item or a whole new suite. Others renewed as they moved into another house with a bath which was very stained or when their own one had become stained.

(e)   Five in the sample built extensions or converted a small room or recess to complete a bathroom or second bathroom. These operations were often undertaken at a time in their lives when they felt they could afford to do so, or needed to do so for convenience.

(f)   Some of the older couples changed their suites in order to modernise or take advantage of a coloured suite and to take advantage of modern design improvements, such as hand rails, low sides, etc.

(g)   One or two couples had to put a new bathroom in as a Building Society mortgage stipulation.

(h)   A few informants had rebuilt their bathrooms as they were too small and had increased the accessories to include a shower unit or a bidet.

Various stimuli acted as catalysts to the decision at a particular time. The tiling needed doing as the tiles looked "shabby — so we decided on a new bath as the tiles would show up the bath . . . no, we had already had a new basin (white)". In addition, a modernised, bright bathroom was seen to be a good house selling point.

Some of the women with young children had become very concerned about a cracked lavatory pan, chipped bath or basin and hated old taps, which dripped, had lost their chrome and were difficult to clean. These had suggested change under the aegis of hygiene for the sake of the children.

A good suite was expected to last "a lifetime" — 20—30 years or more, or until one got "fed up" with it in the meantime. But durability and cost were not the only reasons why renewal was such an occasional thing. Most of the sample felt a new bathroom installation was such a great inconvenience and created such a mess that "it wasn't worth it" unless one was changing house; added to which many people thought one of the biggest provisos was finding a good and reliable plumber.

Few of the sample had merely bought a new bath, but where this was so, it was because of mishap to this one item of the suite, or because other items were in very good condition. To the large majority, a bathroom suite was perceived to be rather like other suites of household furniture, and one renewed the suite not individual items. A very good reason for this was put forth by most respondents, that one had, or had heard of people having, difficulty in matching colours, particularly over time: another reason cited was that all advertising had seemed to be for whole suites, to make a bathroom new, modern and luxurious.

There were various complaints that some things were very difficult to colour match, for example, lavatory seats to the pan, soap holders and grouting to the tiles and bath, tiles and bath, and shower curtains.

Taps and accessories were too expensive to renew frequently and so they tended to be replaced at the time of the bathroom suite, or a new bath. Some informants thought they could not put new taps on old equipment as the plumbing materials had changed over the years (the size of bore, for example) and that basins and baths could be cracked trying to change the appliances.

Once the decision had been taken, activity started in terms of finding out as much as possible about baths, plumbers, showrooms, delivery, etc. The DIY men consulted friends, workmates, neighbours about the plumbing, materials, work involved etc, while non-DIY men and the women consulted plumbers or architects, builders, etc. Only one older couple left the decision entirely to the plumber to choose and replace a white bath with another. The rest sought plumbing advice (but did not necessarily take it) and planned with the man when to start the work, how much it would cost and an idea of how much time and inconvenience was involved.

The next step seemed to be to consult brochures and home-making books and magazines, to get an impression of the range of bathroom equipment, designs, colours, materials and prices. Non-purchasers considered they would choose on colour, cost and style. However, some female informants in the sample felt cost was not as important as overall effect. This attitude depended almost entirely on economic status, e.g.:

> "Did we really think about cost? ('I did', said her husband) — no we didn't. We came in here, looked around and said yes, that's the sort of bath we like, and you didn't say anything about cost and the builder then said he could get one for half the price, and we said no, we like that design and that colour."

Informants studied and discussed the suites between themselves and then, in nearly all cases, both husband and wife had gone to one or more showrooms. Nobody felt the choice should be left to what one saw in the brochures and some couples had changed their minds about colour or design once they had seen the actual items:

"I'm not keen on just leaflets — as when you look at it, it's not at all like the picture — so we went off ours completely. We may have been able to order it, but I think you need to *see* it and feel it."

"In the brochures everything looks big, spacious, comfortable and you go and look at it and you find you hadn't noticed that there was a rough edge here and that sort of thing. And it looks more realistic in the showroom, although even that is a bigger space than you've got at home."

The wider the choice, the more the informants liked it, and those who could only choose between two models of a bath were rather disappointed.

There were a number of *restraints on choice*, which respondents became familiar with either from plumbers or at the showrooms. Although a few men had taken their plumber or architect with them to the showroom, the majority leant very heavily on the showroom staff's opinions and knowledge. The Colchester showroom, in particular, was highly praised for its helpful and knowledgeable staff and for the totally relaxed, undemanding, yet efficient atmosphere. The showroom was also the best equipped of the three and had an extensive range of styles, colours, taps, shower units, curtains, screens, accessories, and a "luxury" Victorian bathroom suite. The Edinburgh showroom was smaller, but again its staff were considered to be most courteous and helpful. In Chorley, however, disgruntled informants talked about the lackadaisical attitude of the assistants, their lack of technical and range information and what seemed a lack of interest and motivation to sell or provide service.

A bathroom suite was a large outlay for most people, particularly if new plumbing was involved and they, therefore, wished to find out as much about it as they could before they purchased. Most people considered they only bought one or two such items in their lifetimes and so they had to gain as much information as they could in order to make sensible choices.

The DIY men sometimes required technical information and fitting instructions, which they found were readily obtainable from DIY shops. Women wanted to know particularly about safety, cleaning the bath, the using of additives, whether the materials would crack and so on.

The informants themselves felt the first consideration in choice was colour, then design and materials, then price or a mixture of the former two with the latter (depending on circumstances). Constraints on choice were presented in most cases by the size of the bathroom or the area in which the bath could fit. Thus, although larger, longer, wider baths were the most desirable, the sample had to buy smaller, narrower baths than ideal in order to fit them into allotted space. Further constraints were imposed in some cases by the plumbing, where a purchaser had required taps which fitted, say, on the side and the plumber had advised against this, or where a shower was not possible seemingly because of lack of water pressure.

The colour choice seemed to be subject to personal preference, providing it was seen to be *warm* by the beholder:

"We chose the pampas for its colour. I like browns and mucky colours — you are not as limited for choice of decor, towels etc. The bathroom doesn't look cold nor does the 'loo'. Bathrooms can be so stark — my husband is not a fussy type of person . . . so it's plain, and the tiffany lampshade is my bit of 'frill' — the bathroom should be fitted out like a room I think, like in the brochures . . . not a room to put the bath and tiles in."

White bathrooms were not only considered to look cold to most, but were psychologically lower in temperature than coloured ones:

"The coloured ones look warm and the colour is most restful. You don't see the condensation either."

White was only chosen where the bath itself was all that was required, where economy was the main priority, or where the couple felt white suites were preferable so that one could add colour and pattern to the room by furnishings. Coloured suites were required to colour-match well and to be warm looking, bright and clean. Although a number of the sample had pink, blue, primrose or lilac bathroom suites, the deeper, non-pastel shades tended to be preferred, or the more unusual colours, such as avocado, sun king, pampas, turquoise, honeysuckle, orchid, wine red, deep blues, greens and browns, purple and orange. Younger people and those with more dynamic general attitudes tended to like the modern colours rather than the pastels. Ideally, most of the sample would aspire to blacks, navy, dark blue, dark green, wine, purple and other strong colours for their suites, but felt they would overpower their small bathrooms. Some of the women felt darker colours might show up dirt, soap marks and talcum powder and look perpetually "scruffy".

Most of the sample considered blue, as well as white, to be cold in colour; while some thought green and primrose were also cold, others did not. Pastel shades were considered "nondescript" nowadays and difficult in terms of matching furnishings and towels, while colours like avocado were described as "softly relaxing colour, warm and cosy, and it looks lovely with a variety of coloured towels". The marbled effect baths were described as looking dirty, and as if the scum had not been washed out, or the items were cracked.

Nearly all the informants who had bought new bathrooms pointed out that one of the major factors in choice was one totally outside their control. This was *delivery*. Once having made their decision on style, colour, size and price range, and returning to the showroom or informing the plumber, they were then tremendously disappointed to be confronted with delays of anything up to a year or more. Those with white suites did not have this problem. Only a few had been lucky enough to order coloured baths (in pastel shades) which had been in stock and delivered almost immediately. Some of these, even so, had to wait a very long time for panels.

One man pointed out that it was because a pigment making factory in Wales had burnt down, so that the pigment for the coloured suites had been long delayed. The rest felt it was utterly dishonest for showrooms and advertising to create a demand which they could not meet. A number in the sample had spent a lot of time and money in really scouring showrooms and merchants for many miles around in order to avoid installation delays.

The purchasers had been extremely disappointed to find that after having come to their initial decision to go ahead with the bathroom and then to have spent a lot of time and effort choosing the desired suite, that they were then forced to wait for unreasonable periods for the items. Most people claimed to have "booked" a plumber or decorator and then faced the delay. Those who, for example, were having several plumbing jobs done simultaneously chose something else, which was in stock. Some couples had had to change their minds over colour or design four times because it was necessary to have the suite quickly. Others decided to "stick it out" and wait for what they wanted.

Among those who were lucky enough to have their suites delivered promptly were a number who had to send pieces back or suffer chips, bad surfaces, wrong handles, etc. or wait another 6 months or more for the replacement. One or two had been delivered complete in the wrong suite colour; another had pieces which did not match, another had the wrong size delivered and three had handles fitted in the wrong way round — "there being no room to get your fingers round".

*This case was prepared by
Jules Goddard of the
London Business School.
© Jules Goddard, 1980.*

CASE 6

John D. Wood

"Dr Quine?"

"Yes, speaking."

"Good morning, Dr Quine. It's Robert — Robert Rorty. You may not remember me . . . I graduated in 1977 . . ."

"Robert! Of course I remember you. How could I ever forget you! How *are* you? What are you up to these days . . .?"

"Well, in a sense this is what I'm 'phoning you about. I'm in a bit of a fix. I've just taken a job with John D. Wood, the estate agents. As advertising director. I know next to nothing about property. You may remember that when I left L.B.S. I took a job with Phillips . . ."

"Oh yes, the auctioneers."

"Yes. I worked with them till just a month ago. Setting up their publicity department and trying to build a bigger name for them."

"Well, you seem to have succeeded. You've put them on the map. It's not just Sotheby's and Christie's now — it's Phillips' as well. I suppose you now want to do the same thing for John D. Wood?"

"Well, I'm not sure. You see, John D. Wood is pretty well-known. It has 5 offices in London and many branches in the country, particularly the south of England and now in the West Country. And it advertises every week in the quality Sundays and, of course, in *Country Life*. In the residential market, we're the fifth biggest."

"Who's bigger?"

"Knight, Frank & Rutley. Easily the biggest. With Savills, Strutt and Parker, and Chestertons between them and us."

"So how can I help?"

"Well, why don't we have croissants and coffee in Serafino's in Mount Street tomorrow morning at nine? Perhaps you could help open my mind to the possibilities of the job. At the moment, I feel I'm in danger of sinking without trace."

"My fees are exorbitant, Robert, even for John D. Rockefeller! I'll see you at nine. Till then, Robert, goodbye."

"Goodbye Patrick"

Patrick Quine, Lecturer in Marketing at London Business School, put down the 'phone, leant back in his chair and gazed out of the window, admiring Robert's nerve at fixing a breakfast appointment at 24 hours' notice. The M.Sc. Programme can't be all bad, Patrick mused, if graduates have such little respect for the value of a professor's time.

His mind then turned to the issue at hand. What *should* John D. Wood do with someone of Robert's talent? What should *Robert* do with an estate agent of John D. Wood's standing? Improve the advertising? How, for heavens sake? Or were there deeper, more strategic problems and opportunities?

Patrick wandered into his secretary's immaculate office to get some coffee.

"Sally, what would *you* do if you were an estate agent?"

"How do you mean?"

"Oh, never mind! But if you're not busy, could you get hold of a selection of estate agency ads from a recent *Sunday Times* and *Country Life*. You know the sort, 'A most attractive listed period house in lovely elevated rural position, with superb detached triple garage and studio flat over.'"

By 10 o'clock, Sally had gathered a selection of recent advertisements for the five leading estate agents. These were John D. Wood's:

JOHN D WOOD

FINAL REMINDER AUCTION SALE ON 19TH MAY, ACACIA ROAD, ST. JOHN'S WOOD, NW8

EXCEPTIONAL DOUBLE FRONTED DETACHED HOUSE. CARRIAGE DRIVE. SOUTH FACING GARDEN. 8 BEDROOMS. 5 BATHROOMS. 2/3 RECEPTION ROOMS (DRAWING ROOM 40ft. x 18ft.). RECEPTION HALL. DOMESTIC QUARTERS. DOUBLE GARAGE. EYRE ESTATE LEASE.

103 PARKWAY, REGENT'S PARK, N.W.1. 01-267 3267

BRYANSTON MEWS WEST, W1 £117,500
Attractive modern house off Bryanston Square, built some 15 years ago to a high specification with spacious accommodation in a quiet residential location. 3 bedrooms, bathroom, double reception room, kitchen, double garage, CH. Lease 105 yrs.

EATON MEWS SOUTH, SW1 £157,500
Bright modern South facing mews house, specially designed for present owner, with good sized first floor reception room in quiet mews close to Eaton Square. 4 beds., 2 baths., 2 recep. rms., kitchen, cloakrm., garage. CH. Lease 38½ yrs.

ST. JOHN'S HOUSE, SMITH SQUARE, SW1 £152,500
Very spacious light and bright maisonette ideal as family accommodation (for M.P. etc. 3 mins. walk from Houses of Parliament. 7 beds., 2 baths., 2 recep. rms., large kitchen, CH. Porter. Lease 40 years.

EATON PLACE, SW1 £55,000
A delightful quiet 2nd floor flat in good decorative condition in well converted period property in heart of Belgravia. Double bedroom, bathroom, reception room, kitchen, CH. Lift, caretaker. Lease 55 years.

23 BERKELEY SQUARE, MAYFAIR, W.1. 01-629 9050

MALLORD STREET, SW3 £167,500
Just in the market a low built family house on ground, first & second floors only with a south facing garden and garage. 5/6 bedrooms, 2 bathrooms, drawing room, dining room, study, nursery, kitchen. Garage. Gas CH. F'hold.

CHELSEA GREEN, SW3 £145,000
An attractive freehold house on ground & 2 upper floors with a sunny roof terrace with an open aspect to the south and west. 3/4 bedrooms, 2 bathrooms (1 en suite), Drawing rm., dining rm., study, fitted kitchen, Gas C.H. F'hold.

SOUTH KENSINGTON, SW7 £129,500
A superb small house with a sunny garden facing west & a garage. 5 bedrooms, bathroom, cloakroom, attractive drawing rm., dining rm., excellent fitted kitchen & full CH. Ready for immediate occupation. Freehold.

HURLINGHAM, SW6 £145,000
A most attractive and well modernised family house with a 50ft. garden facing south-west. 6 bedrooms, 3 new bathrms., drawing rm., dining room, study, superb fitted kitchen and breakfast room, cloakroom. Full gas CH. Freehold.

FIRST FLOOR OVERLOOKING GARDENS, SW3 £130,000
Elegant flat with superb entertaining space in good decorative order. 4 bedrooms, 2 baths. (1 en suite), drawing room, dining room, very large hall, fitted kitchen, lift. Caretaker. Ind. gas CH. Recommended. 65 years.

CRANMER COURT, SW3 £175,000
Seventh floor flat of exceptional light & space in this prime block 5 minutes from Sloane Sq. & Sth. Kensington. 4/5 bedrooms, 2 bathrooms, sep. w.c., drawing room, dining room, study/bed., 6, large kitchen, Lift, C.H, C.H.W. Porter. 92 years.

REDCLIFFE SQUARE, SW10 £65,000
Attractive second floor flat with impressive views over square gardens & gardens of The Little Boltons. 3 bedrms., bathroom, large reception room, kitchen, Entryphone, use of square gardens, very low outgoings, 55 years.

HARCOURT TERRACE, SW10 £65,000
Ground floor flat which has been modernised and redecorated in this very popular and attractive street of period houses. 2 bedrooms, bathroom, reception room, bathroom, Ind. CH & HW. Very low outgoings. 71 years.

9/11 CALE STREET, CHELSEA, S.W.3. 01-352 1484/7701

HEREFORD ROAD, W2 £135,000
An early Victorian family house of great character. Recently modernised and in good order. 3 reception rooms, large kitchen, 4 bedrooms, 2 bathrooms, cloakroom, utility room. Delightful garden. CH.

BOLINGBROKE ROAD, W14 £67,500
A robust and spacious Edwardian house, well maintained, with 2 high ceilinged reception rooms, 4 bedrooms, kit., bathroom. Large area in basement ideal for playroom opening on to a good sized garden.

LEDBURY ROAD, W.11 £33,000
Attractive newly decorated first floor flat just north of Notting Hill. L shaped reception, kitchen, double bedroom, bath. Low outgoings. New fitted carpets. 97 years.

CHENISTON GARDENS, W8 £72,500
Light & cheerful 2nd & 3rd floor maisonette. Good reception room (19ft. x 19ft.), kitchen, cloak., 3 bedrooms, bath. Quiet position just south of Kensington High Street. 90 years.

ABBOTSBURY ROAD, W14 £157,500
Holland Park entrance yards away. In exceptionally good order, this 4 bedroom, 2 bathroom house has a playroom, super kitchen & large dining room all on the ground floor opening into a delightful sunny garden. CH. 80 years.

HILLGATE PLACE, W8 £110,000
South facing sun terrace amongst flowering cherry trees, a super principal bed and bath en suite, 2 good recep. rms. and a big well fitted kit. 2 more beds and bath. Good order. CH.

WEST KENSINGTON COURT, W14 £49,500
A cheerful ground & first floor maisonette with a well proportioned drawing room in excellent decorative order. 3 bedrooms, bathroom, kitchen, porter, CH. 95 years.

GLOUCESTER TERRACE, W2 £45,000
On the 3rd floor of a well modernised period house a 2 bedrm. flat in good order with a 21ft. x 16ft. recep. rm. Balcony. Lift. CH. 92 years.

162 KENSINGTON CHURCH STREET, W.8. 01-727 0705

ROWENA CRESCENT, SW11 £47,250
Fully modernised and well decorated Victorian terraced house in this popular quiet road close to Battersea Park Road. Double recep. 25ft. x 13ft., kit./breakfast rm., 3 beds., bath, Garden. Gas CH.

ADJACENT TO BATTERSEA PARK, SW11 £105,000
Superb family house in excellent condition with spacious, well arranged accommodation in a quiet road within minutes of the Park, and extremely close to Chelsea. Dbl. recep. rm., dining rm., 5 beds., 2 baths., kit. Sunny gdn. Gas CH.

ROSENAU CRESCENT, SW11 £85,000
Fully modernised Victorian terraced house in superb decorative order close to Battersea Park with an elegant drawing rm., 27ft. x 13ft., skillfully designed fully fitted kitchen/dining rm., 2 baths. Cellar. Gas CH. Garden 21ft. x 18ft.

URSULA STREET, SW11 £67,500
Situated in this very popular residential area close to Battersea Park, an extremely well decorated house benefitting from a double recep. rm., 26ft. x 13ft., french windows lead to a large west facing gdn. 3 beds., bath., dbl. recep. rm., kit./b'fast rm. Front/rear gdn., car port. Gas CH.

201 BATTERSEA PARK ROAD, S.W.11. 01-228 0174

JOHN D WOOD

SOUTH NORFOLK
Diss 9 miles. Norwich 15 miles.
Ipswich 30 miles. London 115 miles.

TO BE LET UNFURNISHED—A CHARMING
COUNTRY HOUSE, QUIETLY SITUATED OVER-
LOOKING FARMLAND.
Entrance hall, hall, dining room, kitchen/break-
fast room, rear lobby, utility room, small annexe
room. 4 bedrooms, 1 small bedroom, bathroom.
Garage. Small Garden. Swimming Pool. Well
situated with fast road and rail links to London.
Ideal for Company Executive or Private Residential Use.
Berkeley Square Office (Ref. AHBS)
23 BERKELEY SQUARE, LONDON W1X 6AL.
01-629 9050   Telex 21242

From: *The Sunday Times*

COUNTRY LIFE—NOVEMBER 27, 1980   SUPPLEMENT—9

JOHN D WOOD
In The West Country

John D. Wood are pleased to announce the formation of a
West Country Partnership with Gribble, Booth & Taylor, who have
eleven offices in Devon and Somerset.
The new Partnership will be

JOHN D. WOOD, GRIBBLE, BOOTH & TAYLOR

The local partner is Patrick Sellar,
who will be dealing with prime
Country properties and estates in
The West Country.

The new partnership will be at
61 East Street, Taunton, Somerset;
Telephone: Taunton 78111/2.

23 BERKELEY SQUARE, LONDON W1X 6AL. 01-629 9050
TELEX 21242

Also in The City of London, Chelsea, Kensington, Regents Park,
Southampton, Edinburgh, Harpenden, Winchester, Battersea and Paris.

Martin & Pole, John D. Wood   are in the Thames Valley

1   *100 Great Adver-
tisements*, edited by Barry
Day; Times Newspapers,
Mirror Group Newspapers,
Campaign, 1978.

"What do you think of them, Sally?"

"A bit plonky, aren't they? And they're all the same as their competitors."

"Do you remember those marvellous Roy Brooks ads? Brilliantly written. There's one in this book[1] . . . yes, here it is:

ROY BROOKS ADVERTISEMENT

£5,995 FHLD! Broken-down Battersea Bargain. Erected at end of long reign of increasingly warped moral & aesthetic values it's what you expect - - hideous; redeemed only by the integrity of the plebs who built it—well. Originally a one skiv Victorian lower-middle class fmly res. it'll probably be snapped up by one of the new Communications Elite, who'll tart it up & flog it for 15 thou. 3 normal-sized bedrms & a 4th for an undemanding dwarf lodger, Bathrm. Big dble drawing rm. B'fast rm & kit. Nature has fought back in the gdn - - & won. Call Sun 3-5 at 21 Surrey Lane, S.W.11. then Brooks.

. . . they don't make them like that any more, do they?"

Patrick's coffee was now cold. Sally stoically went to make him another cup. He now remembered having recently filed a press cutting on American plans to bring franchising into the real estate market in Britain. He retrieved it. It was from 'Marketing Week' on August 28, 1980:

Franchising comes to UK real estate
By Hugh Tompson
First it was take-away food, then it was money shops and now the American franchise machine is about to hit another great British institution — the estate agent. In October, Realty World will begin its television launch in the Granada area. If that succeeds, the Realty bandwagon will roll into the Yorkshire and Southern areas.

Tom Collins, who hails from Michigan but has been a successful corporate insurance salesman for eight years, has researched the prospects for over a year. "As the property market goes down, our timing becomes even better", he says. "For right now, estate agents have time to listen and are worried about the future. Franchising is the answer."

Estate agencies' real costs are in promotion and office management. Franchising will offer the individual estate agent the lowest cost per thousand advertising tool, television. As well a packaged and taught management system.

In the States, 40 per cent of all homes are bought and sold through franchises, as are 30 per cent of all retail goods. It has been estimated that in five years the top ten real estate franchises will have completely sown up the market. Century 21 is the market leader, with 7500 outlets, and seven year old Realty World is one of the next biggest, with 2800 offices in North America. They are expanding at a rate of 60 a month.

Tom Harrison is leading the Realty team in the UK. Already, a training school has been set up in Leeds and "various parties are talking seriously. We will offer a better service with computer matching, eventual nationwide coverage and a one-year guarantee on all our houses, covering everything including the plumbing and wiring," Harris says. "In America, Realty goes further and offers a surveying, finance and insurance package."

"We are only interested in successful agents, ones with a share of the market to build on and protect. And they are the ones who are most interested in us. They didn't get successful by being blind to new ideas," says Harris. The company hopes to launch with 40—50 outlets.

Already, large estate agency chains such as Fox and Sons in the South West, Whitgates in Yorkshire and Mann and Co. have shown the smaller estate agents the marketing power and consumer confidence which can derive from being part of a larger group. But a spokesman from the RICS the main professional body for British estage agents, says: "I can't see it working. Commission in the States is 10 per cent, while here it is only one-to-three per cent. The cake isn't big enough to cut up. Selling houses is not like selling hamburgers. A completely different and individual service is necessary."

Replies Tom Collins: "If the commission was higher then agents wouldn't need us. The big image, the projection, brings customers to the customers. Although we demand certain standards the agent keeps his individuality. Its not a case of wall to wall Realty."

In America, even legal services are being franchised. And in Britain it is accepted that in banking, another serious service area, the large image is the most successful. Overheads, if nothing else, will force the paper-intensive agents to look to ways of plugging into bigger computerised systems.

Other American franchises with equally high hopes have come to Britain (Orange Julius and Dunkin Donuts, for example) and failed. It has not always been the story of the triumphant McDonalds gravy train.

"Per capita, there are five times more estate agents in the States," says Tom Harris. "The competition demands franchises. Because there are less market tools being used in Britain — billboards, press and television — we expect our units to be much more profitable." Realty World is also looking at South America, Mexico and Japan.

The introduction of franchising, Realty hopes, will raise the ante for would-be estate agents and thereby help protect the franchises. In America, they pay between $7000 and $12000 for the privilege.

Universal McCann were chosen as the agency to run the Granada launch. "In advertising, all that matters is the lift-off the launch gives. It's immaterial what the product or the industry is," says Harris. "One sure thing in franchising is that if you are the first to successfully launch, then no-one ever catches you up."

On re-reading this article, Patrick became convinced that the estate agency business was ripe for structural change. He reflected that it was one of the only service industries in Britain to have gone through the '70s unscathed by the kind of dramatic changes that had hit retailing, banking, restaurants, cinemas, and many other services.

2 *Charges, Costs and Margins of Estate Agents*, Price Commission, Cmnd. 7647, HMSO, August 1979.

Excited, but not convinced that franchising was the answer, Patrick walked down to the library to see what he could find on the economics of the estate agencies. In no time he found himself browsing through a 1979 Price Commission report on the industry.[2] He soon realised that this was what he was looking for. It was broken down into nine main sections:

1.   The Market
2.   Consumer Attitudes
3.   Competition
4.   Services Provided by Estate Agents
5.   Methods of Charges

6.   Levels of Charges
7.   Estate Agency in Other Countries
8.   Comparison of Sole Agency and Multiple Agency
9.   Profitability

In Patrick's view, the most relevant findings in each of these nine sections were as follows:

1.   The Market

1.   Estate agents operate mainly in the market for second-hand houses which has three principal characteristics — long-run growth, uneven flow of business in the short term and rising prices.

2.   In the long term, estate agents are operating in a growing market. As a proportion of all dwellings in England and Wales, owner-occupier dwellings have increased from about 10 per cent in 1914 to over 55 per cent. Between 1951 and 1976 the number of owner-occupied dwellings rose by 156 per cent. Similarly, the number of second-hand houses coming on to the market each year throughout Great Britain, rose from 685,000 in 1971 to 710,000 in 1976. Further growth to 790,000 by 1981 and 860,000 by 1986 is expected.

3.   The underlying growth in the market is overlaid, in the short term, by considerable fluctuation in the volume of transactions. One reason for this is a seasonal pattern, under which house sales often dip in the first quarter of the year. The second and more important reason is a cyclical variation: for much of the time there is either a buyer's market or a seller's market but, at certain points, a substantial supply of houses for sale is matched by demand and a surge in transactions occurs. These peak periods, which bring high income to most estate agents, typically last only a number of months.

4.   The incomes of estate agents are directly affected by movement in house prices as well as by fluctuations in the volume of house transactions. This is because most estate agents adopt some form of *ad valorem* charging, so that as house prices rise the fees charged by estate agents also rise.

5.   There appears to be a long-term tendency for house prices to rise in relation to the general price level. In the short term, however, there are considerable fluctuations in the relationship between house prices and retail prices. For example, over the 10-year period 1969—78 house prices increased by 233 per cent and retail prices by 187 per cent, but between 1973 and 1978 retail prices rose by 111 per cent compared with a 52 per cent increase in house prices.

6.   There is no reason to believe that estate agents have any effect on the general level of house prices in the long term, although they may affect the speed with which prices adjust to a new, stable level after a change. The sharp increase in house prices in 1972 to 1974 was not a purely speculative boom engineered by estate agents, but was caused mainly by increased personal disposable income.

7.   We estimate that, at the present time, there are about 6,600 firms of estate agents with some 11,500 branches in England and Wales and that estate agents as a whole have about 70 per cent of the market for housing transactions. Most other house sales are accounted for by the do-it-yourself vendor, with the commonest method of finding a buyer being personal contact or newspaper advertisement.

8.   There are two main forms of estate agency; sole agency and multiple agency, and the country is sharply divided (by a line between the Severn and the Wash) according to the relative importance of each of them.

9.   *Sole Agency*: the vendor places the property for sale with one firm of estate agents, with or without a sole agency agreement under which the vendor

undertakes (usually for a specified period) not to instruct any other agent to sell the same property. The vendor is not liable to pay commission if he sells the property privately, unless he has also granted *sole selling rights* to the agent, in which case commission is payable however the property is sold.

10.   *Multiple Agency*: the vendor places the property for sale with two or more agents separately and the whole of the commission is payable to whichever agent effects the sale, the others receiving nothing. If, meanwhile, the vendor sells the property privately, he is not normally liable to pay commission to any of the estate agents instructed.

11.   There are two other relatively unimportant methods of estate agency. *Joint Sole Agency*: the vendor instructs two principal agents to act for him in co-operation with each other. The fee, which can be more than the fee payable to a single agent, is shared between them. *Sub-Agency*: normally the vendor places the property with one (principal) agent, who appoints one or more sub-agents to co-operate with him. If a sub-agent is instrumental in effecting a sale, he shares the commission with the principal agent in proportions agreed between them.

13.   The largest organisations representing the interests of estate agents are:

> The Royal Institution of Chartered Surveyors (RICS)
> The Incorporated Society of Valuers and Auctioneers (ISVA)
> The National Association of Estate Agents (NAEA).

For membership of the RICS and the ISVA, it is necessary to pass prescribed examinations. All three associations require members to have a degree of practical experience. The majority of practising estate agents are members of one or more of these organisations, which all have rules of conduct which reflect an awareness of the need to maintain high standards of behaviour in business dealings.

14.   In addition to the three main ones, there are several much smaller associations: nevertheless a large number of practising estate agents do not belong to any representative body.

15.   Sales of domestic (residential) property provide the major source of income of estate agents (nearly 60 per cent of total income in our sample), but some agents handle commercial property also and many provide a variety of other services such as structural surveys and valuations, property management, auction sales, letting, planning and development, compulsory acquisitions and architectural design services.

2. Consumer Attitudes (amplified in Exhibit 1)

16.   Our consumer survey showed about three-quarters of buyers and sellers operated through estate agents. The majority of buyers and sellers said they were likely to use estate agents again. Further questioning of sellers, who pay the estate agents' fees, showed that over 70 per cent were satisfied with various aspects of the services they received, except with regard to the value for money obtained, with which only 45 per cent were satisfied.

17.   Estate agents were thought to play an important role in recommending prices, but a lesser role in advising on the acceptance of an offer. It was apparent that the property-selling public is not very well-informed on the length of time needed to sell property — either to the 'acceptance of offer' stage or to the point when contracts are exchanged.

18.   The main services estate agents provided were seen as preparing descriptions of properties, advising on prices and the dissemination of this information

to prospective buyers by various methods. Only a small proportion of purchasers were actually accompanied by estate agents when viewing properties, or were provided with additional advice.

19.   The great majority of sellers had the terms of business explained by their agents and three-quarters were finally charged as quoted, most of the remainder receiving no quote. The majority were charged a percentage fee which ranged from under 1 per cent to over 3 per cent of the selling price. If no sale was effected through the agent most clients expected to pay no fee, but 27 per cent expected to pay an expense of some kind. More surprisingly, 12 per cent of buyers were charged a fee by their agents although most did not know what this charge represented.

3.   Competition

20.   In 1969 the Monopolies Commission established that, in over 90 per cent of cases, estate agents charged the scales of fees laid down by national or local associations. The Commission made recommendations which led to the discontinuance of such scale charges, with the intention of encouraging price competition. Recognising that many agents would not easily set aside a long tradition, the Commission looked to new entrants to provide competition and warned against the creation of institutional restraints on entry.

21.   It is relatively easy to set up in business as an estate agent. There is no regulation of numbers of estate agents or of their qualifications and initial capital requirements remain modest. We estimate that about 20 per cent of estate agents now in business started during the past five years. Building up a secure position in a local market is, however, a more difficult matter. The reputation of existing agents makes it difficult for newcomers to attract vendors and the cyclical pattern of house sales also inhibits successful entry.

22.   Our study suggested that there has been an increase in the number of offices or branches in the last decade. Some of these are a result of established firms opening new branches, or experienced employees or partners leaving existing agencies and setting up in business for themselves. Far more effective in terms of increasing local competition are entirely new firms which bring professional marketing skills into estate agency. Commercially orientated new entrants actively seek vendors, using more aggressive sales techniques which are often contrary to the spirit, if not the letter, of national professional and local association rules. Since rules apply only to members of the professional associations, these practices are spreading and successful entry is becoming easier.

23.   Competition between agents takes three main forms: fees, promotion techniques and service. The first of these is not very common. Usually we found that each local market has its fee norm which is effectively a maximum and, where competition is weak, a minimum. Where competition does occur, fees are frequently subject to negotiation. Some firms under-cut the local norm and this is a fairly common tactic for new entrants. Competition on promotional techniques is more widespread. In areas where traditional estate agency practice prevails, agents normally compete only on service.

24.   Although common scale charges have been discontinued, competition between many estate agents is still influenced by the terms of membership of the national and local associations to which they belong. There is a clear distinction between the rules of the ISVA and the RICS on the one hand and those of the other representative bodies. The former can be divided into two groups: those providing a measure of consumer protection and those which affect competition (such as rules on advertising, soliciting and supplanting).

25.   Thirty-four local associations have agreements registered with the Office of Fair Trading. Many of their terms are similar to, or taken verbatim from, the rules of the ISVA or RICS. (A number of other unregistered local agreements exist.) Examination of the registered agreements suggests greater attempt to regulate competition than is contained in the rules of the national associations; e.g. by restrictions on charging, advertising, supplanting, canvassing, co-operation with other agents and restraints on opening hours.

26.   There is, however, little doubt that competition in estate agency has increased during the present decade, since the 1970 Order[3] against common scale charges and the growth of commercially orientated firms. But the degree of change and consequently the current strength of competition varies widely from one local market to another.

3   The Restriction on Agreements (Estate Agents) Order 1970; SI No. 1696 (1970).

4.   Services Provided

27.   Over the UK as a whole, we did not find much variation in the type of service given by estate agents. Except in Northern Ireland and, to a lesser extent in Scotland, most agents confirm in writing their own terms of business and the instructions received from a vendor. The great majority, throughout the UK, inspect a property and take details of its description and measurements. Most agents include a photograph of the property in the details provided for purchasers, although this service is notably less common in London than elsewhere.

28.   Most agents advise on the method of sale and on the asking price, but by no means all are prepared to show potential purchasers around a property. Arranging appointments to view and handling negotiations are services normally available from the bulk of agents, although sole agents are less likely to arrange viewing appointments than those operating on a multiple basis.

29.   Except in Greater London and, to a lesser extent in Scotland, local press advertising is usual. National advertising is significant only in London and in Scotland, where advertisements by agents in the Scottish national press are fairly prevalent. 'For Sale' boards are a common feature in some regions, but not in others.

30.   Most estate agents send lists of individual schedules of properties to potential purchasers, although this service is less common in Scotland and Northern Ireland. Window display of property is a normal feature of the services provided, but again is less frequent in Scotland than elsewhere.

31.   Assistance to purchasers consists mainly of advice on such matters as mortgage facilities, a suitable solicitor and insurance problems. Very few agents are instructed to find a property.

5.   Methods of Charging

32.   Nearly all estate agents (95 per cent) throughout the UK use a method of charging which is directly related to the selling price of the house — *ad valorem* fees. There are two main forms: a simple *ad valorem* fee (e.g. 2 per cent of the selling price) and a tapered *ad valorem* fee (e.g. 2.5 per cent of the first £10,000 and 2 per cent of the excess over that figure). The permutations of percentages and cash bands in tapered tariffs can vary considerably. The remaining 5 per cent of agents use one of a variety of methods which include a fixed fee, a mixture of fixed fee and *ad valorem* charge and, in a few cases, the agent has no 'normal' charge but negotiates each fee separately.

33.   Over the UK as a whole the proportions of agents using simple and tapered *ad valorem* charges are about 55 per cent and 40 per cent respectively,

and these proportions do not vary a great deal in most regions. However, in Greater London and Scotland, around 90 per cent use simple *ad valorem* and in Northern Ireland 96 per cent use a tapered tariff. In the northern sector of the country (including Northern Ireland) advertising is charged for separately in most cases, whereas in the southern sector the fee is usually all-inclusive.

34.   When a vendor agrees to give his agent sole selling rights it means the agent's fees and expenses are payable even if the property is sold privately. In other cases, the vendor may have to meet the agent's expenses only. This arrangement is a lot more common in the north than in the south, where the great majority of agents operate on the basis of 'no sale no fee'.

6.   Levels of Charges

35.   In the first quarter of 1979 the average estate agent's fee ranged from a low in Scotland of 1.5 per cent of the selling price of the average house, increasing progressively on the journey to the south where it was 2 per cent, and reaching a high of 2.4 per cent in Greater London. This means, for example, that a vendor in Greater London selling a £23,000 house (the average house price in London at the time) would typically pay his estate agent approximately £565. The amount would have been lower if sole agency was used and higher for multiple agency. In the south more people use multiple agency than sole agency, although the charge for the latter can be nearly ½ per cent less.

36.   The first quarter of 1979 was a seller's market. In a buyer's market, when it is more difficult to sell houses and more money has to be spent on advertising, the amounts would increase. These increases will, however, tend to be lower in the south than in the north. Some agents are prepared in certain circumstances, particularly where local competition is strong, to negotiate fees below their normal level.

7.   Estate Agents in Other Countries (amplified in Exhibit 2)

37.   Comparisons with estate agencies in other Western countries are difficult, since practices, charging methods, services provided and other costs associated with selling a house vary considerably from one country to another.

8.   Sole and Multiple Agency

38.   The kinds of service which are likely to be offered under sole agency and multiple agency are qualitatively different. A sole agent, relatively sure of obtaining a commission, is usually prepared to risk larger outlays on a broad service to the vendor; under multiple agency, expenditures are more cautiously incurred and the service is correspondingly more selective — speed of sale may become the most important consideration.

39.   We are unable to conclude that one form of agency is better value for money than another. Multiple agency is more costly to provide and consequently more expensive for the vendor, but it has certain advantages which may lead to a quick sale. The choice between the two, where it is available, may depend on local market conditions. However, the choice is not freely available in many parts of the country. The contrast between the south, where both methods are used, and the north, where agents practise sole agency almost exclusively, is as striking today as it was ten years ago. The reasons for this are neither simple nor easily explained, but we believe that, if there is a consumer demand for multiple agency, it should not be frustrated.

9.   Profitability

40.   We measured profitability in terms of net profit per principal (by 'principal' we mean directors as well as sole traders and partners). Return on capital employed has not been used as a measure of profitability since it is inappropriate for a service industry employing relatively little capital.

41.   Firms of estate agents were divided into three categories, namely: single office firms ('small'); other firms with an income in 1978 of up to £½ million ('medium'); and those whose income in 1978 exceeded £½ million ('large').

42.   The average income for the small firms was about £39,000 in 1978 of which 60 per cent was derived from fees earned on the sales of domestic properties. The average net profit per principal for the small firms was £8,600 in 1978 compared with around £6,000 in 1976 and £7,000 in 1977. In 1978, over two-thirds of these firms had a net profit per principal of less than £10,000.

43.   The medium-sized firms had an average of some 3.5 offices per firm and the average income per firm in 1978 was about £162,000; about 55 per cent of the income was derived from sales of domestic property. The average net profit per principal for the medium-sized firms was £12,200 in 1978 compared with around £9,000 in both 1976 and 1977. Nearly one-third of these firms had a net profit per principal in 1978 of over £15,000 and about one-quarter were between £10,000 and £15,000.

44.   The large firms had an average of nearly ten offices per firm in 1978, and an average income per firm of just over £1 million. A little under half the income came from fees on the sale of domestic properties. The average net profit per principal for the large firms was £23,300 in 1978, having been £21,500 in 1977 and £17,800 in 1976. In 1978, one-third of the firms achieved a net profit per principal between £20,000 and £30,000 and another one-third £30,000 or more.

Patrick sauntered back to his office wondering, as he went, whether the material Sally and he had gathered contained within it the seeds of a solution to Robert Rorty's problem.

Only when he sat down at his desk again did he realise that his most pressing problem was to dispose of a second cup of cold coffee without Sally knowing.

Exhibit 1
Consumer Attitudes Extracts from the Price Commission Report.
The Survey

To establish more clearly the attitudes of the public to estate agents, we commissioned the British Market Research Bureau Ltd (BMRB) to carry out a consumer survey in early 1979.

They interviewed 699 buyers and 499 sellers of domestic properties in England and Wales who had effected property transactions during the previous three years. It was established during prior group discussions and pilot interviews that respondents generally had an excellent recall of events and a high level of interest and cooperation was obtained. Below we summarise the main points. Some tables of percentages do not add up to a total of 100 per cent either because respondents were offered multiple choices, the results are rounded or we have only selected the most significant answers.

Sellers
Methods Employed

Four hundred and ninety-nine sellers were asked which methods they used and which were successful.

Per cent

	Total trying method (%)	Proportion successful (%)	Proportion unsuccessful (%)
Estate agents	80	73	7
Personal contacts	20	14	6
Private newspaper advertisements	21	9	12
Private 'For Sale' boards or posters	17	2	15
Other methods	3	2	1

Source: BMRB report

It appears that people tend not to be enterprising when selling their homes, as over two-thirds (68 per cent) tried one method of selling only.

It is interesting to note that nearly one-half of those using private advertising were successful in selling their property. Nearly three-quarters of those using personal contacts were also successful, but no doubt personal contacts were used mainly when good opportunities occurred. Although private 'For Sale' boards and posters were little used, a one-eighth success rate was achieved with this method.

Selling without estate agents tended to be more prevalent where the property was cheaper, under £10,000.

Reasons for Using Different Methods of Sale

Users of estate agents were asked their reasons for doing so. Replies were widely spread, including:

	Per cent
Convenience	27
Speed of transaction	19
Coverage/access to buyers	17
Is the normal/only way	13
They are well-equipped/know what to do	10

Source: BMRB report

When those who had not tried estate agents were asked why, the main answers were that 'they were not necessary/we sold quickly' (59 per cent) or economy/expense (30 per cent).

When the majority who did not advertise privately were asked for their reasons, most of the answers reflected inertia:

	Per cent
Left everything to the agent	27
Too much bother/inconvenience	22
Not necessary/sold quickly	22

Source: BMRB report

Of those who sold by private newspaper advertising, 52 per cent gave economy (avoiding having to pay agent's fees) as their reason. The rationale for other selling methods was not clear.

In order to cause respondents to think more deeply about their choice, a number of factors were listed which, from the results of group discussions, seemed to be important. All sellers were asked which of the factors were the more important. The answers were:

Per cent

	Those using estate agents	Those selling privately
Speed of finding a buyer	61	40
Getting a good selling price	43	35
Convenience of negotiation	28	14
Time taken up with negotiation	7	4
The cost incurred	3	21
The financial rates involved	2	1
Other factors	2	4

Source: BMRB report

Speed and a good selling price clearly emerged as the main considerations, although the cost factor was important to many of those selling privately.

What Do Estate Agents Do? Those who had sold through estate agents were then asked what services have been provided. The responses were:

Per cent

	Provided	Not provided	Not sure
Drawing up property description	92	6	2
Suggested and agreed-on price	87	12	1
Newspaper advertisements	77	18	5
Help with negotiations	74	22	4
Display of details in office	63	15	22
Provision of 'For Sale' board	62	36	2
Circulation of details via waiting list	60	16	24
Showing prospective buyers round property	30	64	6

Source: BMRB report

It is significant that agents tended to provide more services for the more expensive properties, including showing buyers around. This service was also more common in the South where, of course, house prices are also higher. 'For Sale' boards are used more frequently for cheaper properties.

How are Prices Fixed? The fixing of property prices and the agent's role in this important activity were then explored further. All sellers who sold through an estate agent were shown a card of alternative responses. This obtained the following results:

Per cent

No estate agent involvement	13
Agents suggested price — vendor accepted	42
Vendor and agent agreed price together	28
Agents suggested price — we raised it	11
Agents suggested price — we lowered it	3
Agents involved in some other way	3

Source: BMRB report

Thus the agent has a very important influence on asking prices. Only 14 per cent of these sellers positively changed the agent's suggested price, although 28 per cent claimed the price was jointly agreed.

Further probing showed that 38 per cent of sellers said they compared their properties with others in deciding the price, 23 per cent said they decided what it was worth, and 9 per cent had a valuation carried out. Forty-two per cent said they just accepted the agent's advice.

Success in Obtaining the Desired Price

Nearly two-thirds (62 per cent) of sellers through estate agents claimed they obtained the price they wanted, and 36 per cent did not. The remaining 2 per cent were not sure.

Expectations and Realisation of the Time Taken to Sell

Among those selling through agents there was a very wide range of expectations as to the length of time it would take to obtain a satisfactory offer and to exchange contracts. Extreme optimists hoped for success in a week or so and pessimists expected a delay of over six months in each case.

Per cent

	Time expected to be taken	
	To acceptance of offer	From acceptance of offer to exchange of contracts
A month or less	31	19
One or two months	19	43
Three months	18	19
Four to six months	15	5
Over six months	3	1
Not sure	14	13

Source: BMRB report

In the event a significant proportion were disappointed, particularly in the time taken to secure exchange of contracts.

Per cent

	Time actually taken	
	To acceptance of offer	From acceptance of offer to exchange of contracts
More time than expected	33	45
Less time than expected	38	11
Same time as expected	15	32
Not sure	14	12

Source: BMRB report

Estate Agents' Charges

There appears to be some ignorance among the public about estate agents' charges. Most people (86 per cent) who sold through an agent had the terms of business explained to them by the agent, and of these only 11 per cent were offered a choice of terms. Eleven per cent said no explanation was given. Agents charges were said to be calculated as follows:

	Per cent
Simple *ad valorem* percentage of price obtained for property	63
Others	27
Don't know	10

Source: BMRB report

Three-quarters of those selling through estate agents were finally charged as quoted, most of the remainder receiving no quote.

Two-thirds of those who were charged on a simple *ad valorem* basis could remember how much they paid.

	Per cent
1% or less of selling price	11
1¼% or 1½% of selling price	22
1¾% or 2%	29
2¼% or 2½%	27
2¾% or 3%	3
Over 3%	7

Source: BMRB report

If no sale was effected by the agent, 58 per cent thought they would pay no fee and 27 per cent thought they would pay expenses, a registration fee or some unspecified charge. Fifteen per cent did not know. The no sale no fee concept (contingency charging) varied by regions.

Percentage Expecting 'No Sale No Fee'

Total	North	Midlands/Wales	South	London*
58	34	47	71	82

* Small sample
Source: BMRB report

It is interesting to compare the costs incurred by those who sold property privately; 41 per cent of these sellers spent money on advertising as follows:

	Per cent
Less than £10	48
£10 to £29	24
£30 to £39	7
£40 plus	7
Don't know	14

Source: BMRB report

Satisfaction with Estate Agents

Sellers through estate agents were then asked whether they were satisfied with the services offered. The responses were listed under five headings:

Per cent

	Very or quite satisfied	*Mixed feelings*	*Not very or not at all satisfied*	*Did not reply/don't know*
Sales effort before offer	78	10	9	1
Advice on price	79	6	8	5
Effort after offer	70	6	16	6
Overall services	73	14	12	—
Value for money	45	21	32	—

Source: BMRB report

On most aspects the level of satisfaction was high — 70 per cent or more. Clients were less satisfied in terms of value for money, where less than half were very or quite satisfied. Two-thirds of those dissatisfied with value for money said the charges were not justified or that it was a lot of money for a little work. A minority of clients expressed dissatisfaction with the advice given on prices and success in obtaining them, while others said that little interest or effort was shown or that poor results were produced.

Probably the final test is the likelihood of sellers using estate agents again in the future. The answers below indicate that well over half the people asked, including those who did not use agents, will probably use estate agents' services next time, but a third are unlikely to do so.

The likelihood of using an estate agent for next sale	*Per cent Sellers*	
Very likely	34	} 60
Quite likely	26	
Not very likely	20	} 34
Not at all likely	14	
Not sure	6	

Source: BMRB report

Buying   The 699 people who had bought property during the previous three years were asked a different set of questions to establish their attitudes and practices.

How Property was Found and Bought

How Found	*Per cent*	*How Bought*	*Per cent*
Estate agents	60	Estate agents	74
Through personal contact	15	Direct from vendor	22
Private newspaper advertisements	11	Others	4
Calling at 'For Sale' boards	8		
Other/not stated	6		

Source: BMRB report

Estate agents are the main method used by buyers to find and buy a property. Their significance is particularly great in London and the South of England, and for those buying more expensive properties. However, some 40 per cent of properties were not found through estate agents and, indeed, 20 per cent of buyers did not use estate agents at all. The number of people not using estate agents was high in the North, the Midlands and Wales and where the value of the property was less than £10,000.

Reasons for Using Estate Agents

When those who found their houses through estate agents were asked why they did so the answers were as follows:

Per cent

Better choice of properties	32
Convenience	16
Agent had particular property we wanted	14
Moving to new area	9
Knew agent before	7

Source: BMRB report

As with sellers, the same group of buyers were shown a list of reasons derived from group discussions, in order to probe further their reasons for using estate agents:

Per cent

Speed in finding properties	46
Getting a good property for the money	34
Convenience of negotiation	34
Direct contact with the vendor	9
Financial risk involved	6
Costs incurred	4
Not stated	5

Source: BMRB report

It seems these buyers felt that estate agents can provide a range of houses quickly and efficiently and this is their main reason for using them.

Number of Agents Used

The number of agents used varies greatly and the difference between regions is of particular interest:

Per cent

Number of agents supplying details	Total	Midlands and Wales	North	South	London
1	21	20	38	13	20
2	12	19	10	10	8
3—5	31	30	30	37	24
6—9	19	15	9	27	18
10+	15	10	10	16	26
Don't know	3	6	3	1	4

Source: BMRB report

Buyers who had found their house through an agent were asked what services he had provided for them.

Per cent

Details by post	48
General details of all properties	37
Details by telephone	25
General advice on prices	20
Accompanied visits to empty properties	20
Accompanied visits to occupied properties	15
Looking for property	15
Introduction to solicitor	13
Introduction to a mortgage	12
Introduction to a surveyor	10
Advertising specifically	3
None of these	15

Source: BMRB report

Clearly the main function of estate agents, as far as buyers are concerned, is to supply details of properties, and other functions were performed only by a minority, a fifth or less, in each case. The extent to which buyers are accompanied on visits to properties is low and the number of introductions made to other professional help, particularly in connection with mortgages, is less than might be expected, and indeed shows this is less important than the Commission were told by the professional bodies.

Estate Agents'
Charges

The majority (83 per cent) of buyers who found their houses through estate agents were not charged by agents for their services but, perhaps surprisingly, 12 per cent were charged a fee. Most (66 per cent) of those charged did not know what the charge was for, and the remainder mentioned specific searches, telephone expenses, advertising and valuations.

Once an offer to purchase had been accepted, over half (56 per cent) of these buyers paid the agent a deposit, but two-thirds of the deposits paid were less than £200. Interest was rarely, if ever, paid on the deposit by an estate agent.

Future Intentions

Finally, all buyers were asked about their future intentions for using estate agents to buy their next home:

Per cent

Very likely	42	} 76
Quite likely	34	
Not very likely	10	} 17
Not at all likely	7	
Not sure	7	

Source: BMRB report

Buyers in the A/B social grade were more likely than average to use agents as were buyers of more expensive property and buyers living in London and the South. Conversely, the least likely were those in the lower social grades, those aged over 44 and those living in the North. However, nearly half (47 per cent) who bought without using an agent last time are likely to use one next time.

The main reasons given for deciding to use an agent in the future were:

Per cent

	Per cent
The number/range of properties available	23
Speed of transactions	20
Agent helpful and informative	10
Have (always) used agent before	7

Source: BMRB report

Exhibit 2 *Estate Agents in Other Countries*

Levels of Charges

Level of Charges in Other Countries

Country	General level of charges %	Structure of ad valorem charge
USA	6—7	simple
Canada	5—7	simple
Germany (FR)	5—6	simple
France	4—8	tapered
Italy	6	tapered
Belgium	3—5	tapered
Switzerland	3—5	mix of simple and tapered
New Zealand	2.5—5	tapered
Sweden	3—5	simple
Denmark	1.5—4.5	tapered
Spain	2—3	simple
Irish Republic	3.5 Dublin 2.5 elsewhere	simple
UK	1.5—2.5	mix of simple and tapered
Netherlands	1—2	tapered
Norway	1—2	tapered

There appears to be a strong tendency for the rates in all countries to conform to 'norms', frequently under the influence of trade associations or because of legal control. In France and the Irish Republic, for example, the rates generally charged are legal maxima. The rates in New Zealand are set by a statutory licensing authority, whilst those for Belgium and the Netherlands are the scale fees of the national trade associations. Trade associations in the USA and Canada also have a long history of rate fixing and, although the practice is now illegal in both countries, the standard charges have generally been maintained through informal mechanisms.

A number of points should be noted when considering the table above:

(a) We have been led to believe that the high charges in the USA and Canada are related to the high quality of service given. (In the USA title insurance greatly reduces the cost of conveyancing.)

(b) In the Netherlands it is common practice for both the vendors and purchasers to be charged commission by the agent, although this practice is being examined by the Ministry of Economic Affairs. Payment of the agent's fee is frequently divided between vendor and purchaser in some of the German provinces and, indeed, in a seller's market, the whole commission is often paid by the purchaser. In France, also, fees are sometimes split between vendor and purchaser.

(c) Contingency charging (i.e. the 'no sale — no fee' practice) is common in other countries.

(d) In some countries, for example Denmark, Belgium and Norway, a minimum fee is charged.

(e) The cost of advertising is included in the fee in Germany (FR), France and Sweden, and sometimes in the Netherlands.

(f) Auctioneers sell the majority of domestic properties in the Irish Republic.

Operating Methods

The main function of an estate agent is to transfer information from sellers to buyers. The most interesting method of doing so revealed by our international comparisons is through the Multiple Listing Systems operating in the USA and Canada. Under a Multiple Listing System (MLS) a number of firms in a particular local market contribute details of the properties coming on to their books to a central pool. A list of all the properties in the pool is periodically drawn up and distributed to the participant agents. Where the agent who finds the buyer is not the agent who found the seller, the commission is split between the two.

In the USA and Canada, MLSs are generally administered by local associations, or real estate boards. Over the last 30 years these local boards have developed considerable power to inhibit competition by denying new entrants access to the central pool of listings. Anti-trust action has, on occasion, been taken to curb such behaviour in the USA and similar proceedings are in prospect in Canada.

The argument in favour of the MLS approach is that it raises the efficiency with which information is transmitted from vendors to prospective buyers by increasing:

(a) the exposure given to listed properties; and

(b) the scope for computerised data handling. Given the localised nature of real estate markets, economies of scale in data handling can only be exploited to the full where different agencies in the *same area* cooperate to pool their listings. This is the kind of cooperation found within a MLS. In the UK, on the other hand, the pooling of listings (and therefore the use of computerised techniques) has been limited mainly to single firms with a string of offices in *different* local markets. The potential gains from cooperation of this sort appear far more limited.

It is arguable that market efficiency would be increased still further if sellers and buyers had direct access (for a reasonable fee) to MLS listings. This is one of the proposals currently being considered by the US Federal Trade Commission. Its implementation would substantially reduce the role played by estate agents and an alternative method of administering the system would be needed.

Industrial Structure and Franchising

In each of the countries for which detailed information was obtained, estate agency has traditionally been a highly fragmented industry, dominated by sole traders and partnerships. In North America, however, the position has begun to change rapidly in recent years, with the growth of:

(a) national real estate brokerage chains; and

(b) franchising organisations.

The main force behind the emergence of national chains has been the existence of economies of scale in advertising and promotion. These economies have become increasingly important as families have become more mobile; local brokers have been less able to rely on referred and repeat business, and advertising has become a more vital source of trade.

The franchise movement represents a response by small brokers to increased competition from national and regional chains. Each franchisee must pay an initial franchising fee (ranging from $1,000 to $10,000 in the USA), plus annual charges calculated as a percentage of gross income. In return for the fee, the broker receives:

(a) the benefit of national advertising;
(b) training at the schools run by the franchising companies;
(c) access to particulars of the properties listed with other firms under the franchise umbrella.

Many US brokers believe that the structural changes taking place in the industry are such that, in another five years, 70—80 per cent of the sales of single family homes will be controlled by fewer than ten big companies.

This case was prepared by
Shiv Mathur, of the
London Business School. It
was written with the
cooperation of
Dexion management. Facts
and figures have been
disguised to preserve confidentiality. Financial support was provided by The
British Overseas Trade
Board.
© London Business
School, 1976. Revised
1981.

CASE 7

Dexion Overseas Ltd

In November 1975, Mr John Foster, recently appointed Managing Director, and Mr Keith Galpin, Marketing Manager, of Dexion Overseas Limited (DOS), were attempting to give new direction to Dexion's overseas activities. Dexion had, over the years, grown substantially but somewhat haphazardly in its export markets and it seemed to the two managers that it was time for a full review of the company's present position and future overseas activities. They were particularly concerned with DOS's operations in Africa and the Middle East as these regions characterised the changing political and economic conditions in most of Dexion's overseas markets.

**Dexion-Comino
International Ltd**

Dexion-Comino International Ltd, was founded before the Second World War to manufacture slotted angles invented by Demetrius Comino as a solution to the recurring need for easily erectable and demountable industrial structures. What was initially jokingly referred to as "industrial meccano" soon acquired wide acceptance. Mr Comino's initial investment of £14,000 in a 4,000-square foot factory in North London had by 1968 grown into a 200,000 square-foot site at Hemel Hempstead producing well over 50 million feet of slotted angles. By 1973 Dexion was well established as a worldwide name with wholly owned subsidiaries in North America, Europe and Australia, with exports accounting for over 60 per cent of the UK factory's total turnover.

Product Range

As the group's turnover and geographic coverage had increased, so had the company's range of products. What had started as ordinary slotted angles (known as DCP — Dexion Catalogue Products) that could be erected by almost anybody, had gradually grown in sophistication. By 1975 Dexion was a world leader in manufacturing and installing complete materials handling systems.

In the developed countries the continuing search for more efficient techniques of storage and materials handling resulted in a rapid growth of the "unit load concept" (various small parts being containerised for efficient storage) — and in particular the use of pallets. Dexion systems like "Speedlock" adjustable pallet racking were developed to meet this need. The Speedlock range permitted vertical storage to a height limited only by the height of the building itself. When fitted with wheels the racks, then known as "Poweracks", could be mounted on steel rails permitting the closing down of an aisle and opening up of a new one at the touch of a switch.

By 1975 Dexion manufactured a whole family of products that served particular applications. "Apton" square tube framing had been designed for the smarter display of goods; "Clearspan" and "Impex" shelving for better storage of hand-loaded goods; and "Maxi" for storing small items. The basic

DCP range was also modified and extended to meet entirely new applications. For example, DCP products that were usually used for storage had been modified to facilitate the construction of prefabricated housing units in developing countries. The growth of new products in many instances had also produced growth for DCP products as they constituted basic ingredients of the more advanced designs.

Overseas Activities   Until 1970 overseas growth of Dexion's activities had been largely organic. As Dexion products had gained popularity, the company had set up subsidiaries in North America, Europe and Australia. In other countries of the world Dexion had appointed distributors to stock and retail the products. Where local demand was fairly substantial but import restrictions prevented direct export and circumstances did not justify a subsidiary, local manufacturers had been licensed to produce and sell some products in the Dexion range. By the early 1970s Dexion had licensing arrangements with manufacturers in various parts of the world (Exhibit 1), although few were in Africa and the Middle East.

Exhibit 1   *Licensed Product Sales, Royalty Income and Products Licensed*

Country (year of agreement)	Licensee 1974 Sales (£s)	Royalty Rates*	Products Licensed
Spain (1957)	650,000	£13,000 per annum (fixed sum)	DCP, pallet racking
Portugal (1957)	620,000	2%	DCP, Apton, Speedlock
New Zealand (1959)	210,000	2%	DCP
India (1960)	420,000	Profit participation agreement	DCP, Apton
El Salvador (1961)	50,000	4%	DCP
Canada (1964)	1,950,000	£25,000 per annum (fixed sum)	DCP and accessories
Mexico (1964)	1,170,000	2%	DCP, Apton, Speedlock
Brazil (1966)	490,000	4%	DCP, Apton, Speedlock
Argentina (1966)	160,000	4%	DCP, Speedlock
Peru (1967)	230,000	£4,000 per annum (fixed sum)	DCP
Jamaica (1968)	87,000	4%	DCP
Nigeria (1970)	490,000	4%	DCP and accessories
S. Africa (1971)	325,000	4%	DCP, Apton, Speedlock
Hungary (1971)	650,000	£65,000 (lump sum royalty)	DCP

*Expressed as percentage of turnover unless otherwise indicated.

The actual agreement varied from licensee to licensee and reflected the company's attitude at the time the agreement was actually signed. Agreements usually specified a royalty income based on a percentage of turnover, often with a minimum annual payment. Dexion had little control over the pricing and marketing policies of its licensees, though sometimes restrictions were placed on their export activities. As the majority of licensees were mainly concerned with building up strong positions in their home markets, pressure to export to third countries in competition with Dexion's own direct export activities was not a major factor. The problems as seen at Dexion headquarters were not so much of licensee exports to third country markets, but of ensuring that they developed their home markets and that licensee income due was in fact repatriated. Since many of the licensee markets had recurring balance of payment problems the actual collection of royalties was of continuing concern.

Competition with Dexion products both in the UK and overseas had multiplied. Dexion, however, had maintained its market leadership in the UK. Overseas, in adddition to budding indigenous manufacturers, Dexion was facing growing competition from Italian and Continental exporters and lately the Japanese and Indians. But Dexion products were well established and the company prided itself on having a much more comprehensive product range and better design and other back-up services than the non-European competition. Cheaper British steel gave Dexion exports a very real advantage, but it seemed that the position was gradually changing. Mr Foster was getting increasingly concerned about Japanese and subsidised Indian competition in the Middle East and the gradual erosion of the cost advantage of using steel made in Britain.

Dexion Overseas Limited

In 1970 Dexion-Comino International Ltd had set up Dexion Overseas Limited (DOS) as a separate company within the organisation to look after and coordinate its entire overseas export and licensing activities. Markets where Dexion had established subsidiaries or associates were excluded. In order to supervise distribution closely, DOS had divided the overseas market into five regions and appointed regional sales managers (RSMs) located in London to oversee Dexion's interests in each of these areas. The five regions were: (1) the Middle East and North Africa, (2) Europe, (3) the Rest of Africa, (4) the Far East and Southeast Asia, (5) the Caribbean and South America. Exhibit 2 gives DOS results for 1973 to 1975 and Exhibit 3 gives a breakdown of 1975 results by region.

Direct exports and involvement in the Far East and Central and South Europe were comparatively small. Dexion's operations in Europe were mature in nature and the increasing similarity between the UK and continental Europe in terms of competition, products and customers had gradually resulted in most of Western Europe being treated as an extension of the home market, at least so far as the existing product range was concerned. With UK entry into the EEC in 1973, this similarity between the home market and continental Europe was becoming even more obvious, although differences in channels of distribution remained.

Keith Galpin had carried out a detailed analysis of the various international markets that could provide it with substantial business in the future. This analysis had incorporated not only informed views within the company but also interpreted demographic and economic data. The attempt was to

Exhibit 2 *DOS Operating Results (£000s)*

	1973	1974	1975
Invoiced sales	5,672	6,444	6,914
Gross profits*	1,076	1,770	2,088
Variable distribution costs	156	221	290
Gross profit (after distribution costs)	920	1,549	1,798
Home office and regional expenditure	565	560	703
Operating profit	355	989	1,095
Miscellaneous income (including royalties)	94	122	136
Interest	(13)	(75)	(75)
Profit before tax	436	1,036	1,156

*After deducting transfer prices payable to Dexion-Comino International Ltd.

Exhibit 3 *Allocation of 1975 DOS Results by Region (£000s)*

	Invoiced Sales	Gross Profit	Regional Expenses
Middle East and North Africa	3,016	1,006	96
Europe	1,829	378	33
Africa	1,090	408	42
Far East	257	61	26
Caribbean and South America	426	142	49
Miscellaneous	296	93	13
Total	6,914	2,088	259
Variable distribution expenses		290	
Gross profit (after distribution)		1,798	
Less:			
Regional expenses	259		
Central expenses	133		
Marketing and promotion	104		
Administration and rent	130		
Technical	77		
Total		703	
Operating profit		1,095	

highlight not only those markets which would continue to grow, but also select those which could become major profit generators in future. This exercise had brought to light some Southeast Asian and Middle Eastern countries which could be the target for more concentrated attacks.

DOS was of the opinion that during the next five years the company's business in the oil-rich countries of the Middle East and North Africa would expand much more rapidly than elsewhere. This called for a strategy that took into account the prominent position of the region. But the company felt that such a strategy would be applicable in principle to most overseas activities of the company, and Africa generally might follow the developments in the north.

DOS's International
Policy
Markets and
Organisation

Galpin divided the Dexion market in Africa and the Middle East roughly into three kinds of buyers. *Bazaar buyers* were customers who bought mostly DCP-type products to erect small and fairly crude storage and other structural units. Though DOS had no hard data on the buying behaviour of these customers, it was generally believed that they designed their requirements themselves or with some help from local Dexion dealers. Their main criteria for buying Dexion products in preference to those of other suppliers were price and availability. The demand was more for the less sophisticated Dexion products and an important characteristic of the buyer was his lack of awareness and perhaps need for more sophisticated storage and material handling systems.

The second group were *installation buyers*. Installations could vary from small simple racking units (similar to those put up by the bazaar buyer himself) to complete warehouse units made up of products such as Speedlock pallet racking and Impex hand-loaded shelving. This type of business was invariably handled by local distributors, sometimes with the help of Dexion staff, and often required detailed designs and site construction. This design and construction service was increasingly being provided by the local distributor, although Dexion's UK-based units assisted with jobs which were outside the resources and capability of a particular distributor.

There was occasional demand for relatively large and sophisticated systems requiring special resources such as system analysis, structural design, subcontracting, contract negotiation, financing, project management, etc., outside the scope of any distributor. DOS referred to this third type of business as *project business* and it invariably involved sales and implementation resources not available locally from a distributor even when supported by a local Dexion salesman. Support of the local distributor for this type of work was by the payment of a negotiated commission.

In order to serve the growth in both installation and project business, DOS had established in London a technical services cell (see Exhibit 4 for organisation chart). The regional sales managers could refer their design problems to this unit and the cell itself undertook some marketing activities. It stayed in touch with UK-based architects, specifiers and designers to influence them to use Dexion equipment in projects they were associated with. The cell had developed over the years the expertise to quote for and supervise a wide variety of overseas projects. Its links with the regional sales managers were close.

As part of its central marketing function the DOS staff at headquarters attempted to coordinate the advertising and sales promotion campaign for Dexion products in national markets. Films, pamphlets and information material in various languages had been prepared. The marketing department together with regional staff undertook to arrange seminars in various overseas capitals aimed at specific audiences. The marketing department

Exhibit 4 *DOS Organisation Chart*

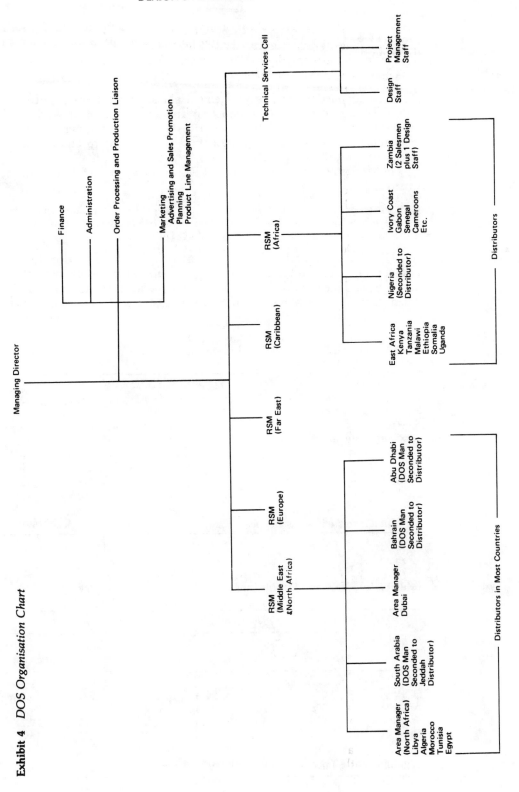

NB: Full-time distributor staff looking after DOS sales and design in Kuwait, Oman and Lebanon.

also looked after the promotion of individual products and retained staff product managers who coordinated the activities for a particular product in the regions.

Pricing DOS was supplied by the plant at Hemel Hempstead at a transfer price that reflected the direct costs of production and an allocation of works and general overheads. DOS, in turn, set prices for its distributors by adding a percentage markup to cover the cost of its own operations and provide a satisfactory profit.

In Mr Foster's view, the essence of DOS's policy on distributor pricing was:

> A question of competitive activity — we should evaluate what price competitive products are selling at and adjust our margins to account for the comparative advantages and disadvantages of Dexion goods.

Distributors in national markets were quoted different prices to take into account expected local distributor mark-up, the prices of competitive products, and the local customers' ability to pay. For example, during 1974, when transfer prices charged to DOS rose by 15 percent (Exhibit 5 (*a*)), there

Exhibit 5 (*a*)   *Increase in Transfer Price to DOS, 1974*

	Cost Increase		Percentage Costs	Increase
Steel	− 5%	on	40%	− 2.0%
Auxiliary material	20	on	35	7.0
Accessories	10	on	10	1.0
Other costs	0	on	15	0
Volume down				
30% on budget				9.0
Total increase in transfer price				15.0%

Exhibit 5 (*b*)   *DOS Product Margins (excluding project sales) (£000s)*

	1973			1974		
	Sales	Gross Profits	Percent	Sales	Gross Profits	Percent
DCP	2,079	610	29.3	2,530	874	34.5
Apton	305	120	39.3	481	164	34.1
Speedlock	1,120	238	21.3	1,347	393	29.2
Others	590	108	18.3	570	107	18.8
Total	4,094	1,076	26.3	4,928	1,538	31.2

was no corresponding across-the-board increase in prices charged to customers. European customers were charged only an extra 5 percent, while Middle East prices went up the full 15 percent in sterling prices. When the devaluation of sterling had been accounted for, however, the local prices ended up lower.

As a result of the policy of value pricing, the markups charged distributors on various Dexion products differed considerably. Exhibit 5 (b)) gives an indication of gross margins by product category. Though DOS informally indicated to its distributors in various national markets the price at which they should retail their products, it did not, and in management's view could not, lay down firm directives. This policy had both its advantages and disadvantages. The company did not retain any firm control on its prices and occasionally found distributors in well-protected or prosperous markets charging exorbitant markups. But with its flexible pricing policy, DOS had built for itself an extensive distributor network. Distributors, it was hoped would in turn set retail prices to maximise their own and consequently DOS's profits. That this did not always happen was seen as a largely unavoidable consequence of using independent companies as part of the distributor system.

Africa The Regional Sales Manager (Africa) had for administrative convenience divided the countries south of the area of Arab influence into four areas: East Africa, Zambia, Nigeria, and the erstwhile French West Africa. The four areas were roughly equal in terms of market potential and four area managers were based in convenient local capitals. Though Dexion had a distributor in virtually every African capital, choice had been limited and determined more by the distributor's general business standing and connections with the local government than by previous experience of selling products related to storage and materials handling.

Apart from South Africa and Nigeria, the region was comprised largely of developing countries with foreign exchange problems and complicated systems of tariff and exchange controls. Often there was no dearth of demand for Dexion products but a noticeable lack of buying power for foreign products. This was in the regional sales manager's view the single most important impediment in exporting to the African market. There were few areas where concentrated marketing effort could be justified. Not only was the entire region plagued by controls but it was also in a state of constant economic and political flux.

Many suppliers besides those in the developed countries had found it possible to meet the less sophisticated level of African demand. Continental, Japanese, and Indian exports abounded, but Dexion with its wide and well-established network of distribution had a firm grip and in some countries like Tanzania had almost wiped out the use of competitive products. In virtually all markets, small local manufacturers making a restricted range of generally low quality products were a continuing threat. In the regional sales manager's opinion, what Dexion had and the competition did not, were the local contacts and a name for quality and service that was well established.

It was not the overseas exporters who provided the major threat in African markets but the growing desire in most developing countries to set up their own production units. As the outlay for such a project would be about £500,000 it was well within the reach of most governments, if not

Exhibit 6 *Africa: Orders Received (£000s)*

| | 1973 | | | 1974 | | | 1975 | | |
	DCP	Other	Total	DCP	Other	Total	DCP	Other	Total
Ethiopia	32	—	32	25	2	27	16	—	16
Ivory Coast	12	—	12	5	3	8	38	7	45
Kenya	26	—	26	18	5	23	55	8	63
Nigeria	44	61	105	60	79	139	103	109	212
South Africa	3	8	11	11	9	20	16	56	72
Sudan	44*	—	44	—	—	—	—	—	—
Tanzania	—	—	—	5	—	5	18	—	18
Zambia	74*	35*	109	61*	71*	132	140*	279*	419
Zaire	5	13	18	1	2	3	—	—	—
Others									
Cameroons									
Gabon									
Ghana									
Gibraltar	85	26	111	72	29	101	49	8	57
Senegal									
Niger									
Etc.									
Total	325	143	468	258	200	458	435	467	902

* Project activity.

individual entrepreneurs. It was possible that the small African markets would not support economic production units. But there was always the possibility of some countries getting together to come to tariff arrangements to form a quasi common market or to look actively for regional exports. Some countries in East Africa and French West Africa had shown just this sort of inclination and this was seen as the thin end of the wedge at DOS headquarters.

The richer countries of Africa — Nigeria, Zambia, and South Africa — were different in their purchasing behaviour. Areas of industrial concentration had resulted in a demand for a host of Dexion products and services. To South Africa and specially Nigeria, in spite of the presence of local licensees, Dexion directly exported the more modern systems, which were not manufactured locally. In Zambia, the company had obtained a large contract to design, supply, and erect a complete materials handling and storage system. The Zambian case characterised an obvious trend in buying behaviour. Developing country governments keen to put up large industrial complexes, often with the help of overseas funds, increasingly contracted for the complete supply, design, and erection of turnkey projects.

Middle East and North Africa

The regional sales manager (Middle East) described his region:

In spite of popular beliefs it's not all gold. For us there are three to four countries that contribute most of the sales. And it would be fair to say that in most countries the results are directly proportional to the effort we put in. When I

Exhibit 7 *Middle East and North Africa — Orders Received (£000s)*

	1973			1974			1975		
	DCP	*Other*	*Total*	*DCP*	*Other*	*Total*	*DCP*	*Other*	*Total*
Abu Dhabi	73	7	80	155	25	180	285	33	318
Dubai	32	11	43	78	3	81	85	27	112
Iraq	147*	—	147	478*	2	480	209*	4*	213
Libya	377*	21*	398	356*	17*	373	252*	60*	312
Oman	18	15	33	58	80	138	130	104*	234
Saudi Arabia	65	48	113	134	247	381	257	369†	626
Bahrain	18	9	27	35	34	69	25	21	46
Qatar	9	—	9	17	3	20	25	—	25
Algeria	—	1,235†	1,235	—	47*	47	—	—	—
Others Cyprus Egypt Iran Jordan Kuwait Lebanon Malta Pakistan Syria Tunisia Yemen	94	14	108	294	29	323	91	9	100
Total	833	1,360	2,193	1,605	487	2,092	1,359	627	1,986

*Project activity.
†Projects not broken up by product groups.

say "we", I mean "we" — the local distributors have far too much on their plates and are often so badly organised that they need all the assistance we can give. The real selling force is frequent visits and resident expatriate staff — people who are willing to live in Arab countries and promote the Dexion name. And they are harder to find than you would imagine.

In spite of the massive oil revenues there was a growing inclination in some Arab countries to ban foreigners from setting up purely trading companies. The United Arab Emirates, Iraq, Iran, and Algeria had formulated, or were in the process of formulating, controls for limiting the activities of foreigners. Others like Libya, who were at that moment big customers of DCP products, had already outlined their intention to set up their own slotted angle plants to reduce the economy's dependence on imports.

Everywhere there was an explosive industrialisation underway. All over the Middle East new plants were being constructed and the host countries, while embarrassingly rich financially, lacked human skills and infrastructure to cope with the growth. Even Iraq and Algeria, while attempting to lower their reliance on foreign companies, recognised the necessity to permit foreigners to bid for and undertake large projects. In fact, almost all Dexion's business in Iraq, Algeria, Iran, and a substantial portion of that in Saudi Arabia had been obtained by negotiating large contracts. (See Exhibit 7)

Though the growth in project activity was generally welcomed by Dexion management, it had created some organisational problems. Contract negotiation took a comparatively long time and resulted more often than not in "next year's sales and this year's expenses". The regional sales managers were always under considerable pressure to maintain expenditure within agreed budgets and treated project activity with mixed emotions. However, when the organisational problems, both within DOS and with the local distributors had been overcome, the profits were very welcome. Gross profits on successful tenders in the Middle East were broadly similar to those obtained on the sale of hardware alone.

Competition in the Middle East was strongest from the Japanese, Italians, and Indians in the supply of DCP-type hardware and from Japan and Germany in the project market. The Japanese and Germans often had a slight edge on Dexion as they had been able to quote for complete turnkey projects. In Libya, DOS's distributor had established very good links with the local government and Dexion products had reached a large market share, but only by pricing below DOS's normal markup to offset the price advantage of Italian products. In Saudi Arabia and the U.A.E., which still constituted the bulk of the hardware business, DOS's response to competition had been first to pare margins and second to promote slightly more advanced systems like Speedlock. In spite of overseas and local manufacturers crowding these markets, there was still ample opportunity for all. Saudi Arabia and the U.A.E had five-year plans that budgeted a threefold increase in public expenditure — justification enough for the most forceful of selling efforts.

Alternative Possibilities With its target of achieving a 15 percent annual increase in sales and profits, DOS management was aware that a series of long-term strategic decisions had to be made. These decisions would have to encompass almost all the activities of the company and would have to bear in mind that 100 percent owned subsidiaries would be difficult to establish overseas. They included:

1. Should the company continue to license overseas manufacturers to produce the DCP range in areas of high tariffs and foreign exchange problems, or should the licensing policy be extended to cover more products and markets? In particular, should DOS agree to permit the manufacture of the Speedlock and Apton range in Nigeria?
2. If licensing was not a viable option, in view of local government hostility to royalties, should DOS look to joint ventures?
3. Another possibility could be to discontinue all overseas manufacture and cancel where possible the existing licensing arrangements and manufacture and export from the U.K., or another suitable European base.
4. Which markets should be focused on and with what products?
5. Should the existing policy be changed?
6. Was there any need to restructure the distribution strategy?

The list of issues which needed to be questioned and sorted out seemed endless. DOS management was also aware of the fact that it would be impossible to put hard figures on many of these options but Mr. John Foster felt that the data he had were reliable, in the sense that they were indicative of the situation. He was particularly aware that the issues were interrelated (e.g. the company could not have a production policy that required licensing arrangements and a marketing strategy that required distributors) and the direction that DOS's total strategy took should at least be compatible within itself.

Assessing Buyer Motivation

This case was prepared by Jules Goddard and Kenneth Simmonds of the London Business School.
© *Kenneth Simmonds, 1981.*

CASE 8
Hirondelle

First launched as a brand of wine in 1969, Hirondelle was an outstanding success. Sales grew from 23,000 cases in 1969 to 750,000 in 1974. A *Sunday Times* quality survey in December 1973, titled "The Good, The Bad and the Undrinkable", placed two of the three Hirondelle styles top and the third style second, after tests on 350 cheap wines. Using a base wine from Austria, liberally laced with Rumanian and Bulgarian wines, Hedges and Butler, the wine merchant subsidiary of Bass Charrington Ltd, seemed to have hit on a perfect taste for the British palate.

Basic wine sources had to be changed from time to time for supply reasons. Indeed, the very success of Hirondelle had meant that only a short while after the *Sunday Times* verdict, Hedges and Butler were switching to Italian sources merely to keep pace with the demand. Nevertheless, with strict attention to the quality and "finish" of the wine, a consistent Hirondelle taste had been maintained. Hedges and Butler had, in fact, shaped a new category of wine for Britain, a standard of quality brand; not *chateau* perhaps, but certainly not plonk either.

The Advertising Brief

The success of Hirondelle had been attained without any media advertising at all. But in 1976, in a reaction to a flattening sales curve, the account was placed with J Walter Thompson Company Ltd. The brief that Hedges and Butler gave JWT included the data given in Exhibits 1 to 6 and the following rationale for putting advertising muscle into the brand.

Early Success

At least four reasons can be given for Hirondelle becoming joint brand leader (with Corrida) of the table wine market without advertising support:

Exhibit 1 *Historical Performance in a Market Perspective*

	Hirondelle Sales[1]	UK Clearances of Still Table Wines[2]		Table Wine Penetration,[3] All Adults
	Cases ('000s)	Cases ('000,000s)	Increase (%)	(%)
1968	0	7.4	22	
1969	23	7.3	−1	
1970	88	7.1	−3	
1971	164	9.4	32	33
1972	510	11.5	22	33
1973	696	16.0	40	35
1974	757	16.3	2	43
1975	678	16.0	−2	46

Source: 1. Hedges & Butler
2. Customs & Excise
3. T.G.I.

Exhibit 2 *Hirondelle User Profile*

	Hirondelle (%)	All Table Wine (%)	Heavy Users of Table Wine (3+ bottles per month) (%)	Total Population (%)
SEX				
Men	50.6	48.8	71.9	48
Women	49.4	51.2	28.1	52
SOCIAL CLASS				
AB	41.2	22.2	40.3	11
C1	32.0	30.0	33.7	23
C2	18.5	29.1	15.4	33
D	6.2	14.3	8.7	22
E	2.0	4.4	1.9	11
AGE				
15—24	24.1	19.1	21.0	19
25—34	28.4	21.6	27.9	17
35—44	17.9	16.2	17.1	15
45—54	13.8	17.9	17.3	16
55—64	10.5	14.0	10.8	15
65+	5.2	11.3	5.9	18

Exhibit 3 *Hirondelle Competitive Position*

Table-Wine Brand	Sales[1] Bottles (%)	Sales[1] £ (%)	Awareness Levels, All Adults[2] Spontaneous (%)	Awareness Levels, All Adults[2] Prompted (%)
Hirondelle	4.2	4.1	5	20
Corrida	4.4	4.0	4	24
Don Cortez	3.7	2.9	3	28
Mateus Rosé	2.7	2.8	12	35
Nicolas	1.9	2.0	1	7
Charbonnier	0.9	1.2		
Baton	0.6	0.5		
All Other	81.6	82.6		

Source: 1. Nielsen Dec. 75/Jan. 76
2. N.O.P. 1976

Exhibit 4 *Table Wine Advertising Expenditure, 1975 (£)*

	TV	Press	Total
Blue Nun	—	89,300	89,300
*Corrida	101,900	300	102,200
†*Langenbach	108,600	—	108,600
Mateus	—	186,000	186,000
Goldener Oktober	—	86,700	86,700
Others	175,500	686,700	863,300
Total for Group	386,000	1,049,000	1,435,600

*London and Southern only
†Final quarter only

Source: MEAL

Exhibit 5   *Hirondelle Distribution: Percentage of Outlets Serviced*

	Total Outlets	All Off Licence	Pubs	Restaurants/ Residential	Clubs
Dec. '72	9	24	5	9	2
Dec. '73	10	25	7	9	2
Dec. '74	13	30	9	14	3
Dec. '75	12	32	7	10	3

a)   The introduction of Hirondelle coincided with the advent of grocery off-licenses and with the formation of a grocery sales force at Hedges and Butler.

b)   In its early years, before it had its imitators, Hirondelle offered unique value for money.

c)   The rapid growth in popularity of table wine has coincided with a rapid growth in grocery/supermarket distribution, for which Hirondelle was explicitly designed.

d)   The 1973 *Sunday Times* survey provided excellent free publicity for the brand.

Why Advertise?   In common with nearly all other alcoholic drinks, the table wine market reached a peak in early 1974, since which it has declined. This recession has been a problem for Hirondelle, but other factors also argue for advertising weight to be put behind the brand:

a)   The number and quality of Hirondelle's competitors, particularly Corrida, Don Cortez and Nicolas, have improved, thus narrowing its lead as the best value-for-money table wine.

Exhibit 6   *Off Licence Distribution and Sales*

	Total Off Licence Outlets	Grocery		Specialist
		Total	Multiples Only	
Number	31,500	18,500	3,900	11,300
Per cent selling:[1]				
Any wine	92	90	100	98
Hirondelle	32	34	82	31
Corrida	20	21	42	21
Don Cortez	23	27	38	19
Mateus Rosé	54	43	75	74
Nicolas	15	13	38	20
Per cent of total wine sales:[2]				
All wines		30	20	
Hirondelle		64	58	

Source: 1. Stats MR Dec. '75
2. Nielsen Dec. '75/Jan. '76

b)   The major retail chains, such as Sainsbury and Marks and Spencer, are developing their own lines of table wine.

c)   If, as some evidence suggests, Hirondelle's brand leadership is due more to its distribution share than to its rate of sale per outlet, then growth in the future can only come from becoming more competitive on the shelf, since its retail penetration would appear to be at a maximum.

d)   The consumer is becoming more sophisticated and requires some justification for Hirondelle's premium price over other branded wines.

e)   Corrida, its major competitor, has just begun to advertise.

Summary   Faced with this dilemma — a static market and increasing competition, especially on price — how can Hirondelle increase its share? In the past share growth has come from increased penetration which is now levelling off; thus we must go for higher sales per outlet through an improved consumer franchise.

Low awareness of Hirondelle and lack of reassurance about its quality are fundamental barriers to increased trial and loyalty. Currently Hirondelle, in common with other non-advertised brands, is not a well-recalled name.

We believe that awareness and reassurance can be improved by advertising. Furthermore, advertising can begin to differentiate Hirondelle from other cheaper products in a way that is less easily imitated than product quality or price.

The Advertising Plan   In response to this brief, JWT produced four advertisements, two of which are shown in Exhibits 7 and 8. Their rationale was as follows:

Objectives of the   In line with the client's diagnosis of Hirondelle's current problems, the aims
Advertising   of any advertising for the brand must be:

a)   To stimulate trial by increasing awareness of the brand name.

b)   To reinforce repeat buying of current users by reassuring them of the quality and pedigree of the brand.

c)   To differentiate the brand from other cheaper products, thereby justifying the price premium.

Advertising Target   ABC1 wine drinkers and under 45's account for around 60% of Hirondelle
Group   usage, and potential heavy users of Hirondelle are thought to come from the same group, though generally younger.

The target group for the advertising is therefore: ABC1, aged 20—45.

Advertising   In ten group discussions of twelve advertising ideas, those which have met
Approaches   with the most favourable reactions are those that:

a)   Clearly position the brand as a mid-market "everyday" wine — not a plonk, nor (in any way) a fine wine; a table wine.

b)   Communicate that it is consistent and reliable, so you can be sure of what you are buying every time.

Exhibit 7

ITS ABOUT AS LIKELY AS A DUFF BOTTLE OF HIRONDELLE.

In 1973, in a comprehensive survey of the less expensive wines, *The Sunday Times* found that Hirondelle was "excellent value for money."

In fact, of more than 350 wines tasted, Hirondelle came top in two of its three categories (medium-dry white and rosé wines) and a close second in the third (vin ordinaire).

In 1975, the *Daily Express* also described Hirondelle as "excellent", and, in a survey conducted last year, placed it first in the 1½ litre category of red table wines.

These surveys only serve to reflect the public's view of Hirondelle over the years, a wine that's not only good, but one that's consistently so.

Hirondelle is selected and shipped by Hedges & Butler, wine merchants since 1667. It is available in red, sweet white, medium-dry white and rosé.

Hirondelle.
Every bottle is guaranteed.

Exhibit 8

ITS ABOUT AS LIKELY AS A DUFF BOTTLE OF HIRONDELLE.

In 1973, in a comprehensive survey of the less expensive wines, *The Sunday Times* found that Hirondelle was "excellent value for money."

In fact, of more than 350 wines tasted, Hirondelle came top in two of its three categories (medium-dry white and rosé wines) and a close second in the third (vin ordinaire).

In 1975, the *Daily Express* also described Hirondelle as "excellent," and, in a survey conducted last year, placed it first in the 1½ litre category of red table wines.

These surveys only serve to reflect the public's view of Hirondelle over the years: a wine that's not only good, but one that's consistently so.

Hirondelle is selected and shipped by Hedges & Butler, wine merchants since 1667. It is available in red, sweet white, medium-dry white and rosé.

Hirondelle
Every bottle is guaranteed

c)   Endorse the fact that it tastes good — for instance, the *Sunday Times* survey of cheap wines in 1973 voted it top.

d)   Talk in a sensible, down-to-earth way about a sensible, down-to-earth brand (avoiding references to wine lore and preciousness).

e)   Indicate that it is available as a range.

Target Responses   This leads to the following responses being sought:

a)   I will never be disappointed with Hirondelle: it is consistent *and* good (evidenced by the *Sunday Times* saying so).

b)   Hirondelle is a no-nonsense, straight-talking branded wine (not plonk, not a fine wine).

c)   It is a wine which has the tradition and history of real wine without the pretension or pomposity.

d)   It comes in red, white (dry and sweet) and rosé.

Media Selection   Press has been chosen as the medium to be used, since it is considered vital that the copy, which tells people in more detail about Hirondelle, should be read. This would not be possible on posters, and television is too costly.

Publications have been selected to avoid making Hirondelle look like a grocery brand, although it is intended that it should be bought primarily in supermarkets. To this end, therefore, publications which are adult/general interest orientated have been selected, and not those that are housewife/food orientated. (JWT's proposed media schedule is given in Exhibit 9, and Exhibit 10 shows the comparative cost analysis of press alternatives that were considered.)

Creative Interpretation   Given the need to communicate directly the consistent and reliable nature of Hirondelle, the "Unlikely Situations" campaign is proposed, with the headline, "It's about as likely as a duff bottle of Hirondelle".

Development of the Campaign   One of the strengths of the "Unlikely Situations" idea is that it lends itself to unending variations on the same theme. Consumers will be curious to see the "latest joke" in the series, much as they do with Guinness advertising. But since there is a host of "unlikely" subjects which, however original in conception — and humorous to some, might offend more readers than they're worth, the folllowing creative guidelines have been put forward to control the development of the campaign:

a)   Each subject should be designed to involve, amuse, delight and startle, rather than unpleasantly shock and upset for the mere sake of it.

b)   Nothing in the emotional values of an individual advertisement should run the risk of alienating consumers by association with that which is clinical, cold, off-putting or down-market.

c)   Whilst it is important that the ideas become more involving and subtle as the campaign moves on, each subject should be fairly quickly comprehensible.

Exhibit 9

(JWT) **Media Department** London

CLIENT HEDGES AND BUTLER LIMITED   PRODUCT HIRONDELLE   PERIOD 1976/77   AREA NATIONAL

1976-77

Week commencing Monday	July	August	September	October	November	December	January	February	March	April	May	June		SUMMARY
Sunday Times Mag		O	O	O	X	O			O	O	X	O	£51050	
Observer Mag.		O	O	X	X	X			O	O	O	O	£29867	
Daily Telegraph		A	A	A	A	A			A	A	A	A	£23017	
Readers Digest			O	O	O					O	O		£12800	
Evening Standard			A	A	A	A			A	A	A	A	£10120	
Punch		O		X	O	O			O	O	X	O	£ 9196	
Cosmopolitan			O	O	O	O				O	O	O	£ 8855	
Country Life		O	X	O	X	O			O	O	O	O	£ 6730	
Illustrated London News			O	O	O	O			O	O	O	O	£ 5760	
Mayfair			O	O	O	O			O	O	O	O	£ 5700	
Geographical Mag.			O	O	O	O			O	O	O	O	£ 4088	

Production

Reserve for
rate increases

NOTES O = Page 4 colour bleed   X = Page B/W bleed

A = 33 cm + 5 col

	Heavy Wine Users	Hirondelle Users
		£167,183
		7,000
		5,817
		£180,000
Coverage	87%	88%
Average OTS	16.0	17.0

Exhibit 10 *Comparative Cost Analysis of Alternative Press Media*

	Cost per Page 4-colour bleed[1] (£)	Heavy Users of Wine Coverage[2] (%)	Cost per '000 (£)	All Hirondelle Users Coverage[2] (%)	Cost per '000 (£)
Mayfair	950	17.1	3.23	13.6	2.61
Penthouse	980	16.2	3.53	13.2	2.76
Geographical Mag.	511	8.0	3.72	8.9	2.14
Men Only	1100	16.7	3.83	13.1	3.13
Illustrated London News	720	8.2	5.07	5.8	4.64
Good Housekeeping	1584	12.7	7.25	15.4	3.83
Punch	968	7.5	7.50	8.9	4.08
Harpers and Queen	667	4.9	7.94	5.8	4.30
Homes and Gardens	1375	10.0	7.99	11.7	4.36
Readers Digest	3200	23.3	8.00	31.0	4.86
She	1485	10.6	8.15	14.8	3.74
Observer Magazine	3097 (2047)[5]	21.9	8.23 (5.44)	25.0	4.62 (3.05)
Observer	— (1980)	19.0	— (6.07)	26.2	— (3.48)
Country Life	745	5.2	8.27	5.0	5.60
Cosmopolitan	1771	12.2	8.43	14.3	4.62
House and Garden	1339	8.7	8.98	8.5	5.87
Field	385	2.4	9.16	1.4	10.13
New Scientist	759	4.6	9.60	3.5	8.07
Daily Telegraph Magazine	4194 (2829)[5]	25.3	9.66 (6.51)	26.1	6.00 (4.05)
Daily Telegraph	— (2557)	23.6	— (6.31)	25.0	— (3.82)
Ideal Home	1595	9.4	9.90	10.0	5.95
Evening Standard	2250[3] (920)	13.2	9.95 (4.07)	9.7	8.68 (3.55)
Sunday Times Magazine	5470 (3190)[5]	31.6	10.09 (5.88)	33.0	6.18 (3.60)
Sunday Times	— (3052)	35.2	— (5.05)	34.7	— (3.28)
Vogue	1552	8.6	10.48	12.4	4.67
Tatler	550	2.9	11.00	2.7	7.63
Radio Times	7900 (4200)[5]	36.7	12.53 (6.66)	38.6	7.64 (4.06)
TV Times	6743	30.9	12.69	27.6	9.12
Tit Bits	1450	6.4	13.18	4.2	12.83
Economist	1050	4.3	14.18	3.2	12.20
Weekend	3080	10.0	18.01	8.5	13.44
Guardian	3300[3] (1402)	10.7	18.03 (7.66)	9.6	12.79 (5.43)
Daily Mail	5250[3] (1750)	16.2	18.88 (6.29)	17.2	11.36 (3.78)
Financial Times	4250[3]	12.9	19.23	6.5	24.56
Woman's Journal	935	2.7	19.89	6.9	5.08
Times	4202[3] (1732)	10.7	22.83 (9.41)	7.3	21.32 (8.79)
Woman and Home	2662	5.9	26.35	15.1	6.57
Brides	1224	1.4	48.96	2.5	18.26

Notes: 1 Bracketed prices = black and white for 33 cm + 5 c or equivalent in tabloid.
2 TGI 1975
3 ½ page 4-colour/equivalent.
4 Full page.

Exhibit 11   *Users and Non-Users of Hirondelle Wine*

	All Users				Solus Users				Major Users				Minor Users				Non-Users
	'000	% down	% across	index	'000	% down	% across	index	'000	% down	% across	index	'000	% down	% across	index	'000
1972:																	
ALL ADULTS	1219	100	3.0	100	146	100	0.4	100	463	100	1.1	100	611	100	1.5	100	13538
MEN	661	54	3.4	114	88	61	0.5	127	242	52	1.2	110	331	54	1.7	113	6469
WOMEN	558	46	2.6	88	57	39	0.3	75	221	48	1.0	91	280	46	1.3	88	7069
15—24	306	25	3.9	131	34	24	0.4	123	125	27	1.6	141	147	24	1.9	126	2648
25—34	346	28	5.1	172	30	20	0.4	123	146	32	2.2	191	170	28	2.5	168	2730
35—44	215	18	3.4	114	23	16	0.4	101	72	16	1.1	101	120	20	1.9	127	2373
45—54	189	16	2.8	96	18	13	0.3	78	73	16	1.1	97	98	16	1.5	99	2467
55—64	115	9	1.8	61	30	20	0.5	130	32	7	0.5	44	54	9	0.8	57	1974
65 OR OVER	48	4	0.7	23	11	8	0.2	44	15	3	0.2	18	23	4	0.3	22	1346
AB	543	45	10.6	355	63	43	1.2	345	231	50	4.5	397	249	41	4.9	326	3087
C1	417	34	5.2	175	38	26	0.5	132	149	32	1.9	165	229	38	2.9	192	3853
C2	187	15	1.2	42	32	22	0.2	59	62	13	0.4	36	94	15	0.6	41	4435
D	67	5	0.7	25	12	8	0.1	35	19	4	0.2	18	37	6	0.4	27	1789
E	5	0.4	0.1	5	1	1	*	12	3	0.6	0.1	7	1	0.2	*	2	375
1974:																	
ALL ADULTS	2678	100	6.5	100	309	100	0.7	100	1126	100	2.7	100	1243	100	3.0	100	16646
MEN	1355	51	6.9	106	147	48	0.7	99	556	49	2.8	104	652	52	3.3	110	8066
WOMEN	1322	49	6.1	94	162	52	0.7	100	570	51	2.6	97	590	48	2.7	91	8580
15—24	645	24	8.5	131	71	23	0.9	124	280	25	3.7	135	293	24	3.8	128	3037
25—34	761	28	10.6	163	83	27	1.2	155	338	30	4.7	172	340	27	4.7	157	3405
35—44	480	18	7.7	119	51	16	0.8	109	172	15	2.8	101	257	21	4.1	137	2654
45—54	370	14	5.5	85	43	14	0.6	84	161	14	2.4	87	167	13	2.5	82	3094
55—64	282	11	4.6	71	39	13	0.6	85	108	10	1.8	65	135	11	2.2	74	2415
65 OR OVER	140	5	1.9	29	22	7	0.3	41	67	6	0.9	33	51	4	0.7	23	2041
AB	1103	41	20.4	316	90	29	1.7	223	448	40	8.3	305	565	45	10.5	349	3189
C1	857	32	9.3	144	102	33	1.1	148	361	32	3.9	144	395	32	4.3	143	4946
C2	496	19	3.6	56	77	25	0.6	75	234	21	1.7	62	185	15	1.3	45	5127
D	167	6	1.8	28	31	10	0.3	45	61	5	0.7	24	75	6	0.8	27	2589
E	54	2	1.4	22	8	3	0.2	30	22	2	0.6	22	23	2	0.6	21	795
1976:																	
ALL ADULTS	2794	100	6.7	100	260	100	0.6	100	1099	100	2.6	100	1435	100	3.5	100	16092
MEN	1339	48	6.7	100	115	44	0.6	93	495	45	2.5	94	728	51	3.7	106	7714
WOMEN	1455	52	6.7	100	144	56	0.7	106	604	55	2.8	105	707	49	3.3	94	8378
15—24	606	22	7.9	118	79	30	1.0	165	233	21	3.0	115	294	20	3.8	111	2794
25—34	1025	37	13.9	207	45	17	0.6	98	442	40	6.0	227	539	38	7.3	212	3355
35—44	433	15	6.9	103	39	15	0.6	99	135	12	2.2	82	259	18	4.2	121	2811
45—54	369	13	5.5	81	39	15	0.6	92	146	13	2.2	82	185	13	2.7	79	2975
55—64	221	8	3.7	55	31	12	0.5	83	84	8	1.4	53	106	7	1.8	51	2181
65 OR OVER	140	5	1.8	28	27	10	0.4	58	59	5	0.8	30	53	4	0.7	20	1976
AB	860	31	17.4	259	53	21	1.1	174	347	32	7.0	266	460	32	9.3	270	3035
C1	1099	39	11.2	166	103	40	1.1	168	428	39	4.4	165	568	40	5.8	167	5032
C2	591	21	4.4	65	70	27	0.5	83	232	21	1.7	65	289	20	2.1	62	4879
D	199	7	2.2	33	24	9	0.3	42	71	6	0.8	29	105	7	1.2	33	2274
E	45	2	1.1	16	9	4	0.2	36	21	2	0.5	19	14	1	0.3	10	873

d)   The subjects should be highly original.

e)   Because the nature of the material, and its quality, is so much at the mercy of subjective opinion, it might, when opinion is divided within, be worth relying on the *vox populi* without.

f)   And, to end at the beginning, each subject must be not only highly unlikely, but as unlike the preceding one as we're ever likely to get.

Exhibit 12 *Terminology Employed in Target Group Index Surveys*

User Classifications

All Users:	Have drunk in the past 6 months.
Solus Users:	Drink only the one brand (of all brands of table wine).
Major Users:	Drink the brand most often but also drink other brands.
Minor Users:	Have drunk in the past 6 months but drink another brand most often.
Non-Users:	Drink the product but have not drunk the brand in the past 6 months.
Adult Users:	Aged 15 or over.
Social Grade:	Social grade is normally based on the occupation of the head of his or her household. It is assessed by the interviewer when attempting to place the questionnaire and is therefore based on information given personally and verbally by the respondent. Interviewers are supplied with a list of occupations within industry to guide them in their assessments.

Social grade	Social status	Head of household's occupation
A	Upper middle class	Higher managerial, administrative or professional
B	Middle class	Intermediate managerial, administrative or professional
C1	Lower middle class	Supervisory or clerical, and junior managerial, administrative or professional
C2	Skilled working class	Skilled manual workers
D	Working class	Semi and unskilled manual workers
E	Those at lowest levels of subsistence	State pensioners or widows (no other earner), casual or lower-grade workers

The Advertising Decision

It fell to Vern Johnson, the senior brand manager of Hirondelle, to prepare a response to JWT's advertising proposal. As it happened, he had just received the latest Target Group Index (TGI) Survey published annually by the British Market Research Bureau (BMRB). One of the statisticians in the company had extracted Hirondelle usage figures from the 1976 survey and compared them with figures for 1972 and 1974. These are given in Exhibit 11, with definitions of the terms used by TGI given in Exhibit 12. (Fieldwork for the TGI survey is conducted in the spring and early summer of the year in which it is published.) Vern wondered, as he cast his eye over the TGI data, whether JWT's creative solution and media strategy were consistent with these latest findings and whether, more generally, the right message was being communicated to the right people at the right time.

This case was prepared by Kenneth Simmonds of the London Business School © Kenneth Simmonds. 1981.

CASE 9

Piper Books Ltd

Shortly after the beginning of the firm's financial year on 1st February, Vernon Martin was promoted from a financial accounting post in Piper Books Ltd to the position of publisher for children's books. Early in March he was asked by the editor responsible for children's annuals to approve a proposal to produce a boy's annual on Great Sporting Achievements in time for the Christmas market. The mock-up of the annual appealed to Mr Martin, but the specification of the market for the annual was rather hazy and he found that no formal market research backed up the proposal and in fact no research had ever been carried out in the children's book group. Mr Martin decided to call in outside research consultants, but before he did so he was considering the questions that he would need answered most urgently.

Piper Limited was one of Britain's two largest publishers of trade books and had maintained a high rate of growth for ten years. While the past two years had been no exception, profits had shown no increase over this period. The lag had been attributed primarily to excessive stocks of titles printed in greater quantities than needed within their peak demand period, and top management had begun to place increasing emphasis on stock reduction. Mr Martin's appointment from accounting and his predecessor's departure were concrete evidence of their intentions. For the children's book group in particular, the end of year stock figure had been £400,000 against an annual turnover of just over £800,000, with the year's net profit before taxes showing no increase at £60,000.

Mr Martin was determined to improve his stock position and when the proposal for the sporting annual was presented, he was concerned that it might produce the opposite effect just in time for next year's balance date. The editor, John Attwood-Reilly, explained that he had already had several long sessions with the sales manager and his assistant discussing the mock-up of the annual and the probable sales level. They were now both satisfied with the proposal and were agreed on a budgeted sales figure of 11,000 copies. While sales could vary from this figure, the minimum would be 7,000 barring a major recession. This would allow for minimum orders from the buyers in the major chains and only scattered orders from smaller outlets. On the other hand, if the publication was received very well, then a higher volume of initial orders and repeat requests could bring the figure to 15,000, or even more if stocks were immediately available.

As the cost of printing extra copies was marginal, requiring little more than the paper cost at under £0.05 a copy, Mr Reilly recommended a print run of 15,000. Only 10,000 copies would be assembled and bound in the first instance and if the volume of first-round orders was high, a further batch could then be bound.

The price was set at £1.50 with a 33.3% discount to retailers and a further 15% to wholesalers. Mr Reilly and the sales executives felt that any attempt to change from the usual price for this sort of annual would be self-defeating. While the market might not be particularly sensitive to price changes of 15% in either direction, any increase in price might lead the trade buyers to classify the annual as too expensive and to switch the emphasis of their orders to other titles.

The number of major outlets in the United Kingdom for this sort of publication was about 7,500, and of these some 3,000 belonged to three chains: W.H. Smith, John Menzies and Boots. Each of these worked through a central purchasing office and probably 50% of the orders for the sporting annual would come from here — at wholesale prices. The Piper sales representatives were in frequent contact with the buyers and could expect them to make their selections for their Christmas line by late August with delivery in October—November. In addition to orders for their own chain, W.H. Smith also bought as wholesalers to other newsagent chains. Before Christmas particularly, there would be numbers of the country's 50,000 newsagents who added a few books to their line. The remainder of the outlets were comprised of some 800 department stores and 3,000 independent bookstores. Even though half the department stores belonged to chains, each store invariably purchased separately. Orders from this second grouping would be placed with the Piper field sales staff, or be sent in direct after their calls or as a result of direct mailings sent regularly to all outlets.

Unless Mr Martin made an exception and authorised sale-or-return offers, all sales for annuals of this sort would be firm. Sale-or-return, however, would induce buyers to increase their orders by as much as 30% when they were uncertain as to the saleability of a title.

Mr Martin could see that sales of 11,000 copies would produce a good profit, given the figures presented to him by Mr Reilly. These are set out in Exhibit 1. General overheads were running at about 10% of revenues and payment for the costs of the project would be made on the average only three months before receiving payment from customers. Beyond this, the only drain on his group's capital would be stocks of any unsold copies. A few might possibly be sold during the following year, but any quantity would

Exhibit 1   *Great Sporting Achievements Annual*

	£
Estimated Revenue	
11,000 copies @ £0.90	9,900
Estimated Costs	
Text, copyrighted graphics & editorial overheads	2,700
Typesetting and proofing	1,000
Paper and printing (15,000 print run)	2,500
Assembling, binding, packing & delivery (11,000 @ £0.2)	2,200
General Group Overheads (10% of revenue)	990
	9,390
Profit	510

have to be disposed of as remainders at little more than the material cost — say £0.15.

What gave Mr Martin real cause for hesitation was the total lack of any concrete market facts when he questioned Mr Reilly. Nothing seemed to be known about what sort of customers bought the type of annual that was proposed — whether it was the younger readers themselves, mothers, fathers or other relatives — the social class distribution of customers, or where they regularly purchased and how frequently. Nor was there any basis for calculating whether the proposal might not simply switch customers from other titles. In these circumstances, Mr Martin could feel little confidence in the sales estimates and he determined that he should make a first step towards more scientific management decision by commissioning some research into the market.

The best starting point seemed to Mr Martin to be the basic motivation of purchasers of annuals. After that, with the mock-up already available, he felt that competent market researchers should be able to pin-point the likely sales more accurately than the estimates put forward which allowed a 30% fluctuation in either direction. Further questioning within the children's book group had revealed a complete absence of any research results concerning consumer motivation, and Mr Martin felt that once the immediate problem had been covered it would be well worthwhile to start collecting a bank of basic motivation research in the children's trade book field.

This case was prepared by Kenneth Simmonds of the London Business School. © Kenneth Simmonds. 1979.

CASE 10

Dornbusch Corporation

On completion of his B.A. in marketing through the sandwich course at Midland Polytechnic, Graham Stoddard was particularly pleased when he was recruited as UK product manager (electric razors) for the Dornbusch Corporation. Dornbusch had a world-wide name in the consumer electrical products field and its brands had been aggressively promoted for many years. The firm had a reputation as a leader in marketing practice and as an excellent training ground for senior marketing posts later in an executive's career.

To Graham's growing astonishment when he started his new job, he could find from internal Dornbusch records no hard data about what was happening in the user market for electric razors and very little on the outlet market. Large retail chains had been demanding and obtaining special deals and it was not clear where, and even at what price, Dornbusch razors were being sold. Promotion costs were running at 20% of revenue, but there appeared to be a very low correlation between promotion and sales patterns over the years.

Dornbusch's current sales were around 210,000 razors per annum — all aimed at the male market. Estimates from the IPC Marketing Manual put the UK market two years previously at 1.6 million units, of which around 10% were probably women's shavers. Dornbusch's estimated 15% of the men's segment placed them well behind Philips with an estimated 800,000 units and Braun with possibly 400,000.

Stoddard knew he could obtain more precise estimates of current sales from A.C. Nielsen surveys of outlets, but he decided that it was more important to find out where the future potential really lay. There had been years of expanding demand and much switching and upgrading by users. Was the future potential in first purchase, replacement or second use? Or was there little potential left at all? Of 20 million male shavers it had been estimated that 70% were still wet shavers. After a little questioning around, Graham was fairly certain that he would get immediate clearance for a research commitment of up to £10,000. On such a budget he estimated he could finance a survey of 2,000 adult males, provided he arranged for the analysis of the results internally and kept the data requested fairly short. He accordingly drew up the following five open-ended questions to be asked of 2,000 randomly selected males aged between 20 and 55:

> What type of razor do you now own?
> How long have you had it?
> What type of razor did you have before this one?
> Have you ever owned any other kind?

When did you switch and why?

Graham hoped that armed with this information he could pull more through from internal sales records and fairly firmly establish the need for an ongoing feedback system.

Audit Answers Ltd had been recommended to Graham as young, keen and hungry. His approach to them confirmed that they were what he was looking for. They were well prepared to carry through the national survey for £10,000 and turn over the interview sheets to Dornbusch for analysis.

This case was prepared by Mr David Jobber of Bradford University Management Centre and Dr John Saunders of Warwick University.

CASE 11
Haskins Engineering

Haskins Engineering was a medium-sized engineering company situated in the Midlands. Founded in 1948 by Frank Haskins, the company had built up a reputation for reliable engineering of low value components for the car industry. As the car industry grew during the 1950s and 1960s, so did Haskins Engineering. By the early 1970s the company had expanded to employ almost 250 people. The company suffered like many other engineering firms in the Midlands during the recession of the early 1980s. Unlike many others, Haskins Engineering survived, through a combination of good reputation, cost cutting and good fortune. By 1985 the workforce had declined to 120 and with foreign competition penetrating its traditional markets the future looked bleak.

The company was now run by Peter Haskins, the eldest son of Frank. Trained as an engineer, Peter had been groomed to take over from his father, and with the announcement of the retirement of Joe Biggs, Haskins' sales manager for 25 years, he took the opportunity of appointing a new manager with some marketing experience. Barrie Everitt fitted the profile exactly. Aged 32, Everitt had worked in the marketing department of a large Midlands-based engineering company before joining a major lock manufacturer as sales manager.

One of the tasks assigned to Everitt was the assessment of potential markets for new products which could be manufactured and sold by Haskins Engineering. Under consideration was a product developed by one of the company's production engineers. Many of the components manufactured by the company required the drilling of holes of various diameters. Consequently the company possessed a number of boring machines. In order to speed up production and improve accuracy, a feed mechanism had been developed which automatically presented the work-piece on to the machining bed for boring and then removed it after the work was completed. The mechanism had been used within the company for over a year very successfully and Everitt wondered about the opportunities it presented as a product to be marketed to other engineering companies. A major limiting factor was that it could only be used on the type of boring machine used by Haskins — the Asquith 500. The design of other machines meant that the automatic feed mechanism would periodically jam causing severe problems in lost production. The problem was being studied, but it was anticipated that it could be at least three years before the problem was solved.

Everitt wanted to know market potential for the feed mechanism attachment. Approaching Asquiths was out of the question because of the danger that they might copy the design themselves. Everitt knew the answer lay in marketing research but he felt ill-equipped to tackle the job himself. However, one of his salesmen, Mike Bissell, was a graduate in business studies from a local polytechnic and had studied marketing research. Bissell was summoned to Everitt's office to discuss the problem. Everitt told Bissell that he wanted to know the proportion of companies in the metal working engineering sector which owned an Asquith 500, so that an estimate of market potential could be made. Bissell replied that he would ponder the problem, and reply within a week. Four days later, Everitt received the following note:

To: Mr B. Everitt
From: Mr M. Bissell

I have considered the marketing research problem we discussed earlier this week and recommend the following approach: a random sample of 200 of our customers to be taken and a mail questionnaire sent to them asking for the information you require. I estimate that around 40% will respond if a follow-up letter and questionnaire is sent to non-responders to the initial questionnaire. This will give a sample size of 80 which is quite large enough to estimate the proportion who own an Asquith. Statistically, any sample over 30 can be regarded as large. The mail questionnaire has the advantage of simplicity and speed and can easily be organised by your assistant. You should have the answers within four weeks.

Everitt, at first, felt delighted with Bissell's recommendations. They were administratively convenient and highly practical. However, upon reflection, Everitt felt uneasy. The new product could mean salvation for his company and he did not want to risk mistakes. Would Bissell's suggestions really provide reliable information which he could present to Peter Haskins in support of the project?

This case was prepared by Professor Kamran Kashani as a basis for class discussion rather than to illustrate either effective or ineffective handling of an administrative situation.
© IMEDE (International Management Development Institute), Lausanne, Switzerland, 1981. Reproduced by permission.

CASE 12

Mediquip, SA

On 18 January 1981, Kurt Thaldorf, a sales engineer for the German sales subsidiary of Mediquip, SA, was informed by Lohmann University Hospital in Stuttgart that it had decided to place an order with Sigma, a Dutch competitor, for a CT scanner. The hospital's decision came as disappointing news to Thaldorf, who had worked for nearly eight months on the account. The order, if obtained, would have meant a sale of DM 1,580,000 for the sales engineer. He was convinced that Mediquip's CT scanner was technologically superior to Sigma's and overall a better product.

Thaldorf began a review of his call reports in order better to understand the factors that led to Lohmann University Hospital's decision. He wanted to apply the lessons from this case to future sales situations.

Background The computer tomography (CT) scanner was a relatively recent product in the field of diagnostic imaging. The medical device, used for diagnostic purposes, allowed examination of cross-sections of the human body through display of images. CT scanners combined sophisticated X-ray equipment with a computer to collect the necessary data and translate them into visual images.

When computer tomography was first introduced in the late 1960s, radiologists hailed it as a major technological breakthrough. Commenting on the advantages of CT scanners, a product specialist with Mediquip said, "The end product looks very much like an X-ray image. The only difference is that with scanners you can see sections of a body that were never seen before on a screen — like the pancreas. A radiologist, for example, can diagnose the cancer of pancreas less than two weeks after it develops. This was not possible before the CT scanners."

Mediquip was a subsidiary of Technologie Universelle, a French conglomerate. The company's product line included, in addition to CT scanners, X-ray, ultrasonic and nuclear diagnostic equipment. Mediquip enjoyed worldwide a reputation for advanced technology and competent after-sales service.

"Our competitors are mostly from other European countries," commented Mediquip's Sales Director for Europe. "In some markets they have been there longer than we have and they know the decision makers better than we do. But we are learning fast." Sigma, the subsidiary of a diversified Dutch company under the same name, was the company's most serious competitor. Other major contenders in the CT scanner market were FNC, Eldora, Magna and Piper.

Mediquip executives estimated the European market for CT scanners to be in the neighbourhood of 200 units per year. They pointed out that prices ranged betweeen DM 1—2 million per unit. The company's CT scanner sold in the upper end of the price range. "Our equipment is at least two years

Exhibit 1 *Mediquip, SA Account Management Analysis Forms*

Key Account: _____

ACCOUNT MANAGEMENT ANALYSIS

The enclosed forms are designed to facilitate your management of:

    1   A key sales account

    2   The *Mediquip* resources that can be applied to this key account

Completing the enclosed forms, you will:

- Identify installed equipment, and planned or potential new equipment
- Analyze purchase decision process and influence patterns, including:
  - Identify and prioritize all major sources of influence
  - Project probable sequence of events and timing of decision process
  - Assess position/interest of each major influence source
  - Identify major competition and probable strategies
  - Identify needed information/support
- Establish an account development strategy, including:
  - Select key contacts
  - Establish strategy and tactics for each key contact, identify appropriate *Mediquip* personnel
  - Assess plans for the most effective use of local team and headquarters resources

KEY ACCOUNT DATA

☐   Original (Date: _____)   Account No.: _____   Type of Institute: _____

☐   Revision (Date: _____)   Sales Specialist: _____   Bed Size: _____

                                          Country/Region/District: _____   Telephone: _____

1. CUSTOMER (HOSPITAL, CLINIC, PRIVATE INSTITUTE)

Name: _____

Street Address: _____

City, State: _____

2. DECISION MAKERS — IMPORTANT CONTACTS

INDIVIDUALS	NAME	SPECIALITY	REMARKS
Medical Staff			
Administration			
Local Government			
State Government			

This exhibit presents a condensed version of the forms, which comprised eight 8½ × 11 inch sheets for entry of relevant information.

3. INSTALLED EQUIPMENT

TYPE	DESCRIPTION	SUPPLIED BY	INSTALLATION DATE	YEAR TO REPLACE	VALUE OF POTENTIAL ORDER
X-ray Nuclear Ultrasound RTP CT					

4. PLANNED NEW EQUIPMENT

TYPE	QUOTE NO.	QUOTE DATE	% CHANCE	EST. ORDER DATE 1980	EST. ORDER DATE 1981	EST. DELIVERY 1980	EST. DELIVERY 1981	QUOTED PRICE

5. COMPETITION

COMPANY/PRODUCT	STRATEGY/ TACTICS	% CHANCE	STRENGTH	WEAKNESS

6. SALES PLAN   Product: _____   Quote No: _____   Quoted Price: _____

KEY ISSUES	Mediquip's PLAN	SUPPORT NEEDED FROM:	DATE OF FOLLOW-UP/REMARKS

7. ACTIONS — IN SUPPORT OF PLAN

SPECIFIC ACTION	RESPONSIBILITY	DUE DATES ORIGINAL	REVISED	COMPLETED	RESULTS/REMARKS

8. ORDER STATUS REPORT

REVISION DATE	ACCOUNT NAME AND LOCATION	ISSUES/COMPETITIVE STRATEGY	ACTIONS/ STRATEGY	RESPONSI- BILITY	% CHANCE	EXPECTED ORDER TIMING	WIN/LOSE

ahead of our most advanced competition", explained a sales executive. "And our price reflects this technological superiority."

Mediquip's sales organisation in Europe included eight country sales subsidiaries, each headed by a managing director. Within each country, sales engineers reported to regional sales managers who themselves reported to the managing director. Product specialists provided technical support to the sales force in each country.

Buyers of CT Scanners

A sales executive at Mediquip described the buyers of CT scanners as follows:

> Most of our sales are to what we call the public sector, the health agencies that are either government-owned or belong to non-profit support organisations such as universities and philanthropic institutions. They are the sort of buyers who buy through formal tenders and who have to budget their purchases at least one year in advance. Once the budget is allocated it must then be spent before the end of the year. Only a minor share of our CT scanner sales goes to the private sector, the profit-oriented organisations such as private hospitals or private radiologists.
>
> Between the two markets, the public sector is much more complex. Typically, there are at least four groups who get involved in the purchase decision: the radiologists, the physicists, the administrators and the people from the supporting agency — usually those who approve the budget for purchase of a CT scanner.
>
> Radiologists are users of the equipment. They are doctors whose diagnostic services are sought by other doctors in the hospital or clinic. Patients remember their doctors, but not the radiologists. They never receive flowers from the patients! A CT scanner could really enhance their professional image among their colleagues.
>
> Physicists are the scientists in residence. They write the technical specifications which competing CT scanners must meet. The physicists should know the state of the art in X-ray rechnology. Their primary concern is the patient's safety.
>
> The administrators are, well, administrators. They have the financial responsibility for their organisation. They are concerned with the cost of CT scanners, but also with what revenues they can generate. The administrators are extremely wary of purchasing an expensive technological toy that becomes obsolete in a few years' time.
>
> The people from the supporting agency are usually not directly involved with decisions as to which product to purchase. But since they must approve the expenditures, they do play an indirect role. Their influence is mostly felt by the administrators.
>
> The interplay among the four groups, as you can imagine, is quite complex. The powers of each group in relationship to the others vary from organisation to organisation. The administrator, for example, is the top decision maker in certain hospitals. In others, he is only a buyer. One of the key tasks of our sales engineers is to define for each potential account the relative powers of the players. Only then can they set priorities and formulate selling strategies.

The European sales organisation at Mediquip had recently put into use a series of forms designed to help sales engineers in their account analysis and strategy formulation. A sample of the forms, called Account Management Analysis, is reproduced in Exhibit 1.

Lohmann University Hospital Lohmann University Hospital (LUH) was a large general hospital serving Stuttgart, a city of one million residents. The hospital was part of the university's medical school. The university was a leading teaching centre and enjoyed an excellent reputation. LUH's radiology department had a variety of X-ray equipment from a number of European manufacturers, including Sigma and FNC. Five radiologists staffed the department, which was headed by a senior and nationally known radiologist, Professor Steinborn.

Thaldorf's Sales Activities From the records he had kept of his sales calls, Thaldorf reviewed the events for the period between 5 June 1980, when he learned of LUH's interest in purchasing a CT scanner, and 18 January 1981, when he was informed that Mediquip had lost the order:

5 June 1980 Office received a call from a Professor Steinborn from Lohmann University Hospital regarding a CT scanner. I was assigned to make the call on the professor. Looked through our files to find out if we had sold anything to the hospital before. We had not. Made an appointment to see the professor on 9 June.

9 June 1980 Called on Professor Steinborn who informed me of a recent decision by university directors to set aside funds next year for the purchase of the hospital's first CT scanner. The professor wanted to know what we had to offer. Told him the general features of our CT system. Gave him some brochures. Asked a few questions which led me to believe other companies had come to see him before I did. Told me to check with Dr Rufer, the hospital's physicist, regarding the specs. Made an appointment to see him again in ten days' time. Called on Dr Rufer who was not there. His secretary gave me a lengthy document on the scanner specs.

10 June 1980 Read the specs last night. Looked like they had been copied straight from somebody's technical manual. Showed them to our Product Specialist who confirmed my own hunch that our system met and exceeded the specs. Made an appointment to see Dr Rufer next week.

15 June 1980 Called on Dr Rufer. Told him about our system's features and the fact that we met all the specs set down on the document. He looked somewhat unimpressed. Left him with technical documents on our system.

19 June 1980 Called on Professor Steinborn. Had read the material I had left with him. Looked sort of pleased with the features. Asked about our upgrading scheme. Told him we would undertake to upgrade the system as new features became available. Unlike other systems, Mediquip can be made to accommodate the latest technology. There will be no risk of obsolescence for a long time. He was quite impressed. Also answered his questions regarding image manipulation, image processing speed and our service capability. Just before I left he enquired about our price. Told him I would have an informative quote for him at our next meeting. Made an appointment to see him on 23 July after he returned from his vacation. Told me to get in touch with Carl Hartmann, the hospital's general director, in the interim.

1 July 1980   Called on Hartmann. It was difficult to get an appointment with him. Told him about our interest in supplying his hospital with our CT scanner which met all the specs as defined by Dr Rufer. Also informed him of our excellent service capability. He wanted to know which other hospitals in the country had purchased our system. Told him I would drop him a list of buyers in a few days' time. Asked about the price. Gave him an informative quote of DM 1,900,000 — a price we had arrived at with my boss since my visit to Professor Steinborn. He shook his head, saying, "Other scanners are cheaper by a wide margin". I explained that our price reflected the latest technology which was incorporated in it. Also mentioned that the price differential was an investment that could pay for itself several times over through faster speed of operation. He was noncommittal. Before leaving his office he instructed me not to talk to anybody else about the price. Asked him specifically if it included Professor Steinborn. He said it did. Left him with a lot of material on our system.

3 July 1980   Took a list of three other hospitals of a similar size that had installed our system to Hartmann's office. He was out. Left it with his secretary who recognised me. Learned from her that at least two other firms, Sigma and FNC, were competing for the order. She also volunteered the information that "prices are so different, Mr Hartmann is confused". She added that the final decision will be made by a committee made up of Hartmann, Professor Steinborn and one other person whom she could not recall.

20 July 1980   Called on Dr Rufer. Asked him if he had read the material on our system. He had. But did not have much to say. Repeated some of the key operational advantages our product enjoyed over those produced by others, including Sigma and FNC. Left him some more technical documents.
      On the way out, stopped by Hartmann's office. His secretary told me that we had received favourable comments from the hospitals using our system.

23 July 1980   Professor Steinborn was flabbergasted to hear that I could not discuss our price with him. Told him of the hospital administration's instructions to this effect. He was not convinced, especially when Sigma had already revealed to him their quote of DM 1,400,000. When he calmed down he wanted to know if we were going to be at least competitive with the others. Told him our system was more advanced than Sigma's. Promised him we would do our best to come up with an attractive offer. Then we talked about his vacation and sailing experience in the Aegean Sea. He said he loved the Greek food.

15 August 1980   Called to see if Hartmann had returned from his vacation. He had. While checking his calendar, his secretary told me that our system seemed to be the "radiologists' choice", but that Hartmann had not yet made up his mind.

30 August 1980   Visited Hartmann, accompanied by the regional manager. Hartmann seemed bent on the price. He said, "All companies claim they have the latest technology". So he could not understand why our offer was "so much above the rest". He concluded that only a "very attractive price" could tip the balance in our favour. After repeating the operational advantages our system enjoyed over others, including those produced by Sigma and FNC, my boss indicated that we were willing to lower our price to DM 1,740,000 if the equipment was ordered before the end of the current year. Hartmann said he would consider the offer and seek "objective" expert opinion. He also said a decision would be made before Christmas.

15 September 1980   Called on Professor Steinborn who was too busy to see me for more than ten minutes. He wanted to know if we had lowered our price since the last meeting with him. I said we had. He shook his head saying laughingly, "Maybe that was not your best offer". He then wanted to know how fast we could make deliveries. Told him within six months. He did not say anything.

2 October 1980   Discussed with our regional manager the desirability of inviting one or more people from the LUH to visit the Mediquip headquarters operations near Paris. The three-day trip would have given the participants a chance to see the scope of the facilities and become better acquainted with CT scanner applications. The idea was finally rejected as inappropriate.

3 October 1980   Dropped in to see Hartmann. He was busy but had the time to ask for a formal "final offer" from us by 1 November. On the way out, his secretary told me of "a lot of heated discussions" around which scanner semmed best suited for the hospital. She would not say more.

25 October 1980   The question of price was raised in a meeting between the regional manager and the managing director. I had recommended a sizeable cut in our price to win the order. The regional manager seemed to agree with me. But the managing director was reluctant. His concern was that too much of a drop in price looked "unhealthy". They finally agreed to a final offer of DM 1,580,000.

Made an appointment to see Hartmann later that week.

29 October 1980   Took our offer of DM 1,580,000 in a sealed envelope to Hartmann. He did not open it, but commented he hoped the scanner question would be resolved soon to the "satisfaction of all concerned". Asked him how the decision was going to be made. He evaded the question but said he would notify us as soon as a decision was reached. Left his office feeling that our price had a good chance of being accepted.

20 November 1980   Called on Professor Steinborn. He had nothing to tell me, but "the CT scanner is the last thing I like to talk about". Felt he was unhappy with the way things were going.

Tried to make an appointment with Hartmann in November, but he was too busy.

5 December 1980   Called on Hartmann who told me that a decision would probably not be reached before next January. He indicated that our price was "within the range", but that all the competing systems were being evaluated to see which seemed most appropriate for the hospital. He repeated that he would call us when a decision was reached.

18 January 1981   Received a brief letter from Hartmann thanking Mediquip for participating in the bid for the CT scanner and informing it of the decision to place the order with Sigma.

Adjusting the Marketing Mix

This case was prepared by Kenneth Simmonds of the London Business School. © Kenneth Simmonds, 1978.

CASE 13

Alabaster Soap

It seemed a natural step up for David Brandon when an invitation came through an executive search firm to join Marcelin Greene Ltd of Uxbridge as Marketing and Sales Director. At age 36, he was already one of four national line sales managers for a leading branded food firm and he was ambitious to take full responsibility for the sales and marketing of a single company.

Greene's was a sleepy one-product firm selling its "Alabaster" soap in toilet and bath size packages throughout Britain. Net turnover was about £1.6 million per annum, giving Alabaster around 2% of the national market for toilet soap in tablet form. By using the retail price index as a deflator, David calculated that in real terms Greene's sales seemed to have been decreasing around 5% per annum over the past four years. Nevertheless, the Alabaster brand, with its distinctive white emblem of a Grecian urn, was widely recognised and the firm made a profit before tax of 6% on sales. The brand had been sold for sixty years and had a good quality image. David was confident he could reverse the trend with an energetic sales campaign. He was on a first-name basis with many of the buyers for national supermarket and retail chains, came into frequent contact with them to arrange special deals and promotions, and had entertained and been "out on the town" with a number.

One of David's first actions on joining Greene's was to commission a special Nielsen-type study of Alabaster representation in different outlets and its share of the market through those outlets. The figures are summarised in Exhibit 1. There was some difference from region to region not shown in this summary, but David concluded that a national sales drive aimed at

Exhibit 1 *Market Audits Limited Summary Distribution Study*

Client: Marcelin Greene Limited

Retail Segment	Estimated Total Outlets ('000s)	Proportion of Sample Stocking Alabaster (%)	Alabaster Share of Total Sample Outlet Sales of Toilet Soap in Tablet Form at Retail Prices (9 months) (%)
Grocery Outlets	98	31	1.3
Chemists	13	47	3.9
Other	5	64	2.1

selected supermarket chains where Alabaster was weakest should be his first priority. He would have to build a national sales force, however, to replace Greene's current manufacturers' representatives.

During the Second World War, Greene's had been forced to use general manufacturers' representatives working on commission to cover its accounts. Thereafter, Greene's had never fully returned to an employee salesforce. The firm now operated through representatives in six regions, although its own Sales Director covered a seventh — London Western — operating from the Uxbridge offices. The representatives worked on a 2% commission for all orders from their regions, including national wholesale and retail chains who purchased for delivery to other regions. Greene's then supplied the orders from bulk warehouse stocks which they maintained at four sites and replenished from Uxbridge. The six regions covered by the representatives were London Eastern, Southwestern, Midlands, Northern, Scotland and Northern Ireland.

The recommended retail price for a standard Alabaster toilet bar was 20p. This placed the brand in the upper third by price, among the quality brands, although some soaps were considerably more expensive. For a standard toilet bar, prices ranged from 5p for a very cheap supermarket soap, through 14p for a typical leading national brand, to 25p for a high-quality name brand. Six brands dominated the market with Lux, Palmolive and Imperial Leather enjoying shares of around 11% and Camay, Fairy and Lifebouy shares of about 8%. Fresh and Knight's Castile followed with 4 or 5% each and the remainder of the market was divided equally between "own brands" and "others".

The total marketing expense for Greene's was 15% of its invoiced sales figure net of discounts. Wholesalers were invoiced at list prices less 20% less 10% and the 20% margin was expected to be passed on to the retailer. Very large chains buying directly received both discounts. Warehousing and distribution represented the largest share of marketing expenses, averaging 10% of sales. Advertising took another £40,000 per annum and was spent largely on displays in women's magazines.

Several competitors spent double the Alabaster percentage on advertising, but David was not impressed with advertising as a strategy for increasing share. He referred to the heavy advertisers as "men of the sixties". Virtually all housewives bought toilet soap and some 9% — disproportionately grouped in the 35 to 44 age bracket — were classified as heavy users. To get at these heavy users, David argued there was no substitute for supermarket display. Two-thirds of all soap sales went through this segment when Boots, with 14% of the market, was included with supermarkets and self-service groceries. This left only small shares of 14% from the remaining grocery outlets, 8% from other chemists and 12% from departmental and variety stores.

For the longer term, David had more ambitious goals. He planned to introduce a "bath gel" under the Alabaster brand. He could see that the use of bath gels was still in its early stages in the United Kingdom. Badedas, owned by Beechams, was a widely recognised brand and sold at a very profitable price to a small percentage of the population. Its normal price of 66p for 6.4 fl ozs gave it by David's estimate over 1,000 per cent margin on production cost. While there were also some less well-known brands sold, widespread use of gel as a soap replacement in bath and shower, as had developed throughout France and Germany, was yet to come.

How and why do you think their advertising works?

David had seen a recent survey which disclosed that six per cent of the English population put washing-up liquid into their baths; thus many were not averse to the use of liquid gels. Most of the United Kingdom population, however, were not yet aware that gels could replace soap and were more than just liquid bath additives. Some even associated use of Badedas with upper-class pretensions because of its advertising approach. David retold the story with great glee of the woman who asked in the chemist's for 'Baa-dee-dah'.

David's idea was to launch his new gel as "Alabaster Gold", thus building on the Alabaster name. The new gel would be a rich golden liquid in a golden container with the familiar white emblem. The launch would be based on widespread coverage of supermarkets with a massive introductory point-of-sale display backed up with considerable media advertising. By such a dramatic move within the next year, David believed that he would put Greene's in on the ground floor of the trend towards gels and could establish Alabaster Gold as a generic name for liquid gel.

Advertising and promotion for the initial launch would require a budget of £250,000, but the high margins from a gel would quickly repay the initial investment. A temporary bank loan would be required, but David was sure that there would be ample security from the Uxbridge property. Land values in Uxbridge had escalated a thousandfold since Greene's had purchased their site and the firm was sitting on an investment worth over £3 million.

This case was prepared by Kenneth Simmonds of the London Business School. © INC. Publishing Company, Boston, MA, USA, 1982. Reprinted with permission, INC., June 1982.

CASE 14

Leisure Time Ice

Richard Hendler, owner of Saxony Ice Co. in Mamaroneck, N.Y., had always been impressed when such humdrum products as water, bananas and chicken suddenly became big sellers after they were promoted under brand names like Perrier, Chiquita, and Perdue.

Why, he wondered, couldn't the same marketing strategy work for his own product? All he had to do was come up with a brand name that the public would automatically associate with clear refreshing bags of ice.

Saxony Ice needed just such a boost. The company was founded in 1963 and, by 1975, sales were only $485,000. Hendler's customer base hadn't expanded much beyond the small set of stores that had been with him since the beginning.

Hendler realised early that a company the size of his couldn't afford to launch a widespread and effective marketing campaign singlehandedly. But there was nothing to stop him from joining forces with one or more ice companies to form a trade association which would promote member companies' product under a single brand name.

In 1975 Hendler and Harold Reynolds of A.T. Reynolds & Sons in Kiamesha Lake, N.Y., formed a two-man trade association under the name "Leisure Time Ice".

The name Leisure Time was chosen to convey the convenience of packaged ice over homemade ice. The logo — a snow-capped mountain backed by blue sky and surrounded by green forests — suggested a clean and refreshing product different from traditional ice packaging, which featured scenes from the North Pole — igloos, Eskimos, and polar bears. Hendler and Reynolds had the logo printed on their bags, 10 trucks, and company stationery. Total cost was approximately $5,000.

At first, other ice manufacturers were sceptical of Hendler's idea to give ice new status. "When it's hot, people buy ice", said the owners. "In the meantime, let's continue to advertise in the *Yellow Pages*."

But several months after the trade association was formed, another manufacturer, Richard Feingold of Bacu Ice Co., in Poughkeepsie, N.Y., began to think better of the idea and said he and some of his friends wanted to join the association.

During the next three years, Hendler, now president of Leisure Time Ice, made presentations at regional and national trade association meetings, gathering new members from Maine to Colorado. "The more people we have, the more exposure we get, and the bigger we appear", Hendler explained to each group.

Under the association's licensing agreement, a member company used the name and logo of Leisure Time Ice and contributed advertising dollars. In all other respects, however, a member company continued to operate as a separate entity, with its own buyers, suppliers, and pricing strategy. To join the association, each company paid a membership free based on the number of bags of ice it sold annually.

By 1978, the Leisure Time Ice association boasted 15 members and 60 trucks. Annually, it was selling about 13 million bags of ice with the new name and logo, along with the packager's name printed discreetly at the bottom of each bag. The next step was to hire a public relations firm to tell consumers about the advantages of packaged ice. The firm chosen — Creamer, Dickson, Basford Inc. of New York City — sent out fact sheets and news releases touting the association's message: Packaged ice is taste- and odour-free and is clearer and longer lasting than homemade ice.

The hearts of business writers and food editors from Boston to Los Angeles melted. Serious, lengthy articles were written on ice etiquette, including how many cubes to use with different drinks and how much ice to plan on per person. Hendler himself was interviewed by at least 25 editors and appeared on 15 radio and TV talk shows, holding a glass of clear, pure Leisure Time Ice cubes in one hand and a glass of cloudy, homemade cubes in the other. The *Wall Street Journal, New York Times, Los Angeles Times*, UPI, and Associated Press have all featured items on Leisure Time Ice.

Meanwhile, association members' sales increased by at least 10% a year. Hendler's own company went from $458,000 in sales in 1975 to $1,700,000 in 1981. His new business increased by 40%, and his business with existing customers expanded by 60%. "We were the only ice manufacturers doing any advertising, and this gave us a considerable stature with buyers", Hendler says.

The association spent $50,000 for public relations in 1978, $75,000 in 1979, and $95,000 in 1980. In 1981, ads were placed in regional editions of such magazines as *Newsweek, Sports Illustrated,* and *Time*. One ad — a joint effort by seven members of the association — cost $24,000 to place. "It's very impressive to walk into the office of a buyer and say, 'Did you see our ad in *Newsweek?*'" remarks Hendler.

This summer the 27-member association will spend $100,000 to produce and air 30-second TV spots in areas where it has membership — the Northeast, much of the Midwest, and some of the West and Southwest. The commercial's voice-over explains why Leisure Time Ice cubes are nicer than homemade cubes. Visuals show two beverage glasses — one with cloudy cubes and one with clear cubes.

Like Perrier water, Chiquita bananas and Perdue chickens, Leisure Time Ice may or may not have something special to offer that sets it apart from competitors. But by banding together and using their imagination, a handful of small ice manufacturers with average sales of no more than $500,000 a year have given their product something that the individual ice companies never had — national exposure and a touch of class.

This case was prepared by Kenneth Simmonds of the London Business School. © Kenneth Simmonds, 1984 (revised)

CASE 15
Rediplant

Early in 1981 John Bryant, owner of an English timber products firm, was asked by his close friend Martin Nievelt whether he would consider becoming a commissar of Rediplant NV — a company being formed to exploit the new Rediplant method for packaging bulbs. (Commissars of Dutch corporations are outside directors appointed by the shareholders to oversee the employee directors. They have a number of specific powers and their consent must be obtained for all borrowing by the company.) Martin also wanted John's opinion on the number of sealing machines that should be purchased in advance of the first full season of Rediplant sales. This was a particularly difficult decision for him, as there was little guide as to how much they would sell and most of the packaging would have to be carried out during the month of August.

Martin Nievelt and Walter Praag were owners and joint Managing Directors of Hans Praag & Co., an old established Dutch bulb exporter based in Hillegom, Holland. Before the Rediplant development, Praag had concentrated on bulb sales to France, the United Kingdom, Switzerland and Germany. They sold to nurserymen, wholesalers and large retailers as well as directly to the public through mail order catalogues. There were two seasons each year. The larger was for spring bulbs which were lifted from the bulb fields and distributed in the autumn for planting up to mid-winter. This season represented 70% of the bulb market and covered tulips, crocuses, narcissi and hyacinths.

Recent performance of firms in the bulb business had been poor and there had been numerous failures over the previous two years. The 600 exporting houses all belonged to an industry association and argued the need to hold price levels, but competition amongst them resulted in continual margin cutting. Praag had recorded losses both years, mainly because of low response to its mail order catalogues, attributed by Martin Nievelt to cold, wet weekends that discouraged customers from thinking about gardening. While substantial profits could still be made in a good mail order season, the response rates had been dropping at an average rate of 8% per year. The development of the Rediplant system therefore came at a particularly opportune time and gave Praag an opportunity to differentiate its product and increase its margins. Praag decided to withdraw from the direct mail order side of the business and concentrate on building the broadest possible sales of Rediplant packed bulbs. Sales of the mail order list, moreover, would provide finance for the new effort and avoid surrender of ownership interest which was usually required in order to obtain long-term bank lending for small private companies.

The French, German and Swiss mailing lists were sold to Beinum & Co. late in 1980. Beinum was the largest Dutch bulb merchant, with a turnover of around 100 million guilders (Fl. 100m.) and a mailing list of 5 million

1 The standard abbrevia-
tion for a Dutch guilder, or
florin, is Fl. Exchange rates
were:
£1.00(UK) = Fl. 4.30
$1.00(US) = Fl. 3.00

catalogues.[1] Praag's United Kingdom mail order list and the UK wholesale business were sold to Sutcliffe Seeds Ltd of Norwich. Sutcliffe were moving into the bulb market as an extension to their traditional seed activities and the agreement provided for Praag to supply all Sutcliffe's requirements for Dutch bulbs, whilst retaining the right to go directly to a selected list of retail chains and large stores in the United Kingdom.

Development of the Rediplant System

The idea for Rediplant was first conceived in November 1979 by Walter Praag, who concentrated on the engineering and production side of the business, leaving the commercial side to Martin Nievelt. (See the Appendix at the end of the case for a chronology of Rediplant development.) Rediplant was basically a transparent plastic strip moulded to hold bulbs in equally-spaced blisters open at the top and bottom. It was designed as a usage container that could be planted directly in the soil without removing the bulbs, giving them protection from frost, birds, rodents and slugs, and enabling the bulbs to be easily retrieved for planting in subsequent seasons.

Walter Praag explained the development in this way:

> I got the idea at the end of 1979 and aimed only to make our competitive position easier and to solve planting problems for the buyer. We ran trials and found that it made not only for easier planting but also gave protection and a better flower, though it was not invented for that purpose. We tested a great quantity with a sensitive control test and the packaged bulbs showed up better than bulbs planted by hand. We limited our tests to hyacinths, tulips, narcissi, crocuses and gladioli, because the others have extra difficulties for packaging and these are the main selling items. With gladioli we had some trouble and I had to redesign the pack as the sprouts came out of the side of the bulb rather than the top. When we told people the name of our new pack was Rediplant many remarked that it was not a very good name — but minutes later they would all use the name without any prompting. We decided it must be a very good name.

The bulbs were packed automatically into previously formed plastic strips which were then sealed and fitted into a cardboard sleeve printed with details of the bulbs and planting instructions. After considerable experimentation the new pack was ready for launching and in May 1980 a vacuum forming machine was purchased to make quantities of the strips. At this stage the pack was comparatively crude, with a single coloured cardboard sleeve which totally enclosed the plastic strip which was in turn stapled together to hold the bulbs.

Mr Nievelt did his own market research by asking friends, acquaintances and the general public what they thought of the packs and if they would buy them. On his frequent sales trips to England, for example, he asked customers in garden centres and large stores he visited whether they would buy the packs and they all said they would. The packs contained six tulips with a suggested retail price of £1.30 as against a price of £1.00 for similar loose bulbs. Martin also asked retailers in England what they thought of the packaging. He recalled:

> Large retail chains, Woolworths, Boots, Debenhams and John Lewis liked it and after a while the larger garden centres would say that they would buy it. Small centres and garden stores, however, generally said they did not like Rediplant. They gave few reasons but they seemed worried that it would mean other types of stores would find it easier to sell bulbs.

Martin also persuaded three different outlets to test market the strips — a store on a US air force base at Woodbridge, a seedshop in Ipswich and a garden centre at Ramsey, Essex. Each received one hundred strips, without charge, and each qucikly sold the entire assignment at £1.30 each.

Rediplant packaging was next featured in Praag mail order catalogues for spring bulbs sent out in autumn 1980. These were mailed to some 300,000 customers in Britain, France and Germany at a cost including postage of £0.20 (or equivalent) each. Prices for a Rediplant package of six bulbs were set about 30% below the catalogue prices for a standard quantity of 10 loose bulbs, making the price for a Rediplant bulb 15% higher than an equivalent loose bulb. Rediplant packaging appeared on the cover, and the catalogue started with a two-page spread outlining the Rediplant system and offering a 200% guarantee to replace every non-flowering Rediplant bulb with two new bulbs. The spread also showed how Rediplant strips could be planted in evenly spaced rows or in cartwheel or zigzag patterns. Walter Praag commented that this sort of thing seemed to appeal particularly to the German market, which was also much more concerned with rodent and insect damage than other nationalities. He thought the British tended to be keener gardeners and more knowledgeable about bulbs, while many more potential customers in France and Germany would avoid buying loose bulbs that they did not understand, or else buy some and plant them upside down. With Rediplant packages these customers would find planting much easier. Praag's experience had been, too, that the British tended to be much more price conscious than the others, while the French tended to identify value with the price charged.

As orders began to come in during the early winter months, Praag was very encouraged by the high proportion of Rediplant sales. Final figures were as follows:

Country	Cata- logues Posted	No. of Orders Received	Average Order Size	% of Total Bulbs Ordered in Rediplant Packs		
				Tulips	Hyacinths	Narcissi
UK	150,000	8,056	£14.00	18	20	10
France	101,000	5,581	£20.80	27	32	13
W. Germany	50,000	2,091	£21.80	44	39	39

Examination of 160 UK orders at random showed the average order for Rediplant to be £8.00, representing on average 50% of the customer's total order.

Walter Praag continued work on the Rediplant design. The cardboard sleeve was redesigned with full colour pictures of the blooms and better instructions, and the strips were made narrower and extended to include seven bulbs rather than six in a new pack measuring 40 centimetres. Martin Nievelt thought this might discourage price comparison with loose bulbs sold in dozens. Exhibit 1 shows these new strips on the display stand.

For sales through retail outlets, special units were designed containing 180 strips with wire pegs for each six strips. These pegs could be fitted onto pegboards or specially designed Rediplant display stands for floor or counter displays. The mix of varieties for the units was based on a statistical analysis of the historical proportions of bulb sales and would not be varied for individual orders. The unit contained 112 strips of tulips in 14 varieties, 24 strips of hyacinths in 4 varieties, 12 strips of narcissi in 2 varieties and 32 strips of crocuses in 4 varieties. Large display posters illustrating the planting of Rediplant strips were designed to accompany each unit, which would be boxed with or without a display stand as required.

Patents for the Rediplant system of packaging were applied for and obtained in the Benelux countries, the United Kingdom, France, Germany, Canada and the USA. This patent was granted for a "usage" package and competitors would find it difficult to break through simply by altering the design. Moreover, anyone wishing to compete would find it essential on a cost basis to package in Holland, rather than to ship, pack and then redirect the bulbs — and Praag was sure that they would be advised by the Dutch Customs if their patent was infringed.

Partnership with Van Diemen Bros

In late 1980 Praag was approached by Van Diemen Bros who had seen the packages and wanted to explore ways by which they, too, could use the new packaging method. Discussions led to the idea of a partnership for developing the system. Van Diemen had the largest sales force in the Dutch bulb industry, owned their own bulb fields and research laboratories, and were suppliers by appointment to the Netherlands Royal Family. "The idea went against the mentality of the industry that it is not right to work together", said Martin Nievelt. "We had the idea but the other firm had forty sales people against Praag's two, as well as contacts with wholesalers all around the world. A partnership would provide resources and backing at the same time as it removed one of the major sources of potential competition."

Nievelt believed that the fragmented nature of the industry and the lack of product differentiation were the prime causes of low prices and small or non-existent profits. He hoped that the combined strength of the two firms would enable them to make a much larger impact on the bulb market and eventually claim a significant proportion of Dutch bulb sales at higher margins.

The arrangement worked out on a friendly basis with Van Diemen was that Rediplant NV would be formed as a limited company, with Hans Praag & Co. and Van Diemen Bros each owning 50% of the equity. Rediplant would lease Praag's storage and packing facilities in Hillegom and manufacture for the two sales companies, invoicing them at cost after payment of a royalty to Praag of Fl. 0.04 per strip. Praag would retain the right to all sales anywhere in the world destined for customers via mail order and also to wholesale sales in the United Kingdom, Holland and Switzerland. Van Diemen would cover wholesale sales in all remaining countries. This arrangement meant that there would be little change from past concentration because Praag had very little wholesale revenue from France or Germany. The direct mail market, moreover, accounted for some 20% of Dutch bulb exports for dry sales. Martin Nievelt and the senior Van Diemen agreed to act as commissars for the new firm and to ask John Bryant to act as a third neutral commissar. Solicitors were asked to draw up formal agreements. As of the end of February 1981 the drafts had not yet been received.

Meanwhile, Walter Praag and Dik Van Diemen, son of the Van Diemen president, had agreed to become joint managing directors of Rediplant and had become immersed in detailed planning of the production requirements for the 1981 spring bulb season. The elder Van Diemen had also applied to the Dutch government for a grant to develop the invention and Rediplant had received a non-returnable grant of Fl. 130,000.

Exhibit 1 *Rediplant Display Stand*

Assortment 180s

An exclusive new pre-assembled
Assortment for You!

112 packs of tulips in 14 varieties
       7 bulbs per pack

 24 packs of hyacinths in 4 varieties
       5 bulbs per pack

 12 packs of narcissi in 2 varieties
       5 bulbs per pack

 32 packs of crocus in 4 varieties
       14 bulbs per pack

180 packs in 24 well-chosen varieties

Floor space: 15" × 33"
Height display: 63"
Size display poster: 31½" × 18½"
Weight case: 59 lbs.

This display offers an easy and fast set-
up with a minimum of floor space

Advantages:
REDIPLANT is unique (patent pending)
Honest presentation in see-through packs
Optimal ventilation preserves the quality
of the bulbs
Packs are delivered on pegs, saving
labour in setting up display (except
assortment 180 and 90)
REDIPLANT has been successfully tested
Over a century of successful bulb-
growing experience guarantees a high
quality product
Your Department as well as the Dutch
Dept. of Agriculture inspects all bulbs
before they are exported

REDIPLANT

instant planting-system

minute-planting

protection against: mice, birds, vermin and frost

even

Meeting the Demand The period for selling spring bulbs to intermediate outlets ran from January
through August, but delivery requirements would be very tight. Excluding
mail order business, 55% of all sales had to be packed by mid-August, the
next 30% by the end of August, and the last 15% by the end of September.
All United States sales were included in the initial 55% because of the need to
meet shipping dates, but another week could be saved by air freight although
it would increase the freight cost for a standard shipment from Fl. 43.00 per
"180" unit to Fl. 129.00. After September, mail order business could then be
supplied fairly evenly until early December. Delivery commitments were
regarded as very important by all the Rediplant executives. The retail buying
season was concentrated and a supplier who failed to meet his commitments
would ruin his chance of repeat business. Martin Nievelt considered it would

be better to take a limited amount of Rediplant orders in the first season rather than run the risk of not being able to meet orders on time and ruining the Rediplant name.

The supply of bulbs themselves presented few problems. Most bulbs were bought from the growers on a contract basis in the spring while still in the ground. A buyer would contract to buy all the production of a given acreage at a fixed price per bulb. As he sold to his customers before he knew how many bulbs he would receive from this acreage, he had to buy any additional requirements or sell any excess on the free market where the price could fluctuate wildly depending on whether there was a glut or a poor season. Although the average price of bulbs could usually be predicted within 10%, a given tulip had fluctuated in price between Fl. 28.00 and Fl. 44.00 per hundred over the previous few years. By industry agreement, payment to growers was required promptly on 1 November. For a merchant to retain a good name amongst suppliers payment could not be delayed.

The real problems in supply stemmed from the short packaging season after the bulbs were taken from the fields. Crocuses might not be ready to be packed until 25 July, narcissi and hyacinths a week later, and tulips between 25 July and 10 August, depending on the variety. Packaging, therefore, had to be very carefully planned.

When the bulbs arrived for packaging they would be inspected and sorted before being placed in the PVC strips by semi-automatic filling machines. The strips would then pass along conveyors to an automatic radio frequency sealing machine and from there to a station where they would be fitted with the cardboard sleeve and packed into cartons. While the vacuum-forming machine making the PVC strips could produce only 900 strips per hour, stocks could be built up before packaging began. The sorting machines worked rapidly and could take large quantities of bulbs so they did not limit the output in any way. The speed of the filling machines could also be increased if needed. Four filling machines, moreover, had been built and these could keep at least four sealing machines busy. The limiting factor, then, seemed to be the number of sealing machines. These operated with an output of 900 strips per hour and at Fl. 33,000 were the most expensive items. One machine had been specially designed for Rediplant. Orders for further units would have to be placed immediately as there was a three-month delivery time and orders placed after the beginning of March might not be received in time for the packaging season. The machines were believed to be reliable, but if an electronic component should break down an engineer from the manufacturer would be required.

Praag and Van Diemen were annoyed that the manufacturer of the sealing machine was insisting on payment before delivery, had raised the price to Fl. 33,000 from a verbally agreed figure of Fl. 25,000, and would not make any effort to schedule shorter delivery. They had, therefore, investigated other methods of sealing that did not require expensive equipment. All had major disadvantages. Adhesives and stapling were much slower and stapling spoilt the look of the package, while adhesives attracted the dust from the bulbs and were not 100% effective.

Martin Nievelt argued that only one further sealing machine should be ordered. He pointed out that there was no guarantee that huge volumes of Rediplant could be sold in the first season when the buyers knew it to be experimental; moreover, financial difficulties could limit the opportunity to expand in later years. Hans Praag & Co. had little finance available and this had been a further reason for the partnership with Van Diemen. The total requirement for subscribed capital had to be kept to Fl. 400,000 (see Exhibit 2) if Praag's share in the partnership was not to fall below 50%. There was no chance of credit from the machinery supplier and the bank had said previously that it would advance funds only in exchange for some of the ownership equity.

During the busy season it was usual to work two shifts, seven days a week, using mainly student labour. For the peak period from 27 July until 17 August, Martin calculated that two sealing machines would enable a production of 605,000 strips (21 days × 16 hours × 900 strips × 2 machines). As this period would represent 55% of the season's activity, this would mean a total production limit of 1.1 million strips. To be on the safe side he set a first tentative limit of 4,750 units (855,000 strips) for the season's selling activity.

Exhibit 2 *Rediplant Costings*

	Fl.
Equipment	
Vacuum Forming Plant	84,000
Transformer & Electrical Installation	20,000
Moulds	40,000
Sorting Machines 10,000 × 4	40,000
Filling Machines 7,500 × 4	30,000
Transport Lines	20,000
Sealing Machines 33,000 × 2	66,000
	300,000
Packaging Cost	
Electricity & Maintenance	10,000
Rent	40,000
Labour (25,000 hours @ Fl. 12)	300,000
Other Overheads	100,000
Depreciation @ 20%	60,000
Interest: on Equipment	30,000
on Materials and Working Capital	20,000
	560,000

Packaged Cost (excl. display stands)

	Per Strip	Per Unit (180 Strips)
Bulbs	1.24	223.2
PVC	0.08	14.4
Sleeve	0.12	21.6
Royalties (all sales)	0.04	7.2
Packaging (@ 1 m strips)	0.56	100.8
Carton Packaging including labour	0.08	14.4
Point-of-Sale Advertising (display posters and pegs)	0.06	10.8
Packaged cost	2.18	392.4

Rediplant Sales While Walter Praag and Dik Van Diemen concentrated on the production planning, Martin Nievelt took on the task of coordinating the Rediplant sale commitments. With Van Diemen's agreement, he had in January allocated the tentative target limit of 4,750 units on the following basis:

1,500	United Kingdom
1,000	United States
1,000	Germany
500	Sweden
250	France
250	Holland
250	Switzerland

Martin was quick to admit that these were little more than rough guesses but he felt that the overall demand figures offered even less help. These are shown in Exhibit 3.

Exhibit 3 *Dutch Bulb Exports, 1979*

	Total Exports (Fl. millions)	Exported for Dry Sales* (%)
Germany	236	31
United States	96	70
United Kingdom	70	35
France	68	64
Italy	62	59
Switzerland	42	42
Canada	16	68
Austria	12	64
All other markets	10	55

*Dry sales refer to the proportion of the sales going to the general public either directly or through outlets. Wet sales refer to sales to nurserymen for forcing cut flowers.

By the end of February the sales force was just commencing its main effort and there was still very little sales feedback to go on. One large order of 1,000 units without stands, however, had just been confirmed by the largest garden supply wholesaler in Germany who had placed this initial order against a request that he be the sole German distributor next year. This firm employed a sizeable sales force calling on both garden supply outlets and major retail chains. The price negotiated by the Van Diemen sales force was Fl. 2.66 per strip net ex Praag warehouse. The German retail mark-up was usually 35% on sales and the Van Diemen sales representative had been told that the wholesaler himself would take a 20% mark-up on retail price. Transport costs to be met by the wholesaler would be small and there was no duty into Germany.

There had also been other enquiries for large volume supplies but Martin Nievelt had argued against pursuing these for 1981. For example, Beinum, the mail-order house which had purchased Praag's mailing lists, had enquired about Rediplant. It would supply its own bulbs and purchase only the packing and packaging but the volumes required could be very large indeed. After initial discussions that ranged around a figure of Fl. 1.20 per strip it was decided not to do anything until the following season. A very large US mail order firm, Henry Field Seed Nursery Co. of Iowa, also showed interest, but would have required delivery for September when its mail order packing commenced. Several of the large US retail chains had expressed interest. Other than arrangements for a modified test by A&P, the supermarket chain, however, these were not followed up because the A&P firm alone could absorb all Rediplant output in just one of its regions. This supermarket chain planned to test sales of the product at US$2.69 per strip. Van Diemen's US salesmen were instead concentrating on the suburban garden centres which mainly purchased loose bulbs. One of them had reported that, by chaining the size of the Rediplant order he would accept to the amount of loose bulbs ordered, he had been able to gain a substantial increase in his sales of loose bulbs.

Martin Nievelt felt that he could safely leave the Van Diemen sales effort to Van Diemen management. They were well organized, with a world-wide sales director and four area managers. He had, however, provided sets of Rediplant brochures and price sheets drawn up in five languages. The prices Van Diemen chose were set to allow them around 20% on sales and to meet the usual trade margins in the particular country. In the United States, for example, the standard price for a strip at port of entry had been set at the equivalent of Fl. 3.30 to cover such a margin, 12½% duty, and delivery costs.

Exhibit 4   *Van Diemen Bros — Geographical Performance*

	% of 1979 Turnover	No. of Agents
Sweden	20.1	4
W. Germany	19.7	4
Finland	16.7	1 + 1 agent
France	10.7	6 + 3 agents
Italy	8.2	1
Norway	7.0	1 + 6 agents
United States	4.5	5
Denmark	3.8	1
Switzerland	3.0	1
Canada	1.4	—
Austria	1.2	1
Iran	1.1	—
United Kingdom	0.9	1
Greece	0.4	—
South Africa	0.4	—
Belgium	0.4	—
Japan	0.1	—
Portugal	0.1	—
Hong Kong	0.1	—
Rest of World	0.1	—

Van Diemen salesmen were paid a basic salary of Fl. 35,000 plus a commission of 2% for the first Fl. 800,000 increasing by ½% for each additional Fl. 200,000. Detailed technical training was given and maintained on all aspects of bulb culture, although there was no special sales training. A geographical breakdown of Van Diemen's sales is shown in Exhibit 4, together with the numbers of salesmen concentrating on each country. Scandinavia, with a 5% growth rate, was the fastest growing market, as well as bringing Van Diemen its largest sales.

United Kingdom Market

Having reserved 1,500 units for the United Kingdom market, Martin Nievelt was anxious to meet this figure. He was awaiting news from Jan Straten, Praag's only other salesman, who was currently on a sales trip to Britain. Martin expected him to come back with some good orders for Rediplant, some of which would be test orders from the major chains.

Praag's UK bulb turnover in 1980 had been £360,000, of which £160,000 was direct mail. At this level of activity Praag was 6th or 7th in the ranking of about 300 Dutch bulb exporters to the United Kingdom. It was this entire turnover that Praag had sold to Sutcliffe Seeds Ltd at the end of 1980. As part of the agreement Sutcliffe undertook to purchase all its Dutch bulbs from Praag at an agreed formula, whether sold by direct mail or through outlets. Prices were to be set to cover packing and shipping costs and give Praag a 20% mark-up on the packaged cost. The suggested retail price would then be set at 100% mark-up on the price to Sutcliffe (50% on sales). Sutcliffe would give its outlets a discount of 33.3% off this suggested retail price plus an additional 5% for payment within 30 days.

Sutcliffe had been actively looking for ways of expanding its sales of bulbs. It had recently taken over the garden seed division of Charles Gibb & Sons and now held over 30% of the retail seed market in the United Kingdom. With a total UK seed market of only £24 million, however, further growth would be difficult. Against this, the UK bulb market of around £40 million offered more opportunity and Paul Duke, managing director of Sutcliffe, had set his sights on 10% of this market by 1985. Although Sutcliffe had bulb sales of only £160,000 at this time and there were a great number of competitors, Duke planned to develop into the quality end of the market using Sutcliffe's name and selling only the best Dutch bulbs. Local bulb growing had expanded considerably in recent years and Dutch mail-order firms had been undercut by local suppliers, but there were still many bulb varieties better provided from Holland, and direct container shipment in bulk could off-set almost all the location advantage.

Paul Duke had also asked if Sutcliffe could have an exclusive distributorship for Rediplant in the United Kingdom. Martin Nievelt knew that Praag would not have the resources to set up a significant sales force and had agreed to Duke's proposal, subject to Praag retaining the right to visit a number of its existing outlets and 20 of the largest chain stores and department stores in the United Kingdom. Nievelt undertook not to sell to these outlets at a price lower than Sutcliffe's net price to its outlets less 2% cash discount, on the understanding that Sutcliffe would use the same mark-ups as for loose bulbs.

Nievelt was very pleased with the agreement made with Sutcliffe. He thought that in the first year Sutcliffe's sales force of 60, which called on all the garden centres and hardware and garden stores in the UK, would take orders for somewhere in the vicinity of 600 units. The top salesmen sold between £200,000 and £240,000 of merchandise each year. Sutcliffe planned, moreover, to spend £80,000 on advertising its bulbs in the ensuing year and was planning to hold a cocktail and dinner party to announce its venture, which would be widely covered in the trade papers.

With the major demands of the Rediplant development, Martin had been unable to manage a selling visit to the major outlets he had retained for Praag, and had sent Jan Straten in his place. Jan Straten had started with Praag eight years ago at the age of eighteen and, with the exception of a two-year spell in the Dutch army, had worked with them ever since. He was paid a fixed salary of Fl. 35,000 and received £30 a day to cover his expenses while in the UK. He retained his home in Hillegom, seldom being away from home for more than a month at a time, and had sold £100,000 last year, which Martin Nievelt thought was fairly good for a younger man.

The price at which Jan was seeking Rediplant sales in the United Kingdom was £0.88 per strip delivered to the customer, less 2% discount for payment within 10 days. This price was based on a suggested retail price of £1.32 per strip, which Martin had decided would be necessary to give Sutcliffe the same mark-up as for loose bulbs and still leave a reasonable profit for Praag. Costs of packing, freight, insurance, duty (10%), delivery, etc. would amount to about 20% of the packaged cost although this percentage might be reduced for full container deliveries. Martin would have preferred the retail price to be £1.16, which would have about equalled the price for similar loose bulbs in garden stores, but was convinced that at £1.32 Straten should be able to persuade several of the chains to place orders.

APPENDIX:	Late 1979	- Idea for Rediplant conceived by Walter Praag.
Chronology of	May 1980	- Lab testing of Rediplant complete. Relatively crude pack of six bulbs ready for market launch. Vacuum-forming machine for strip manufacture purchased.
Case Events	Summer 1980	- Test sale in three UK outlets. All sell 100 strips quickly at £1.30.
	Autumn 1980	- Rediplant in "6-pack" featured on cover and 2-page spread of Praag mail-order catalogue.
		- Continued improvements to Rediplant — redesigned sleeve and instructions, switch to 7 bulbs instead of 6.
		- Patent applied for.
		- Hans Praag & Co. goes out of mail-order business.
		- Praag enters marketing agreement with Sutcliffe for UK market covering all Praag products.
	Late 1980	- Praag approached by Van Diemen Bros regarding partnership in Rediplant. Friendly agreement reached, but not yet formally signed.
	February 1981	- Preliminary production and marketing plans for Spring 1981 season.
		- Preliminary selling efforts for Rediplant by Van Diemen salesmen in Germany and US; negotiations for mail order with Beinum.
		- Jan Straten of Praag in UK selling to UK customers not covered by Sutcliffe.

This case was prepared by
Dr. Jules Goddard and
Professor Kenneth
Simmonds of the London
Business School.
© Kenneth Simmonds,
1985

CASE 16
Access

Sean MacShane's pride was hurt. As director in charge of the Access account at J. Walter Thompson, the largest advertising agency in Britain, he had just heard from Adam de Vere, the Access marketing director, that four advertising agencies had been invited to pitch for the Access account in competition with JWT who had held the account since its inception in 1972.

This had come as a surprise to Sean. It was February 1978, and the year's advertising campaign, with which the client had seemed delighted, had only just broken. Sean had always understood that the account was on a particularly firm footing, not just because of the success that Access had achieved in its first five years, but more because of the major part that JWT had played five years earlier in the very conception of the card and how it should be marketed. It was JWT, for instance, who had suggested "Access" as its name, who had designed the red and green symbol for the card and who had launched it with the highly acclaimed slogan, "Access takes the waiting out of wanting".

The Access card was issued directly to their own customers by the four major banks which had jointly established the new credit card. It could be used as a payment card, or alternatively for drawing cash advances direct from a bank. The chief competitor was Barclaycard which had been issued six years earlier by Barclays Bank to both its own customers and those of other banks.

Past Promotion of Access

As the agency for The Joint Credit Card Company (JCCC), the service company which was responsible for the establishment of the Access scheme, J. Walter Thompson was not concerned primarily with the recruitment of Access cardholders. Cardholders were recruited directly by the banks contributing to the Access scheme. JWT's task was more to stimulate the actual use of the Access card — although its campaigns were expected to reinforce the banks' recruiting efforts as a secondary objective.

The launch campaign was an aggressive attempt to expand the use of credit under the slogan, "Takes the waiting out of wanting". Government and other pressures, however, forced a change of strategy. The 1975 campaign featured convenience and positioned Access as "Simply a Better Way to Pay". It was aimed at cardholders who used them infrequently. The following year, the emphasis was moved back towards encouraging users who did not incur interest charges to do so, through a cartoon campaign, "I can buy expensive items".

For the 1977 campaign, the strategy had been to position the card as the ideal way to pay for large, necessary items as a means of both beating inflation and saving through bulk buying. The thinking was that sales of high-value items would lead to more credit taking. The targets were existing cardholders and the campaign slogan was "Access makes the most of your money".

The Brief for the 1978 Campaign

Last year's review of Access advertising had started normally in July 1977 following receipt of the client's marketing brief. Against this brief, the Agency's task had been to prepare an advertising plan for 1978.

The following is extracted from Adam de Vere's brief:

As always our main objective for the forthcoming year is to increase profitability and this gives rise to the following aims:

(1)   To increase the number of active cardholders.
(2)   To increase the frequency of card use by cardholders.
(3)   To increase the interest-bearing element of the outstanding balance.
(4)   To recruit new cardholders.
(5)   To generate discount income in excess of JCCC operating costs.

These are our projected targets and, on the assumption that it will not be until the end of the period that there will be any upturn in economic activity, we feel we shall have to generate the business levels sought:

	1976 Actual (£)	Base 1977 Target (£)		1978 Target (£)	
Turnover	410m.	540m.	(+32%)	700m.	(+30%)
Ticket Volume	30.4m.	38m.	(+25%)	46.7m.	(+23%)
Average Ticket Value (ATV)	13.46	14.20	(+5.5%)	15 min.	(+5.5%)
New Access Accounts				250,000	

You will know that one of the main objectives during the current year has been to position ourselves as a medium of payment for higher value transactions (£20 and above) with the thought that not only would the discount income be increased but that the purchases of higher value items would give rise to greater use of the extended credit facility. The most recent information would indicate that in fact greater profitability is likely to stem more quickly from an increase in interest payable rather than discount and that the high-interest payers among cardholders are the high-frequency users who in fact, have a slightly lower-than-average ATV. It would seem, therefore, that the required growth in ticket volumes will be achieved only by raising frequency of use throughout the year by all cardholders. Higher usage alone, however, cannot be relied upon to achieve the objective of lengthening the present average period of credit and we must present cogent reasons to all groups of cardholders to use Access for credit.

We have, as you will see, come away from the thinking that it is a prime objective to concentrate on higher value tickets, but nevertheless we feel that the reasons we have advanced in the current campaign — bulk-buying credit, better quality credit, bargain credit, beat-inflation credit — are still valid.

It would seem to us that what is required from our national advertising campaign is some slight change of emphasis from the higher value purchase/credit platform to an approach that positions *the card rather than the transaction* as of prime importance and encourages greater frequency of use in the everyday purchases of life, both big and small. I would hope that this could be done with some style and panache because, although I think that our current campaign is communicating the present message effectively, my one slight criticism would be that it lacks conspicuous originality and does not command as much immediate impact as I would wish.

At the same time, it continues to be necessary to emphasise the responsible aspect of the credit card facility and to erode the in-built suspicion of this form of credit taking and, indeed, all other forms of credit.

We shall be supplementing the above-the-line advertising by point-of-sale activity on the same lines as during the current year and, necessarily to some extent, there will be a tendency to concentrate on higher value tickets. We would not propose to alter this strategy, both because of lead-in times and also because of a lack, at present, of sufficient evidence to justify a dramatic switch in emphasis.

The 1978 Advertising Recommendations

In preparing the campaign John Street, the account executive, had available the Access performance statistics and the other market and competitive data set out in Exhibits 1 to 5. The 1977 figures at that time were estimates, though as it turned out accurate ones. He also had available the results of a very large survey carried out for Access by Research Surveys of Great Britain Ltd (RSGB). The survey was based on a national quota sample of 755 cardholders questioned during May 1977 using a 14-page questionnaire. In his new campaign proposal, John wrote,

The last study into cardholders' attitudes towards credit (Image Study 1975) has been discussed in full in previous documents. However, results from the RSGB Survey, July 1977, indicate that:

Exhibit 1   *Access — Performance Statistics*

	1973	1974	1975	1976	1977
Accounts on File (m.)	3.1		2.8	2.3	2.8
Gross Active Accounts During Year (m.)	1.2	1.4	1.7	1.9	2.2
New Accounts (000s)	246	201	264	310	485
First Time Actives (000s)	664	323	358	287	373
Turnover (£m.)	138	172	302	410	542
Average Ticket Value (£)	12.98	11.68	12.26	13.77	14.15
Index (1973 Values)	100	78	65	63	56
Deflated Values		9.11	7.97	8.68	7.92
Frequency of Use (No. of Times Per Annum)	8.8	10.4	14.8	16.4	17.6
Repayments:					
As % of Turnover	72	101	92	95	99
As % of Statement	18	23	27	27	28
Credit Limit (£)		184	240	269	272
Average Credit Balance (£)		67	83	100	106
Balance Outstanding at Year End (£m.)	68	75	112	155	190
Interest-Bearing Element of Outstanding					
Balance (%)	77	66	62	61	62
No. of Interest-Bearing Accounts (m.)		0.85	1.02	1.14	1.32

Exhibit 2   *The Lending Market*

	1974	1975	1976	1977
Total Personal Lending				
(Bank Loans + Hire Purchase)				
End of Third Quarter (£m.)	5,144	4,984	5,338	6,210
At 1974 Values (£m.)	5,144	3,982	3,724	3,819
Index	100	77	72	74
Access Interest-Bearing Balance as %	0.9	1.3	1.7	1.8

Exhibit 3 *Access Use by Major Retail Categories*

	1973	1974	1975	1976	1977
Sales = 100%					
(Excludes Access Cash Advances)					
Clothing/Footwear	25	22	18	17	17
Dept. Stores/Mail Order	19	17	18	18	17
Travel & Entertainment	12	14	16	18	19
Garages	9	13	16	14	16
Consumer Durables	14	14	12	11	14
Furniture/Household	9	8	8	9	9
Miscellaneous	12	12	12	13	8

Exhibit 4 *Access Competitive Position 1977*

		Adult Population	Current Accounts	Access	Barclaycard	Store Cards	Hire Purchase
Total (millions)		42.0	20.0	2.7	3.1	1.2	6.0
Percentages of Total:							
Social Groups:	AB	12	20	33	30	18	6
	C1	24	32	40	39	29	21
	C2	32	29	20	22	31	40
	DE	32	18	7	9	22	33
		100	100	100	100	100	100
Age Groups:	15–24	19	14	8	11	14	20
	25–34	18	21	31	27	22	28
	35–44	15	18	21	20	22	23
	45–54	16	18	22	19	20	17
	55–64	14	14	11	14	11	9
	65+	18	15	7	9	11	3
		100	100	100	100	100	100

Exhibit 5 *Advertising and Ownership*

	Credit Card Advertising (£1000s)				
	1973	1974	1975	1976	1977
Access	480.6	574.9	319.8	336.7	472.0
Barclaycard	150.6	284.5	221.4	247.8	549.5
American Express	45.2	38.0	56.1	308.1	706.2
Total Market	717.9	866.5	628.5	985.8	1,834.1
Access's Share	67%	66%	51%	34%	26%

	Credit Card Ownership							
Year Ending March	1974		1975		1976		1977	
	000s	%	000s	%	000s	%	000s	%
Adults With Any Credit Card	4,653	11.3	5,362	13.0	5,555	13.4	6,892	16.6
Access		4.9		5.5		6.3		6.4
Barclaycard		4.9		6.1		6.1		7.5
Diners		0.2		0.3		0.4		0.4
American Express		0.2		0.3		0.3		0.5
Others (Excluding Eurocard)		n.a.		1.2		1.6		2.9

(a) Frequent card users/major interest payers are also the major users of other sources of credit. A credit card is just one of the sources of finance they use.

(b) These pro-credit people believe credit is a good thing because their repayments can be seen as a means of forced saving. It leaves their savings intact for emergencies.

(c) Credit cards are quite favourably regarded but there exists amongst all but the heavy users the lingering doubt that they are "a temptation to overspend". Light users in particular regard them very much as a safety net to fall back on.

(d) Credit cards are handy and convenient for paying and borrowing in the short term (2—3 months) but they are felt to be more expensive than they actually are. When cardholders were asked what they thought the monthly interest rate was, the average of their replies was 2.4%. (Previous advertising research had shown a similar trend to overestimation, respondents expressing surprise at the apparent low cost of interest in the sample repayment tables, for instance.)

(e) Cards are not used routinely, except by heavy users. Very often it just does not occur to cardholders to *use* their card. They need frequent reminding of the availability of their card.

John Street summarised the market as follows:

- Women and the C1/C2 social classes are becoming increasingly important as cardholders and potential users.
- Those who use their cards most frequently and who therefore tend to pay more interest (i.e. "heavy users") also tend to use other sources of credit.
- "Light users" are not using their cards routinely.
- "Light users" and potential cardholders are confused about the relationship between their Access card and their bank account.
- Potential cardholders don't know the rate of interest they pay. They frequently overestimate it.

He then moved immediately on to his proposals as follows:

Advertising Objectives

(1) Persuade more Access cardholders to use the card routinely for purchases large and small.

(2) Increase Access cardholders' confidence in Access as a responsible and readily available method of finance.

Target Group

(1) People owning an Access card of their own volition. They do not yet use it, however, to the full extent of their credit limit.

(2) They are of either sex, 25—44 years old and of all social classes. There is a bias, however, to the ABC1s.

(3) In all probability they are married, with the responsibility of children and a mortgage.

Advertising Responses:
Beliefs about Access

(1) Access can be used routinely to purchase items of all sizes.

(2) Access is as convenient and easy to use as cash.

(3) Access credit can be paid off in full at the end of the month or at regular monthly intervals, as I choose.

(4) Access is an important means of financial control. It enables me to plan my finances in my own way, to best suit my own needs.

Feelings about Access   (1)   I understand how Access works. I can trust myself to use it sensibly.
(2)   Access is surprisingly inexpensive. I'm not worried about the cost of
using the credit facility.
(3)   Access enhances my reputation. I am happy to be seen using it.

Translating the advertising objectives into media requirements, Street
argued that national newspapers would be the best choice to carry the campaign. The objectives required a highly visible and continual presence
amongst existing and potential cardholders. Television would be too expensive for continual presence, posters would transmit only a simple message or
reinforce elements of the main campaign, and magazines (except for the
Radio Times) would generally provide too low a coverage of the target
group.

With a budget of £600,000, a full colour page in a national daily
newspaper would be possible at least once every week of the year, supplemented by a monthly insertion in the *Radio Times*. The proposed media
plan was as follows:

Daily Mail	12 insertions
Daily Express	12 insertions
The Times	12 insertions
Financial Times	6 insertions
Guardian	6 insertions
Radio Times	8 insertions

This plan would yield coverage and frequency of the following levels:

Social Class		Men	Women
ABC1	— Coverage %	82.0	75.0
	— Average Exposures per annum	10.8	10.1
C2	— Coverage %	61.0	57.0
	— Average Exposures per annum	8.9	8.2

A budget of £600,000 was a considerable increase over the previous
year's budget. Exhibit 5 compares the advertising by credit card competitors
since 1973, and card ownership over the same period. As John Street pointed
out, both Barclaycard and American Express had doubled advertising in the
current year so that in real terms the total spending was about where it was in
1973. Access's share, however, had fallen from 67% to 26%. The effect of
the competitors' increase in media expenditure, John Street wrote, had been
"to reduce Access's share of mind-association in the credit card market".

After a little correspondence and several meetings, the budget of
£600,000 was tentatively agreed and JWT proceeded to develop the advertisements shown in Exhibits 6 to 8.

Exhibit 6

Not as much as you'd think. Especially when you think how useful it can be.

Access is welcome at over 100,000 places throughout the country. It's safer than cash, simpler than cheques, and gives you greater flexibility in the way you spend your money.

So how much will this service cost you? If you've bought goods and services with Access and you settle your account, in full, before the date given on your statement the service need cost you nothing. If you settle your account in part we charge you interest at 1¾% per month on the remainder.

So next time you see that card in the window–reach for your own card. Using it is much simpler than you think–and much less expensive.

Cost of £50 over 4 months:	
Month 1	£12.89
Month 2	£12.89
Month 3	£12.89
Month 4	£12.85
Total	£51.52
Interest payment	£1.52

Use Access to make the most of your money.

Exhibit 7

You probably bring your best china out only once or twice a year. Are you doing the same with your Access Card? If you are, you may be missing out on something. Access could take a lot of stress and strain off your family budget. How?

By taking the load off your bank account. By reducing the need to write out so many cheques. By avoiding the necessity of going into overdraft. All these things cost money in the long run.

You can save money by using Access to snap up bargains as they come along. Things like D.I.Y. and decorating equipment are not going to get any cheaper. Pay for your season ticket with Access–before the next round of fare increases.

If you've bought goods and services with Access and you settle your account, in full, before the date given on your statement, the service need cost you nothing. Or you can spread your payments.

So don't just use your Access Card for special occasions. Use it today and every day and see how much you'll benefit.

Cost of £30 over 3 months:

Month 1	£10.20
Month 2	£10.20
Month 3	£10.21
Total	£30.61
Interest paid	£0.61

Use Access to make the most of your money.

Exhibit 8

Wouldn't you be more comfortable if you weren't sitting on your Access Card?

Sitting on your Access Card may seem, at first sight, the most sensible thing to do.

It appears to offer countless opportunities for getting into trouble. A lifetime of thrift and sensible spending thrown out of the window?

Certainly, an Access Card should be handled with intelligence and care.

Because one of the things about Access is that you won't get much out of it if you don't use it. Access can help you get more real value for money. For example, that overcoat isn't going to be worth much to you if you can't afford it until the spring. Access allows you to buy things when you need them.

Use it to take advantage of bulk buying. You'll find opportunities everywhere, from railway season tickets to frozen food. Pay at the time with Access and then settle with us, when it's convenient.

So if you're sitting on your Access Card, why not think about taking it out a bit more often. You could make your money work a lot harder for you.

Cost of £50 over 4 months:	
Month 1	£12.89
Month 2	£12.89
Month 3	£12.89
Month 4	£12.85
Total	£51.52
Interest payment	£1.52

Use Access to make the most of your money.

The maximum interest payable with an Access Card is 23.1% p.a.
A SERVICE OF LLOYDS, MIDLAND, NATIONAL WESTMINSTER, WILLIAMS & GLYN'S AND CLYDESDALE BANKS, THE ROYAL BANK OF SCOTLAND, NORTHERN AND ULSTER BANKS
For further details, call in at any bank displaying the Access sign or write to: Access, Joint Credit Card Company, at Southend-on-Sea X SS99 0BR

Some Client Unhappiness

The news in February 1978 that the client was not entirely satisfied with the agency's performance did not come as a complete surprise. JWT knew that major marketing discussions had been going on at the JCCC board level for some time.

Indeed, during October, a copy of one of the internal memoranda had been passed to the agency for comment. Here are extracts:

(1)   Over the past two years, the number of Gross Actives has risen by 42% but they use money which has shrunk by 25%.

(2)   Faced with such very large changes, we have looked for a standard against which to assess our performance and selected two: the interest-bearing balance on the average Gross Active account; and the value of the average ticket, because total income basically rests on these two factors.

(3)   Interest income comes from the outstanding interest-bearing balance and this has fallen over the past two years by 9% in real terms for the average Gross Active account.

(4)   Discount income stems from the ticket value, and the value of the average ticket has also fallen in real terms over the past two years, by 13%. But the number of times the average Gross Active account holder uses his card has risen by around 20%.

(5)   Thus, of the four basic sources of income, two, namely the number of active cardholders and the number of times they use their card, have both risen; while the other two, the average interest-bearing outstanding balance and the ATV, have both fallen in real terms.

(6)   In particular, two features cloud the future profitability of the card:

     (i)   Because advertising has failed to arrest the decline in ATV, we are in the precarious position of having more and more transactions falling below the break-even ticket value of £13.50 (i.e. average discount commission of 2½% on £13.50 = £0.34, the marginal cost of processing each ticket).

     (ii)   Because there is a discernible trend for Access users, as they become increasingly "sophisticated borrowers", to take their full six weeks or so of free credit and never bear interest charges, the banks are denied their primary source of card revenue and profitability.

(7)   In other words, our cardholder recruitment has been successful. We, or they themselves, have upped the frequency of use. But our advertising and promotional activities aimed at persuading cardholders to take interest, or to buy larger ticket items, have been far from successful.

(8)   This leads us to suggest a limited number of advertising and marketing experiments: in particular, the skimming off of, say, 10%—15% of the national budget and spending it all in a small area for it to represent a trebling or so of advertising weight. If in this area we do (or do not) influence ATV and/or the average interest-bearing balance outstanding we would know we can do it, though at a price, by conventional means — if we don't, we would have to reconsider our strategy.

(9)   Without doubt, Access has grown enormously and very successfully. In particular, the fall in the processing cost per ticket has been a most powerful push towards profitability. Equally, the banks have done well in cardholder recruitment. But our failure to influence the cardholders' behaviour in the ways we wish — the prime objective of our advertising and merchandising activities — must give rise to doubts about either our methods or the weight we put behind them, or both. I believe we should try next year to discover which — if either.

John Street replied with a long letter refuting the memorandum's figure of 42% as the rise in gross active accounts over two years, and arguing that the increase was more like 34%. Furthermore, a recent calculation of the Access market share of outstanding consumer debt showed the Access share rising from 1.3% to 1.8% over the two years. He continued:

> One would expect new users of Access to use the card less often at first and thus to incur lower interest-bearing balances. The fact that a one-third increase in active users in the past two years has not apparently had such a markedly diluting effect on Access's share of consumers' installment credit borrowings is no small cause for satisfaction.
>
> Research has shown that Average Ticket Value is inversely correlated with frequency of use. This is consistent with what we know of consumer behaviour: initially tending towards occasional use for major purchases and subsequently developing into greater everyday usage for minor as well as major purchases. So it is not particularly surprising, in the light of what we now know, that increased frequency of using the card has been accompanied by a decline in average ticket value in real terms. In addition, the success of the JCCC retailer recruitment must have had some effect on ATV, with stores such as Woolworths and Boots coming into the scheme in recent years. The addition of these kinds of large-volume, low-ticket-value chains to Access's repertoire must have an effect on average ATVs.
>
> But averages conceal as well as reveal. Comparison of July 1977 with July 1976 shows that the number of sales tickets of over £20 (the target specified in the strategy for 1977) increased by 24% year over year, whereas the number of tickets of below £20 rose by only 6%.
>
> As to the fall in the average interest-bearing balance, that is due to a drop in the cash advances taken by cardholders. By contrast, the level of *purchases* bearing interest has risen by about 70% in real terms over the two years — i.e. a real increase of about 28% per active cardholder. Furthermore, the bulk (about three-quarters) of this increase has occurred within the latest year, during which the advertising strategy was more specifically and overtly directed to encourage credit taking.
>
> The criticism that advertising and merchandising have failed "to influence the cardholders' behaviour in the ways we wish" is one that we would resist. Card usage has risen — that was one of our 1976 objectives. *Purchases* bearing interest have also increased. "Credit market share", while a fluctuating yardstick, has risen much in line with the increasing number of active cardholders. We should not be self-complacent about this, but it is hard to agree we have totally failed.

John was not sure how far his reply had circulated within the client group. Whatever had happened, Sean MacShane, as the JWT director responsible for pitching to retain the account, now had to pull together a team to prepare a full client presentation.

Some More Data   The growth of credit card usage was making an obvious impact on buying practices, so the national press frequently featured articles about the two leading competitors. Just as Sean's team began work, the following table appeared in the *Daily Telegraph*:

	Barclaycard	Access
Turnover per Year	£500m.	£550m.
Active Cardholders	£2.3m.	£2.4m.
Sales per Card	£217	£230
Average Debt	£100	£100
Average Credit Period	4 months	4—6 months
Average Retailer Discount	2.7%	2.9%
Income from Retailers	£13.5m.	£15m.
Yearly Lending	£150m.	£170m.
Average Transaction	£11	£14
No. of Transactions Per Year	50m.	39m.

The following report on credit cards also appeared in *Update*, produced by Mintel who had commissioned British Market Research Bureau (BMRB) to question a national sample of 899 adults in January 1977:

The last eighteen months have seen a period of consolidation and pruning to the point where both Access and Barclaycard are working at beyond break-even point and now have a firm base to plan development for the future.

Although both companies have been actively recruiting new cardholders, there has at the same time been considerable pruning of bad debts and those who have held cards but do not actually use them. Now that for the first time both companies were operating profitably during 1976, the concern is to maintain this situation.

However, it is anticipated that, as attitudes towards credit cards change and younger people grow to accept credit cards as a way of life, the number of cardholders — and indeed of active users — will increase steadily. The most receptive market currently for future credit card users is the C2 social class, the AB and C1 classes being near saturation level. However, towards the lower end of the social scale, attitudes are harder to change and so recruiting progress will almost certainly be slower than it has been in the past.

While the actual number of cardholders has not been increasing recently, turnover of the credit card companies has indeed grown to the point where average annual expenditure per cardholder has now reached a level of £250—£300, and total annual turnover of the four big credit cards (Access, Barclaycard, American Express and Diners' Club) now amounts to £1,250 million.

It is not possible to assess the achievement of the companies simply in turnover terms since — in the case of Access and Barclaycard — they have to finance the "free" period between the purchase of the item and 28 days after the relevant account date. Nevertheless, some 80% of such credit cardholders are indeed using their cards as a form of extended credit while only 20% usually pay off the total amount outstanding on each account. The companies would prefer that all their cardholders should use their cards for credit purposes since the commission received from retailers in the scheme by no means covers the cost of the operation.

The number of outlets where purchases can be made by Access or Barclaycard now exceeds 100,000 for both cards — the larger outlets being deliberately recruited by the card companies while smaller high street outlets, such as independent electrical goods retailers and drapers, tend to apply to the companies for inclusion in the scheme.

Table A illustrates purchases with credit cards by type of retailer. It can be seen that department and general stores account for the largest single proportion, followed by sales of clothing and footwear, and by household goods and garages for the purchaser of petrol.

Table A *Credit Card Purchases by Type of Retailer*

	%
Departmental/General Stores/Mail Order	19
Clothing and Footwear	18
Household Goods (inc. Durables)	16
Garages	14
Garden Centres/Photographic/Sports Equipment	9
Service (British Rail, Clubs, Travel, Insurance)	7
Hotels	6
Restaurants	3½
Other	7½
	100

Source: Trade estimates

The proportion of sales by credit cards can vary between retailers by anything from 1% to as much as 30% in some discount houses (where mainly household goods are sold) to even higher levels in some garages. The cost to the retailer varies also, but is commonly around 5% or slightly higher.

Ownership of credit cards is illustrated in Table B. As can be seen, personal ownership has increased very slightly, the increase being accounted for by women.

Table B *Personal Ownership of Credit Cards*

	1975	1976
Base, Adults	933	899
	%	%
All adults	12	14
Men	16	16
Women	8	13

Source: BMRB/Mintel

In terms of area, card ownership in the South of the country has increased to a greater extent than elsewhere — the apparent drop in the Midlands is, in fact, not statistically significant.

The much lower level of ownership in the North is borne out by the experience of the credit card companies who have found the North a much harder nut to crack, attitudes in general being far more entrenched in that part of the country than elsewhere.

Table C *Credit Card Ownership by Area*

	1975	1976
Base, Adults	933	899
	%	%
All Adults	12	14
South	14	20
Midlands	12	11
North	8	10

In terms of social class, the effort made to recruit C2 adults to the card-holding fraternity has certainly paid off, as shown below:

Table D *Ownership by Class* (Base: Adults 1975 = 933; 1977 = 889)

	1975 %	1977 %
AB	29	31
C1	20	20
C2	9	13
D	3	4
E	2	3

Source: BMRB/Mintel

Now that Access and Barclaycard have moved beyond the break-even point there will certainly be a close watch on circumstances and recruitment, and maintenance of existing cardholders will have to be carefully controlled to maximise the profit to be gained. Recruitment will therefore be positive, if cautious.

Exhibit 9 *RSGB Segmentation of Credit Cardholders*

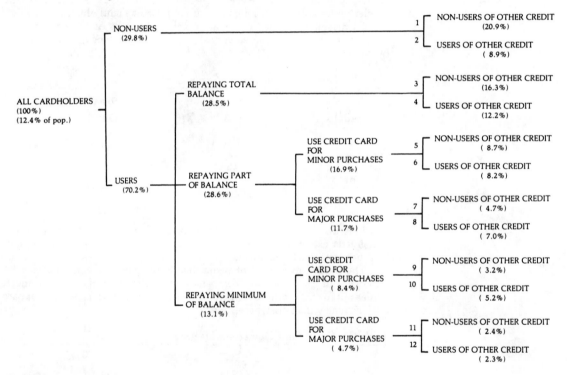

Definitions

Users: those using at least once in the last 12 months.

Users Repaying —

Total outstanding balance: at least twice out of last three occasions.
Minimum outstanding balance: at least twice out of last three occasions.
Part of outstanding balance: those who do not belong to either of the above two categories.

Minor purchases: maximum purchase in last 12 months equal to or less than £50.
Major purchases: maximum purchase greater than £50.
Users of other credit in last 12 months: includes a very small number of people who have used a credit card other than Access or Barclaycard.

The most hopeful sign for the credit card companies for the future of their business was that, when the repayment rate was increased in the Autumn of 1975, it had no discernible effect on the use of cards. There is a theory that card users are more likely to relate the actual cost to them of using the card for credit to the minimum monthly repayment rather than to the long-term interest rates — if so, this bodes well for the future of credit cards.

Certainly any future growth is likely to be steady rather than spectacular, with some natural increase as attitudes change and credit cards become more an accepted way of life. It will be some years, however, before either Access or Barclaycard sees its number of cardholders increase by any significant amount over current levels.

The JWT team also took another look at the RSGB survey. When commissioning the survey, Access management had carefully specified the segmentation of cardholders that would be of most interest to them. The resulting segments are shown in Exhibit 9, along with the definitions employed and the percentages of cardholders falling into each category. This form of segmentation was thought to segregate the main factors contributing to interest taking. However, Trevor Plymouth, one of the JWT research staff, decided to reclassify the data by grouping the classes as follows:

Credit Users	Classes	% of Sample
Inactive	1, 2	30
Light	5, 7, 9	17
Medium	6, 10	13
Convenience	4	12
Heavy	8, 12	9

Exhibit 10   *Card and Credit Usage (JWT Classification)*

		Inactive (N=225)	Light (N=115)	Medium (N=98)	Convenience Users (N=92)	Heavy (N=68)
CARD USAGE						
Av. Frequency of Use Per Month		—	1.6	2.4	2.8	3.2
Used Card in Last Week	(%)	—	16	28	30	46
Approx. Credit Limit	(£)	220	253	227	250	294
Most Valuable Item Bought With Card in Last Year	(£)	—	50	23	49	120
Size of Outstanding Balance, Made Up Of:	(£)		52	71	41	106
1–2 Large Items Only	(%)	—	19	11	21	16
Large and Small	(%)	—	21	23	17	44
Lots of Small Items	(%)	—	44	56	40	32
Other Credit Cards Owned:						
Any Shop Card	(%)	10	12	30	29	37
Amex	(%)	1	5	1	5	10
Diners	(%)	2	—	1	7	6
CREDIT USED IN LAST YEAR						
Access	(%)	—	56	53	64	54
Barclaycard	(%)	—	55	57	46	56
Shop Credit Card	(%)	2	—	18	27	19
Bank Loan/Overdraft	(%)	12	—	53	49	74
HP — Finance Co./Retailer	(%)	9	—	30	19	29
Budget A/c — Mail Order/Retail	(%)	13	—	29	22	29

This classification left out classes 3 and 11 but, as Trevor said, the remaining data gave a clearer indication of cardholder attitudes. Trevor's data are shown in Exhibits 10 to 13. The remaining Exhibits 14 to 18 are taken directly from the RSGB report.

Exhibit 11   *Demographic Profiles of Respondnets (JWT Classification) (%)*

Class	Inactive	Light	Medium	Convenience	Heavy
16—34	30	43	53	49	41
35—54	50	51	37	42	55
55+	20	6	9	9	3
AB	38	49	39	49	42
C1C2	62	51	61	51	57
Head of Household	56	55	61	61	74
Housewife	38	43	36	26	24
Other Adult	7	5	5	13	4
Single/Widowed/Divorced	17	10	14	21	10
Scotland/North	31	23	24	37	20
Midlands	21	25	23	11	18
South	48	51	52	52	62
Cards Held:					
Access Only	41	43	42	48	43
Both	6	16	15	20	19
Barclaycard Only	52	42	43	33	38

Exhibit 12   *Attitudes Towards Finance and Credit (JWT Classification) (% Agreement)*

	Inactive	Light	Medium	Convenience	Heavy
ATTITUDES TO HANDLING FINANCE					
I don't enjoy juggling in finance.	74	62	72	55	63
I think I'm more organised and efficient in my financial affairs than others.	44	41	32	48	43
I often buy things I didn't plan on.	28	36	39	23	19
ATTITUDES TO CREDIT					
With credit there's a great temptation to spend too much.	88	77	77	73	68
I like to pay my way; what you can't afford you've got to work for.	89	79	70	84	49
I don't like things on credit; it's at the back of my mind all the time.	69	50	29	38	22
You don't get the same satisfaction from buying on credit as from saving up.	44	26	16	20	15
Credit is a good thing today.	37	54	63	59	72
Should keep savings for emergencies and use credit to buy things.	21	40	47	41	59
Credit can be used as a sort of forced saving.	42	47	52	36	59
Cheaper to buy now on credit and beat inflation.	40	59	60	60	79
I buy most things, apart from food, on credit; I find it very useful.	3	14	15	23	29

Exhibit 13   *Attitudes Towards Credit Cards (JWT Classification) (% Agreement)*

	Inactive	Light	Medium	Convenience	Heavy
ATTITUDES TO CREDIT CARDS					
Get things cheaper by cheque/cash than c.c.	76	53	55	51	57
More convenient than writing out cheque	36	53	51	65	60
Saves using cheques/bank charges	32	56	47	50	51
Up to eight weeks' free credit	43	53	64	68	72
Like to use for routine purchases only	10	32	46	29	43
Use to spread load/avoid being overdrawn	18	36	45	30	29
I never spend up to limit, in case of something unforeseen	68	63	63	53	54
Nice safe feeling/something to fall back on	70	86	91	74	81
C.C. purchase tends to be spur-of-moment thing	48	34	39	33	32
Too easy to spend the money	76	60	63	44	46
Wouldn't use for meal, can't see benefit after	55	32	27	17	21

Exhibit 14   *Attitudes to Different Credit Sources (RSGB Survey) (% Agreement)*

	Credit Cards	Bank Personal Loan	Bank Overdraft	HP	Shop Account Card	Budget Account With Shop
BASE: All Cardholders (755)						
There is too much checking up on you each time you need to borrow money.	7	17	12	33	8	9
There's a certain snob value attached to borrowing money in this way.	12	11	15	—	11	10
It is difficult to find out exactly how much interest you are paying with this kind of credit.	15	5	7	27	13	12
You can get into difficulties if you miss a repayment when you are borrowing money this way.	21	21	20	57	21	20
With this form of credit you are free to use it in any kind of shop.	61	33	26	4	5	2
You would have to pay a higher rate of interest with this form of credit.	20	13	18	52	6	8
The beauty of this kind of credit is that you know exactly how much you have to pay back each month.	55	50	20	42	19	29
You can use this form of credit for any purpose that you wish.	60	40	31	7	5	5
I would hesitate to try to borrow money in this way, for fear that I might be turned down.	1	13	12	5	2	2
It is a simple, convenient way to borrow money.	74	28	18	12	13	13
You are treated like a responsible adult when you borrow money in this way.	63	57	39	26	28	27

Exhibit 15   *Credit Facility Chosen: Two Hypothetical Purchases (RSGB Survey)*

	Total	Access	B'card	Bank Loan	Bank Overdraft	HP	Shop Acc. Card	Shop Budget Acc.	Would Not Buy On Credit
	755	191	162	15	13	42	20	31	230
REASONS — VACUUM CLEANER (£50)	%	%	%	%	%	%	%	%	%
Convenient/quick/easy to use	35	62	57	40	54	45	55	13	1
Get free credit	12	29	21	—	—	2	—	10	—
Spreads out repayments	3	3	2	—	8	19	5	10	—
More convenient for such small sum	9	14	17	—	8	14	5	10	3
Pay less interest/cheapest	10	7	12	27	23	19	5	42	5
Bank interest cheaper	1	—	—	47	23	—	—	—	—
Shop deals fully with it	2	—	—	—	—	5	25	19	—
Don't like credit	9	—	—	—	—	—	—	—	29
Prefer cash/cheque for this amount	19	—	—	—	8	—	—	3	61
Get cheaper at discount	7	—	1	7	—	—	—	3	22
	755	137	99	55	27	60	29	41	231
REASONS — CARPETING (£100)	%	%	%	%	%	%	%	%	%
Convenient/quick/easy to use	28	61	58	40	37	37	41	15	**
Get free credit	8	28	22	—	4	2	3	10	—
Spreads out repayments	5	3	2	7	11	38	3	2	**
More convenient for such small sum	3	7	5	5	—	3	3	37	2
Pay less interest/cheapest	9	3	10	16	19	18	17	—	—
Bank interest cheaper	4	—	1	42	30	—	—	—	—
Shop deals fully with it	3	—	—	—	—	2	28	29	—
Don't like credit	10	—	—	—	—	—	—	—	32
Prefer cash/cheque for this amount	18	—	—	—	4	—	—	2	54
Get cheaper at discount	7	—	1	7	—	—	—	—	20

** Less than 1%

Exhibit 16 *Beliefs About Relative Expense of Credit Sources: All Cardholders (755)*
(RSGB Survey)

Hire Purchase	%	Bank Loans	%	Credit Card	%
Most Expensive	71	Most Expensive	9	Most Expensive	17
Least Expensive	4	Least Expensive	55	Least Expensive	36
Average	26	Average	37	Average	47

Exhibit 17 *Percentages Who Have Ever Used These Credit Sources (RSGB Survey)*

	All Card-holders	All Card Users	Card Credit Only	Card and Other Credit	Other Credit Only
	755	530	132	166	159
Extended Credit on Credit Cards:	%	%	%	%	%
Access	51	61	57	57	54
Barclaycard as a Credit Card	49	56	57	60	40
Other (Not Shop Cards)	3	5	2	8	4
Bank Personal Loan	42	45	40	67	50
Bank Overdraft	31	36	31	52	38
Hire Purchase Through Finance Co.	32	33	35	41	42
Hire Purchase/Other Extended Credit Through Shop	21	22	20	36	27
Budget Account With Retailer	10	12	10	18	16
Budget Account With Mail Order Co.	21	21	27	33	35
Shop Credit Card — e.g. Debenhams/Burtons/Option Account	19	24	14	32	30
Loan From Employer or Friend	12	13	3	23	19
Electricity/Gas Board Credit	10	11	4	15	16
Loan From Money Lender	1	2	2	2	3
Loan From Money Lending Company	2	2	2	3	3
Cheque Trading — e.g. Provident	3	2	3	4	4
Building Society/Mortgage	4	5	1	6	9
Insurance Policy/Company	1	1	—	1	1
Local Authority	—	—	—	1	1
Bridging Loan	—	—	—	—	1
Other	—	—	—	—	1
None	4	—	—	—	—

Exhibit 18 *Advantages of Other Forms of Credit Chosen By Current Users (RSGB Survey)*

	TOTAL	Bank Loan	Over-draft	Finance Company HP	Shop HP	Shop Budget Account	Mail Order Budget Account	Shop Credit Card	Friend/ Work/ Relative	Card & Other Credit Users	Other Credit Users Only
BASE:	269	91	62	48	34	22	63	48	20	142	125
	%	%	%	%	%	%	%	%	%	%	%
Cheaper	14	20	8	8	15	18	13	19	5	15	12
No Interest	10	5	6	4	15	9	16	13	40	9	10
Less Interest	16	24	24	8	24	14	5	8	—	18	14
Simpler	43	38	55	52	35	59	33	40	35	42	43
Regular Fixed Payments	11	15	8	13	12	18	8	13	—	11	12
Only Source for that Amount	8	5	8	15	3	—	3	6	10	6	10
Get Commission	3	—	—	—	—	—	11	2	—	—	5
Prefer Home Shopping With Mail Order	5	2	—	2	6	9	22	2	5	6	10

Reasons Why Credit Card Not Used Though Considered as Alternative

BASE: All Considering as Alternative Source (18)

	%	
Interest Too High	17	
Not Accepted at Shop	28	
Did Not Want To Increase Balance	17	
Other More Convenient	17	

Reasons Why Credit Card Not Considered As Alternative

BASE: All Not Considering as Alternative	(251)	(88)	(58)	(43)	(30)	(21)	(60)	(45)	(19)	(132)	(117)
	%	%	%	%	%	%	%	%	%	%	%
Chosen Credit Cheaper	18	24	16	14	27	19	17	20	21	17	17
Above Card Limit	20	27	24	23	13	14	12	7	26	21	19
Chosen Credit Simpler	9	8	7	2	7	14	13	4	16	8	11
Card Not Accepted	7	5	7	7	7	19	15	7	—	5	9
Already Had Shop Account	7	1	2	5	3	—	2	29	—	6	8
Relative/Friend Runs Mail Order	9	2	3	7	3	—	35	4	5	7	17
Don't Know/No Answer	32	43	41	40	33	10	15	33	26	36	27

CASE 17
Financial Times Business Newsletters

In July 1976 Keith Foley, Marketing Manager for the *Financial Times* Syndication Department, was reviewing the marketing strategy for *Financial Times* Business Newsletters. The London *Financial Times (FT)* was a leading daily newspaper aimed at top business and financial executives; it had a strong readership and reputation in the UK and overseas, especially in continental Europe. Apart from the newspaper itself, the *FT* group published books and magazines, organised conferences, provided various information and research services, and supplied syndicated articles to other journals on a world-wide basis; newsletters were the responsibility of the Syndication Department.

In Foley's words, "A newsletter is a periodical which seeks to supply current information on a topic in a very concise form, rather than a hotch-potch of features, advertising, etc, like a magazine ... There's no advertising at all". Most newspapers came out weekly, fortnightly or monthly. The fixed production and editorial cost of a newsletter could be as low as £5,000 or up to £10,000 per annum. Since a year's subscription could be in excess of £100, and the incremental copying and postage costs per subscriber were low (around 25p per issue), newsletters were potentially very profitable, depending on how many subscriptions could be generated and with what marketing expenditure. Here are some extracts from Keith Foley's description of how the *FT* marketed its ten Business Newsletters (see Exhibit 1).

> At the beginning of 1976 we had nine established newsletters — we'd just dropped one at the end of 1975, and we hadn't yet launched *World Accounting Report*. I've got a budget of £36,000 for promotion of these established newsletters, £4,000 each. As you'll see, there are some which need more promotional attention and some which need less, but I'm under some pressure to stick to that rule. Still, if I spend, say, £6,000 on a particular newsletter, that's fine as long as I'm adequately covered by revenue ...

> The only way we can maintain profitability is to drop the dead ones and introduce new ones. It would be nice just to bring out new ones of course, but with the department as it is, we couldn't really cope with many more than ten — I guess twelve would be an absolute maximum. Anyway the product life cycle is fairly short: on an annual basis we might weed out two and bring in two, keeping the total constant ... This gives an average life cycle of five years, but with great variability about the average (see Exhibit 2). Of course, one of the problems is knowing why such-and-such a newsletter has come down from its peak: it may be a cyclical effect of the big recession which began in 1973, or it may be that a lot of people were prepared to try it out originally because of the FT's reputation, and that gave it an artificial boost. Finally, the whole field is much more competitive than five years ago. Most of the competition comes from the States, where they've even got a newsletter on newsletters! ...

Exhibit 1 *FT Business Newsletters*   (As at July 1976: £1.00 = $1.88)

EUROPEAN COMMUNITY INFORMATION

(Monthly. £25.00/$65.00 p.a.)

Summarises all the main decisions and new initiatives of the European Commission, the Council of Ministers, the Court of Justice, the European Parliament and the Investment Bank. There are regular sections on: economics and finance, competition, labour matters, regional policies, legal affairs, external relations, associated states, agriculture, and statistics together with background information on the different institutions.

BUSINESS LETTER FROM EUROPE

(Weekly. £70.00/$175.00 p.a.)

The monitoring of key business developments on the continent is the prime aim of this letter. Concise weekly reports cover such key topics as developments and decisions in the Community institutions, duties and tariffs, finance and taxation measures, imports and exports, key business developments within individual European countries, industrial output, labour relations and agriculture; special emphasis is devoted to the key industrial and commercial sectors, with reports on the activities of all major European companies.

TAX NEWSLETTER

(Monthly. £55.00/$140.00 p.a.)

It is international in scope, because the widespread operations of modern business have to take both domestic and foreign tax laws into account. The news which is presented is guided by the principle of concentrating on worldwide developments likely to have a practical impact on business decisions. The newsletter is essential reading for those whose work requires them to keep up-to-date with international tax affairs.

PETRO·MONEY REPORT

(Fortnightly. £120.00/$300.00 p.a.)

Helps fill the growing need for detailed information from the Middle East and the world's financial markets on vital matters arising from the changing direction of oil money flows. The newsletter is primarily about finance and investment, though it does relate the deployment of oil revenues to economic and political developments both in the Middle East and elsewhere.

WORLD COMMODITY REPORT

(Weekly. £70.00/$175.00 p.a.)

Commodities are at the heart of the new relationship that is developing between the primary producers of the Third World and the industrialised economies. This newsletter, therefore, is a broadly international source of information about the weekly trends of the major minerals and foodstuffs. It reports on the production news, consumption trends, crop forecasts, new discoveries and their development, and the politics of commodities. All this is preceded by a regular in-depth look at a topical commodity or a geographical region.

EUROPEAN LAW NEWSLETTER

(Monthly. £55.00/$140.00 p.a.)

Provides vital information on the legal aspects of doing business in Europe. The emphasis of the information is to cast light on the practical consequences of each legal development. Among the decisions analysed are those which affect cross-border investments, marketing arrangements, and co-operation with foreign firms.

EURO · MARKET LETTER

(Weekly. £155.00/$390.00 p.a.)

A confidential report on international and domestic capital and money markets. The letter opens with a news summary of events occurring within the world markets. It usually concentrates on two or three significant items followed by a resumé of the rest of the news. This is normally followed by a section devoted to medium term financing. Under the heading "Eurobonds", details of rates and banking transactions are described, and a list of prices of recent dollar bond issues are also quoted. Detailed reports are given of domestic money markets in the major financial centres. Finally, there is a synopsis of the state of Euro-currencies followed by a short listing of selected Euro-dollar rates.

WORLD INSURANCE REPORT

(Fortnightly. £100.00/$250.00 p.a.)

In both the private and public sectors, those who must take high-level decisions on the insurance of major risks need to be kept well briefed on this unpredictable industry. Regular coverage of: Non life insurance, Reinsurance, Social and employee insurance, Legislation, Management, Company developments. Many other aspects are included. With insurance becoming one of the major financial liabilities these days, this newsletter becomes essential to those with more than a local interest in the subject.

NORTH SEA LETTER

(Weekly. £100.00/$250.00 p.a.)

From both the offshore and onshore developments of the North West Continental Shelf a vast new industry has emerged. The economic impact of North Sea oil will continue to pave the way for further opportunities. The North Sea Letter monitors the progress and the possibilities continually being opened up in this vigorously competitive area. It regularly covers: Exploration, Onshore activities, Offshore supplies, Production, People, Finance, and Politics.

WORLD ACCOUNTING REPORT

(Monthly. £55.00/$140.00 p.a.)

The emergence of the standard-setting bodies in the UK and US, and the trend towards harmonisation in Europe, started the ball-rolling. The rapid growth of the international accounting firms, the creation of the International Accounting Standards Committee, and the proposed formation of the International Federation of Accountants in New York, has further stimulated the need for a comprehensive publication about international accounting. Each month, within a geographical framework, World Accounting Report looks closely at how international accounting procedures have taken on fresh significance.

From these, the largest single collection of business newsletters published in the UK, there may be one or more which will be of particular interest to you. If there is, and you would like to see a specimen, please complete and return the coupon overleaf.

Prices quoted are UK only. Overseas rates are available on request.

We've just done an analysis of our subscribers (see Exhibit 3 for the figures for Euromarket Letter). Our own sales split about 50—50 into UK and overseas, with most of the overseas being continental Europe . . .

Another thing is that if we drop a newsletter, we seem to be able to pick up most of the subscribers on other newsletters. I find this rather surprising, as there isn't an enormous degree of overlap. There is some in the case of *European Community Information* and *Business Letter from Europe*, which gives me a problem with priorities: if I'm given access to a new European mailing list (as happened three months ago) which one do I promote? I can't promote both!

Exhibit 2 *Subscription Levels at 1 January each Year*

Newsletter	1970	1971	1972	1973	1974	1975	1976
BLE	(1)	300	280	260	220	200	196
EML	(1)	130	210	250	240	240	250
A	(1)	80	100	70 (3)			
ELN		(1)	320	470	410	370	380
B		(1)	140	190	100 (3)		
TN		(1)	400	550	520	490	480
ECI			(2)	1290	1030	880	820
C			(1)	240	190	110 (3)	
D			(1)	180	120 (3)		
WCR				(1)	120	150	150
E				(1)	70 (3)		
PMR					(1)	180	200
F					(1)	110 (3)	
NSL						(1)	260
WIR						(1)	190
WAR							(1)

(1) Launched.
(2) Purchased from European Commission with 950 subscribers.
(3) Withdrawn.

Exhibit 3 *Euromarket Letter: Analysis of Subscribers as at 1 July 1976*

	UK	Europe	North America	Middle East	Far East	Rest of World	Total
Banks	65	77	14	7	11	9	183
Finance Institutions	12	2	2	2	1	1	20
Government	2	1	2	2	1	2	10
Mfg. Industry	6	6	2			2	16
Insurance Companies	1	1	1				3
Investment Companies	2	2	1	1			6
Private	1	4	1		1		7
Miscellaneous	4	2				1	7
Unknown	3	6	1		1		11
TOTAL	96	101	24	12	15	15	263

Each editor is in complete control of what goes into his newsletter. Obviously, I take an interest in the editorial content, but I have no control over it at all — after all, I'm not the expert. I respect the editors as journalists, and they respect that my responsibility is the marketing . . . One thing about the production is that subscribers, although they're paying £100 or whatever, want to see something in a fairly cheap form. Because they see it as a kind of confidential service, they think if it's typewritten it's specially for them. So it's first class mail, typed and copied on cartridge paper, never on gloss . . .

The other side of the coin is what we do to increase subscription of current newsletters. Direct mail is by far the most effective way of improving sales, and the cost is still only about £200 per thousand even at today's postage rates. Display advertising doesn't really work, except insofar as we advertise in the *FT* — and we're able to get in — we get the space very cheap. Let's take *North Sea Letter* as an example of the kind of things we do.

As at the 1st of January this year, we had 258 annual subscribers. For historical reasons, a lot of these — 55 altogether — terminated in January. Of these 44 renewed, exactly 80%, which is good — the average over all products is about 65%. We have an automatic system whereby each subscriber gets a renewal reminder two months before termination, with two follow-ups.

In February there was a big government announcement about the landing of the first North Sea oil. Based on that, I did a small mailing to about 1800 people — oil interests out of a directory. I normally do a mailing with three insertions: a letter, an A4 fly leaflet and an order card, all with similar graphics. This is part of the corporate identity we introduced back in November 1975. The leaflet includes a money-back offer for people who originally paid cash, and then decide after six issues that the newsletter does not meet their requirements: apart from the fact that this helps us to sell subscriptions, it improves our cash flow, and in practice hardly anyone decides to drop out.

On that particular mailing I got ten definitely attributable subscriptions — this may not be all, because despite the order card, and a note in the letter, some people insist on ordering with their own order forms or by letter, and we can't tie that subscription in with any particular promotion. This 'miscellaneous'

Exhibit 4   *Subscriptions to North Sea Letter: January to June 1976*

MONTH	JAN	FEB	MAR	APR	MAY	JUN
OPENING SUBSCRIPTIONS	258	248	248	250	255	268
Terminations	(55)	(37)	(20)	(12)	(16)	(11)
Renewals	44	29	18	11	12	8
NET TERMINATIONS	(11)	(8)	(2)	(1)	(4)	(3)
New subs: direct mail	0	5	3	2	11	20
New subs: advertising	0	2	1	2	2	0
New subs: misc	1	1	0	2	4	5
NEW SUBSCRIPTIONS	1	8	4	6	17	25
NET GAIN/(LOSS)	(10)	0	2	5	13	22
CLOSING SUBSCRIPTIONS	248	248	250	255	268	290

category for *North Sea Letter* is 13 so far this year, as you can see from the monthly subscriptions record (Exhibit 4).

In May we changed *North Sea Letter* from fortnightly to weekly, and I did a mailing to over 10,000 people: three different lists, each coded separately. We also did a special offer, a map of the North Sea, showing all the blocks, fields and so on, which you get with your first issue if you take up a subscription — and which we're also offering to previous subscribers if they renew. The map cost just £80 for a run of 500, and it doesn't increase the postal cost of the first issue if someone takes up or renews a subscription. And it gives us something to talk about.

I've also spent a total of £550 this year advertising *North Sea Letter*. The ads are more light-hearted than the mailings, in order to get attention . . . I've done one in the *Petroleum Economist*, one in the *Oil and Gas Journal*, and two in the *FT*. All my ads are couponed, but again, it's hard to relate promotion to sales: as in April, I advertised in the *FT* and received 62 enquiries — but out of that 62 I can only show one definite conversion who used the coded order form. That ad cost me £90 on production, plus £84 for space — that's for a quarter-page. I get the space at 90% discount in the *FT* — when I can get it. Obviously, at that discount I get bottom priority, and I can never guarantee when I'm going to get in: this year, they're being so successful selling space that I'm always getting booted out . . .

There's another thing about advertising which worries me. I suspect that seeing adverts may have a bad effect on existing subscribers — it reduces the feeling of a confidential personalised service . . . In fact I'm seriously thinking of dropping it altogether — it costs a lot to get together, and there's such a hassle getting it into the paper, I'm beginning to think it's not worth the time and trouble. The only time that it is, is when we launch. For example, with *World Accounting Report* we got 450 replies to the first ad in the *FT* . . . But again, the main launch effort for *World Accounting* was direct mail. We did a large mailing in April, to people on seven different lists, that's 30,000 people altogether. And we're hitting another 6,000 in the States this month . . . That makes just over £7,000 I'll have spent on launch mailings, plus £700 on advertising and £200 on a press reception. The response has been very good — over 300 subscriptions to-date and still rising fast . . .

I think *World Accounting* is well-positioned and well-priced . . . What would normally happen is that I would get together with Dick Hall, who runs the Syndication Department, and we'd decide it's about time we introduced something new for profit reasons, and between us we'd put our heads together and think of a field where we think we would have a market. And then I would go into it in more research detail. I would have a number of subject areas to look at. It's a very informal process, which mostly takes place in corridors! Journalists hate meetings, of course, whereas I need them in order to know what other people think . . .

World Accounting was unusual, in that it was dreamt up by the guy who's editor. I did do some informal field research by telephone, using oblique rather than direct questions to check that there was need for such a publication. The object was not to modify the product concept, just to make sure it was viable . . . I did the pricing — talking with the editor, estimating the size of the market and what it would bear, given the competition etc; I also had the likely overheads and promotion costs, and of course our experience with all the other newsletters . . .

What else do we do? Well I don't really do any direct selling, because I'm not qualified to talk about international taxes or European law or whatever . . . I'd always review the content of a brochure, an ad or a letter with the relevant editor. He wouldn't have much direct marketing involvement, but if he was going on a visit he might ask me for some sample copies to give to the people he's interviewing, and then ask me on his return to write to so-and-so and try and sell him a subscription . . .

I've also got a huge stand which either goes as a window display downstairs, or which I set up at conferences. For overseas conferences I just send sample copies to go inside delegates' folders, or alternatively a small stand which goes out with the conference department staff, who of course I know. And obviously, we tend to mention *FT* conferences in our editorial, so we help each other . . .

One other thing we're playing with now is letting subscribers have extra copies of a newsletter at an extra charge of 10% of the initial subscription, for each extra copy . . .

This case was prepared by Professor Kenneth Simmonds of the London Business School. © Kenneth Simmonds, 1986.

CASE 18

Structon Engineers

On 13 November 1984 Structon Engineers of London received a letter from the head office of Chemica Internationale SA (CISA) in Brussels announcing their intention to build an oil-seed extraction plant in Sassandra. Sassandra is a town at the mouth of the Sassandra river in the West African nation of the Ivory Coast and not far from the port of San Pedro. An extract from this letter reads as follows:

> The work to be performed is the erection of the plant and its related facilities. All the necessary materials will be purchased by CISA and delivered at San Pedro harbour.
>
> We are preparing an erection specification in which the requirements for this project will be given and on the basis of which we intend to invite competitive lump sum bids. We should appreciate your letting us know on or before 19th November whether you would be interested in submitting a tender for erection work. We will then send you our invitation to bid together with our erection specification and our proposed agreement.
>
> The tender should be submitted six weeks after the date of the formal invitation to bid. It is intended to award the contract about one month after the tender will have been received, and the construction of the plant will have to be completed on or before 1st June 1986.

Mr M. Bergen, Structon's Sales Director, knew that an expression of interest in this project would not bind the firm to submit a bid but, on the other hand, any later withdrawal or submission of an unreasonably high bid might prejudice CISA against Structon when selecting bidders for other projects.

Structon's Product Line Policy

Structon was an international construction firm specialising in the design and construction of chemical processing plants that required an integration of mechanical, chemical, electrical, structural and civil engineering skills. Headquarters were in London, and all the design and engineering staff were located there.

Exhibits 1 and 2 show the firm's sales pattern over the last five years broken down by type of contract and nature of the process, and according to the location of the construction. These figures represent the value of construction and engineering actually carried out during the year, not the value of orders recorded during the year.

Two-thirds of Structon's business was made up of orders for which the customers provided Structon with information or designs concerning their own processes. This was divided again into work for which the customer arranged the engineering (construction only) and work for which Structon engineered the process based on the customer's data. Structon preferred to use its own engineers. Construction-only work did not add to the engineering capabilities that the firm wanted to build up, and when engineering and

Exhibit 1   *Five-Year Analysis by Type of Contract and Process*

	£ millions				
	1980	1981	1982	1983	1984 projected
Structon Processes					
Industrial Chemicals	5.3	5.1	5.6	8.5	9.1
Agricultural Chemicals	5.0	6.3	8.4	10.2	11.1
Petrochemical Processes	0.8	1.2	1.2	0.3	1.8
Other (Sugar refining, salt plants, textile treatment, etc.)	6.1	6.7	7.7	9.0	10.0
CLIENTS' DATA					
Engineering and Construction					
Industrial Chemicals	15.2	3.1	7.9	11.2	9.0
Agricultural Chemicals	2.9	13.9	7.7	8.6	10.4
Petrochemical Processes	1.3	0.6	0.9	—	—
Other	7.1	12.0	20.1	10.3	11.7
Construction Only					
Industrial Chemicals	6.3	2.1	5.9	8.1	10.3
Agricultural Chemicals	—	—	—	—	—
Petrochemical Processes	14.0	0.3	3.7	8.0	12.0
Other	—	—	7.5	6.0	—
Total					
Industrial Chemicals	26.8	10.3	19.4	27.8	28.4
Agricultural Chemicals	7.9	20.2	16.1	18.8	21.5
Petrochemical Processes	16.1	2.1	5.8	8.3	13.8
Other	13.2	18.7	35.3	25.3	21.7
Total	64.0	51.3	76.6	80.2	85.4

Exhibit 2   *Five-Year Sales Analysis by Geographical Location (£ millions)*

	1980	1981	1982	1983	1984 projected	Estimated Average Rate of Growth of Market Over Next 5 Years
Home Market	25.7	19.3	38.1	24.1	29.2	8%
Western Europe	22.1	14.2	13.2	9.1	15.0	15%
Eastern Europe	—	3.1	—	20.9	16.4	20%
Middle East	—	1.9	—	14.1	11.7	5%
North Africa	6.4	—	14.5	—	—	10%
Rest of Africa	—	5.6	—	—	—	10%
Asia	3.6	—	8.1	—	—	20%
Australasia	—	7.2	2.7	12.0	13.1	10%
Central & South America	6.2	—	—	—	—	?
Total	64.0	51.3	76.6	80.2	85.4	

provision of materials were in the customer's hands Structon had little opportunity to make economies in design or scheduling. Customers who arranged the engineering separately, however, were mainly very large firms or public authorities with a considerable volume of work, not all of which might be already engineered. Large firms were also in a position to license construction firms to build plants for other customers, using their processes. Construction-only work could also add to the firm's output at a time when engineering staff were occupied on other work.

The remaining third of Structon's business was represented by work for which Structon provided all the technology. Structon wished to extend this side of its operations, hoping to get to the stage of being able to offer developing nations and less sophisticated customers inexpensive well-designed plants. Orders for this class of work were less subject to fluctuations and helped to smooth out the troughs between major, one-off contracts. Tender and selling costs were higher but were offset by the higher success rate and higher mark-ups, although the firm had to invest in research and development in anticipation of a market for a particular process.

A preponderance of Structon's production had been in chemical processes, providing industrial chemicals and gases and agricultural chemicals for fertilisers except where these were processed from petrochemical by-products. Although Structon had erected a number of plants in the petrochemical field, it was not a major contractor here. No contract had ever been undertaken for the complete design, engineering and erection of a major petrochemical plant. Structon executives had decided that Structon should begin to move more strongly into this field. With this in mind an agreement had been entered into, in 1984, with an American petrochemical contracting firm, to draw on their engineering experience for work outside the North American market.

Some Structon executives considered that the firm should immediately take steps to enter the bidding on contracts for the complete engineering and construction of major petrochemical plants. Others were against this plan. They pointed out that there were many larger firms already experienced in engineering and erection of petrochemical plants against whom Structon would have to bid. One executive claimed that even with the engineering know-how of the American firm, two or three major contracts might have to be taken at a loss for each type of process before Structon could build up the experience to compete with established firms. Also, the technology was relatively developed and profitability would therefore be quite low. Structon might never recover the initial investment in lost profits. The executives who were against bidding on complete major plants were generally agreed that the firm should put its efforts into less developed areas of petrochemical processing for which Structon could eventually develop its own processes, and which were not confined to large, sophisticated chemical firms as customers.

Geographical Policy Mr Bergen had summarised Structon's geographical policy in his forecast for 1984 by claiming, "Structon is prepared to undertake the right sort of job almost anywhere in the world, provided it fits into the work schedule and the risk is adequately covered". There were, however, advantages from building up contracts and experience in a particular country or area and as a guide for focusing the firm's selling effort, rather than diluting it by attempting to cover the whole globe, Mr Bergen had drawn up a list of geographical priorities.

After its home market, Structon was particularly interested in Eastern Europe. In most Eastern European countries, however, very little of the actual construction was let to foreign firms. Other West European countries were next on the list, although local competition was generally too strong in Holland and Germany. European countries were not too distant geographically and relatively stable. They offered immense scope for plant erection over the next five years.

Structon had recently established a resident branch in Australia and wished to give work there a priority. With a resident construction force it was considered particularly important to develop a steady volume of business, whereas in other countries it was the policy to operate on a job basis and withdraw all resident staff when a major job was completed.

In the Middle East a considerable number of contracts had been undertaken in Saudi Arabia and the Gulf in the past, but the reduction in capital spending was now a major problem for this area. Egypt was listed high on the priority list becuase it offered much opportunity for petrochemical plant, and was extending its production capacity in many fields. Elsewhere in Africa there was little to attract specific concentration by Structon, except for South Africa, and a policy decision had been made to avoid work there.

China, Pakistan and Indonesia were considered worthy of further attention and, although little work had been undertaken in the past in these countries, Mr Bergen was actively following all opportunities to bid there. Structon also had little experience in South America. Political conditions had discouraged the management and no priority was placed on expansion there. Opportunities to bid in Venezuela and Brazil would be considered, but not actively sought.

The Customer   CISA was a large and widely diversified chemical firm operating many chemical process plants in Western Europe, Africa, the Middle East, South America and Australia. All new CISA investment was administered from Brussels and the majority was currently being funnelled into Common Market countries.

CISA normally invited only three or four firms to tender on its plant investments. This brought advantages to both the tendering firms and to CISA. Costs of allocating an order reduced with the number of firms bidding, particularly when those chosen were all experienced and CISA could be relatively certain of their competence. CISA could also ensure effective competition by inviting only those firms that needed the work. A limited number increased the probability that any one competitor would be successful, and made it likely that each firm would be keener to submit its best price and perhaps spend more on pre-acceptance costs.

Structon had not been invited to tender on a major job for CISA for the past ten years, although many attempts had been made to get onto the list of invited firms. In October, Mr Phillips, Structon's Managing Director, had visited Brussels to discuss a conflict of interest with the CISA management, and the plans for the Sassandra plant had been mentioned during the conversation. When asked if Structon would be interested, Mr Phillips had replied that Structon would certainly like to take a look at it. Having expressed an interest and received an invitation to bid, it seemed unwise not to take advantage of it. Even if the bid were unsuccessful, cooperation now might lead to further opportunities later.

Structon also knew that CISA would shortly be building a plastic resins complex alongside a refinery in Australia and successful construction of the Sassandra plant would be a mark in Structon's favour when it came to getting this Australian order which would be many times larger than the Sassandra contract.

There were many advantages in working for CISA. It was a reliable firm and payment was certain. Work would not have been opened for bidding without an intention to proceed, and the engineering plans would be of a high standard. Structon executives were fairly confident that once CISA had made sure that bidders understood the specifications and were in a position to carry out the work at a high standard and within the specified time, the lowest bid would normally be accepted. A contract with CISA would enable Structon to establish itself in a new country without the risks and investment normally associated with working in a developing country.

The Ivory Coast Structon had never previously carried out work in the Ivory Coast. There was a possibility, however, that the firm would obtain a later contract to design, engineer and erect a fertiliser plant outside Abidjan, the capital of the Ivory Coast. This contract might reach £20 million in value. The customer would be the Ivory Coast government, but the successful tenderer on the oil extraction plant would not receive any preference for the fertiliser plant. It was possible that Structon might obtain the government order without competitive bids being called. Some initial negotiations had been entered into with the Ivory Coast authorities concerning this plant, so Structon already knew something of the general conditions in the Ivory Coast.

San Pedro was the second seaport in the Ivory Coast and the cranes available at the port would be adequate for handling the materials for the oil extraction plant. The transport of equipment and material to the site presented few problems, although Structon's commercial section reported that "commissions" were becoming more and more prevalent and some expense of this nature might have to be incurred to facilitate clearance and delivery.

Generally speaking, the political conditions were stable and little political involvement would be necessary, particularly as CISA had a resident company. The country was governed under a single-party system and President Houphouet-Boigny had been in power for some twenty-four years. Another election was due in October 1985 but no political upset was predicted. The country had a sound development policy, although it had overstretched its borrowing capacity over the past two years and Structon did not expect any further major projects for another three to four years.

There were conflicting reports as to the availability of local labour. It was fairly definite that there would be inadequate labour in Sassandra itself, but it was claimed by those who knew the Ivory Coast, and by the local labour office, that men could be brought from Abidjan. On the other hand, the volume of civil and industrial construction planned for Abidjan would call for a greater number of production hours than had ever before been achieved. The labour office stated that a contractor would be given every facility to engage expatriate technicians for "highly technical or other jobs for which he cannot find qualified Ivorians". Although there was increasing urban unemployment, artisans and tradesmen remained scarce and it was feared that those available, if any, would be men found unsatisfactory by other contractors.

Labour troubles had been relatively unknown. Unions existed, but they were not strong nor nationally organised. Unions were company unions including all employees regardless of trade, so labour troubles would not be caused by issues outside the control of the employer. There were no regulations or difficulties regarding firing.

Sassandra was hot all year round with average temperatures of 28 degrees centigrade and constant high humidity. The rainy season, when flooding could interrupt construction, was during May and June.

The Competition

Structon knew that CISA would follow its usual policy of inviting three or four firms to tender. For many years, the Belgian firm of Meerdonk had carried out a considerable amount of CISA's new plant construction and it was highly probable that it would be one of the bidders. Its bids had always been very competitive and its close liaison with CISA might bring some preferential treatment, but this would be hard to gauge.

A large British firm with a chemical engineering division, Weybridge Limited, was also expected to be amongst the bidders. No special advantage was held by Weybridge.

Structon's Current Order Book

In November 1984 Structon had no major overseas construction project scheduled to start in 1985. If the firm was to continue to build up its reputation as an overseas constructor, at least one project was essential. Structon was nearing completion of a major series of construction contracts in the Middle East and would have supervisory staff available from these projects. If the CISA order were not obtained, however, most of these men could be absorbed in other projects.

Exhibit 3 shows the state of Structon's order book as at 31 October 1984,

Exhibit 3 *Order Book as at 31 October 1984 (£ millions)*

	1985				1986		
Quarters in which work is programmed:	Jan Mar	Apl Jun	Jul Sep	Oct Dec	Jan Mar	Apl Jun	Jul Sep
STRUCTON PROCESSES							
Orders on hand, 31 Oct.	6.3	6.2	5.4	3.7	2.2	1.6	2.0
Outstanding Bids*, 31 Oct.	1.9	4.6	8.6	5.2	7.1	4.2	5.0
CLIENTS' DATA							
Engineering & Construction							
Orders on hand, 31 Oct.	9.1	8.7	9.4	4.2	5.0	3.2	0.7
Outstanding Bids, 31 Oct.	3.6	7.5	2.8	16.9	7.3	4.1	2.1
Construction Only							
Orders on hand, 31 Oct.	4.3	4.2	—	—	—	—	—
Outstanding Bids, 31 Oct.	—	5.2	3.9	2.1	—	—	—
Total							
Orders on hand, 31 Oct.	19.7	19.1	14.8	7.9	7.2	4.8	2.7
Outstanding Bids, 31 Oct.	5.5	17.3	15.3	24.2	14.4	8.3	7.1

* Outstanding Bids include estimated figures for bids under preparation, but not yet submitted. All work is apportioned over the quarters in which it would be carried out.

Exhibit 4   *Budgeted Load on Engineering Staff as at 31 October 1984*

	Nov	Dec	Jan	Feb	Mar	Apl
Engineering Section:						
Mechanical	100	100	120	90	80	60
Structural	90	80	70	70	40	40
Electrical	80	90	90	80	50	30
Chemical	95	100	70	65	40	30
Instrumentation	80	75	60	30	20	10

Percentage of Capacity Committed to Firm Orders and Bids Under Preparation

Exhibit 4 the budgeted work load for firm orders and bids being prepared, and Exhibit 5 sets out various statistics concerning Structon's bidding over the previous four years. Structon's estimating section advised Mr Bergen that erection of the CISA plant would require up to fifteen months from commencement, with man-hour requirements spread fairly evenly across months three to thirteen of the erection programme.

Mr Bergen knew that there would be other opportunities for construction work in 1985, but there was no indication as to when and where these

Exhibit 5   *Bidding Statistics: Bids Submitted 1980—1983*

		Structon Processes		Client's Data							
				Under £2 m.		£2—5 m.		£5—10 m.		Over £10 m.	
No. of Opportunities Considered		103		583*		139		238		31	
		Bids Made	Orders Recd	Bids Made	Orders Recd	Bids Made	Orders Recd	Bids Made	Orders Recd	Bids Made	Orders Recd
No. of Bidders	2			12	5	—	—	—	—	—	—
	3			98	20	10	2	33	5	2	1
	4			104	17	27	6	35	5	4	1
	5			57	6	25	4	20	2	3	1
	6			13	1	20	2	9	—	4	—
	7			—	—	4	—	2	—	—	—
		75	39	284	49	86	14	99	12	13	3
Average Value of Bid (£m.)		2.1	2.4	0.9	0.9	3.1	3.0	7.1	7.1	14.1	13.7
Average Mark-Up on Prime Cost + Contingency Estimate (%)		14.8	13.3	13.3	9.7	13.1	11.9	11.9	9.5	9.6	9.1
Average Cost of Submitting Bid**(£000s)		20.0		6.7		15.2		31.0		55.7	

*   Structon had a policy of rejecting all opportunities to bid on clients' data which, after initial consideration, were shown to be under £0.5 million in value.

**   The cost of submitting a bid is not included in the prime cost. This average cost of submission includes an allowance for administrative time and associated overheads. Of these submission costs, 70% are fixed, and the firm's expenditure on these does not vary with short-run fluctuations in the number of bids.

would arise. It would be unlikely that any other major work for 'construction only' could be tendered for and commenced before September 1985.

Profitability of the Order

Structon's estimating section estimated the prime cost of the contract would be roughly £10 million. It was thought that an overhead and profit margin of 10% might be expected. This £1 million mark-up would be after depreciation on plant, but before meeting interest on the capital required. The firm would probably require to spend £2.5 million on new plant at the commencement of the project but the total amount of capital tied up by the project would probably average only £1.25 million for 15 months. Structon used an interest rate of 16% per annum in calculating the cost of finance, and at this rate could obtain the necessary funds.

The accounting section had calculated that only two-thirds of the firm's overheads were applicable to construction work where no engineering was involved, and included in this were the pre-acceptance overheads for estimating, selling and tender presentation. Mr Bergen estimated that it would cost the firm around £60,000 to prepare a bid to CISA. Structon's flexible overhead and profit budget over its likely range of turnover is shown in Exhibit 6.

Exhibit 6 *Flexible Overhead and Profit Budget 1985 (£ millions)*

Sales	50.0	60.0	70.0	80.0	90.0	100.0	110.0
Overhead and Profit Margin —							
10% of Sales	5.0	6.0	7.0	8.0	9.0	10.0	11.0
Overhead Cost	5.0	5.0	5.25	5.5	5.5	5.75	6.0
Profit Before Tax	—	1.0	1.75	2.5	3.5	4.25	5.0
Taxation (at 40%)	—	0.4	0.7	1.0	1.4	1.7	2.0
Profit After Taxation	—	0.6	1.05	1.5	2.1	2.55	3.0

Managing
Competitive
Strategy

CASE 19
Scripto Pens Ltd

In September of 1959 Mr Paul J. Brown, Managing Director of Scripto Pens Ltd of London, England, was evaluating his company's current competitive situation in the British ball-point pen industry. He was particularly concerned about a recent pricing move by the Biro Swan company, Scripto's largest competitor, and was wondering what, if anything, Scripto should do in response to the move.

Background

In 1956 the Scripto Pen Corporation of Atlanta, Ga., USA, purchased the Scroll Pen Company of London and renamed the new company Scripto Pens Ltd. Prior to its acquisition by Scripto, Scroll had traditionally concentrated on the manufacture and sale of ball-point pens in the 'medium' price range. Ball-point pens in this range usually sold at retail for a price somewhere between 50p and £1.30. These pens were designed so that the original ink cartridge, when empty, could be replaced by a refill cartridge, which Scroll also manufactured.

After the 1956 acquisition, Scripto Pens Ltd continued to manufacture a medium-priced line of ball-point pens and ink refill cartridges under the SCROLL brand name. At the same time, however, the company brought out a line of ball-point pens which it marketed under its own brand name of SCRIPTO. Most of the models in this line were also in the medium price range, although the line did include a few higher priced models. As time went on the company began to place major emphasis on the SCRIPTO brand and gradually to phase out the SCROLL brand. As of late 1959, the old line of SCROLL pens was still being manufactured, but only on a limited scale.

Scripto manufactured the ball-point pens which it supplied to the domestic British market in a plant adjacent to its offices in London. The manufacturing process was one of mass production utilizing much specialized machinery. In 1956 the plant had an annual production capacity of 12.5 million ball-point pens and ink refill cartridges and employed over 450 workers.

To sell its products Scripto maintained a force of 24 full-time salesmen. These salesmen sold about two-thirds of the company's total volume to 1,000 wholesalers. Wholesalers, in turn, sold SCRIPTO and SCROLL pens to many thousand retail dealers located throughout the British Isles. These retail dealers included stationers, department stores, drug stores, newsagents, tobacconists, and other miscellaneous outlets. The remaining one-third of the company's sales volume was generated by Scripto salesmen selling directly to 15,000 retailers and to five or six large chain organisations. Generally speaking, both the wholesalers and retailers through whom Scripto sold its pens also carried the pens of competing manufacturers.

Scripto allowed all wholesalers a 25% mark-up on the price at which they sold to retailers. Retailers, in turn, were granted an average mark-up of

161

30% to 35% (depending on the model), regardless of whether they purchased from wholesalers or from Scripto's direct salesmen. Neither wholesalers nor retailers were granted additional discounts for volume purchases.

Despite the fact that Scripto sold direct to a number of retail outlets, the company made an effort to protect its wholesalers as much as possible so as to ensure that these wholesalers would devote maximum effort to the sale of Scripto's products. Thus, Scripto made it a practice never to sell directly to retailers at a price below that being charged by the wholesalers. Moreover, direct salesmen tried not to visit retailers who were already being adequately serviced by wholesalers. In most cases wholesalers did not seem to mind the fact that Scripto salesmen were selling direct to some retailers. Mr Brown, Scripto's Managing Director, felt this was due to the fact that even when a Scripto salesman did visit a retailer directly, he did so only about once every six weeks; consequently his efforts very often resulted in repeat orders for pens or refills for the wholesalers who visited these retailers in the interim; on the whole, Mr Brown felt Scripto's wholesaler relationships were quite satisfactory.

The retailers whom Scripto salesmen visited, in turn, generally welcomed the opportunity to deal directly with the company, the main advantages being that company salesmen offered on-the-spot delivery, in-store display service, and immediate attention to retailer or customer complaints.

To back up the sales plan, Scripto annually budgeted an amount equal to approximately 15% of total factory sales for advertising and promotion. Of this amount, about 12½% was allocated to newspaper and television advertising; the remainder was set aside for promotion of Scripto's products to wholesalers and retailers. Prior to 1959 the company had never used up the total amount of its annual advertising and promotion budget. Approximate actual expenditures since 1957 were as follows:

1957:	£220,000
1958:	£260,000
1959:	£300,000 (estimated)

Trends in the Sales of Ball-point Pens

The English ball-point pen industry had been expanding at an extremely rapid rate for several years prior to 1959. From sales of approximately 11 million ball-point pens in 1952, the industry had grown to the point where, in 1959, sales were estimated at 86 million units, a seven year increase of almost 800%. Meanwhile, sales of fountain pens and mechanical pencils had remained fairly constant. Exhibit 1 presents the trends in unit sales of writing instruments in the British Isles.

In pounds sterling, industry-wide sales of ball-point pens and ink refill cartridges had risen from about £3.7 million in 1952 to an estimated £14.0 million in 1959, an increase of about 375%. Exhibit 2 shows the magnitude of sterling sales of writing instruments between 1952 and 1959.

During this same period, the average price of an individual ball-point pen dropped measurably. An indication of the magnitude of this drop is given in Exhibit 3.

Mr Brown had conducted some informal market research into the public's pen buying habits and had reached some tentative conclusions concerning the reasons why people bought pens. He felt that the primary reason for the tremendous increase in the popularity of ball-point pens was that

Exhibit 1 *Trends in the Unit Sales of Pens in the UK*
   Source: Board of Trade, London

Exhibit 2 *Trends in the Sale of Ball-Point Pens in the UK*
   Source: Board of Trade, London

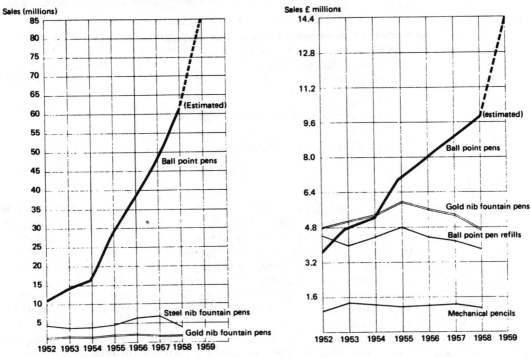

Exhibit 3   *Average Factory Price per Ball-Point Pen*
   Source: Board of Trade, London

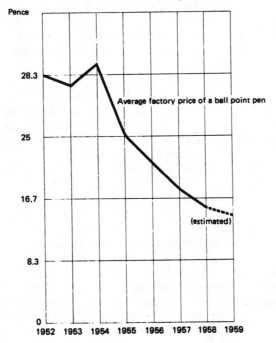

people felt that they represented an ideal compromise between the permanence and attractiveness of an ink writing instrument and the convenience, cleanliness and inexpensiveness of a lead pencil. Generally speaking, Mr Brown felt that a ball-point pen was an impulse purchase. To most people a ball-point was neither a large enough nor an important enough purchase to demand much forethought. Finally, Mr Brown believed, on the basis of his experience, that the following factors, in order of importance, most influenced the sales of a particular brand of ball-point pens:

(a) Quality of pen
(b) Availability of brand in a large number of retail outlets
(c) Price
(d) Appearance and attractiveness of pens and retail display material
(e) Media advertising

Composition of the Industry

1 Refill cartridges manufactured by one company, generally speaking, could not be used in the ball-point pens made by other manufacturers.

2 BIC was the largest French manufacturer of ball-point pens and had almost 80% of France's annual 100,000,000 unit market.

As of 1956, when Scripto bought out the Scroll Pen Company, there was one other major manufacturer of ball-point pens in the United Kingdom. This company, Biro Swan Limited, was the largest in the industry. Biro Swan had about 45% of the 1956 sterling sales volume of ball-point pens and ink refill cartridges,[1] Scroll had about 22% and a number of other small manufacturers together accounted for the remaining 33% of the market.

At the time of Scroll's acquisition by Scripto, all of the above companies concentrated their major efforts on the manufacture of ball-point pens which sold at retail in the medium (50p to £1.30) or high (£1.30 and up) price ranges. They also, of course, manufactured refill cartridges for these pens.

In September of 1957 a controlling interest in Biro Swan Ltd was acquired by the BIC Pen Company of France.[2] Following this transaction it was rumoured within the trade that an overall internal management reorganisation occurred within the ranks of the Biro Swan Company. At the same time it was also rumoured that Biro Swan began a programme to expand significantly its production capacity for ball-point pens. This management re-organisation and expansion of production capacity supposedly continued for about a year.

Introduction of a Low-Priced Line of Ball-Point Pens by Biro Swan

3 'Non-refillable' meant that once the original ink cartridge went dry, it was not possible to replace it with a refill cartridge. Non-refillable ball-point pens were sometimes also known as "throw-away" pens.

Following this year of preparation, Biro Swan made a move which marked the industry's first large scale departure from its traditional emphasis on marketing pens in the medium price range. Thus, in August of 1958, Biro Swan introduced the first low-priced line of ball-point pens to be seen in England. This new line of pens, which was initially launched in the Midlands and then quickly expanded to the rest of England, was sold under the "BIC" brand name. Three pen models made up the line: the non-refillable[3] "BIC Crystal" retailing at 20p; the non-refillable "BIC Clic" retailing at 30p; and the refillable "BIC Coronet" retailing at 40p.

To announce the introduction of its more low-priced line of ball-point pens, Biro Swan made heavy expenditures on consumer advertising. Throughout England extensive use was made of both spot television commercials and advertisements in local newspapers. In this widespread advertising campaign, the company placed major emphasis on trying to create heavy public demand for the 20p "BIC Crystal". To achieve this goal, the company's advertising strongly stressed the price appeal of the new pen.

Biro Swan had little difficulty getting retailers all over England to carry the new low-priced line. In attempting to achieve intensive distribution for the new line, Biro Swan followed its traditional policy of selling both through wholesalers and direct to the retail trade. For its selling activities the company employed a force of "van salesmen" who operated more in the capacity of "order takers" than as "salesmen". Thus, they visited wholesalers and retailers, took orders, and immediately filled these orders from the supply of merchandise which they carried in their vehicles.

One fundamental difference existed in the pricing policies of Biro Swan and Scripto. Whereas Scripto's direct salesmen made it a point never to undersell the company's wholesalers when visiting a retail account, Biro Swan salesmen would grant an additional "wholesale" discount to any retailer who ordered in sufficient quantity.

Biro Swan's venture with the 20p, throw-away pen proved to be extremely successful. As of August 1959, one year after its introduction to the public, production of the "BIC Crystal" had grown to the annual rate of 53 million units. This figure compared with the annual production rate for the "BIRO" medium priced ball-point pen line of seven million units.

Scripto's Reaction to the Introduction of the 'BIC Crystal'

Biro Swan launched its 20p BIC pen shortly after Mr Brown arrived in England from the United States to take over as Managing Director of Scripto Pens Limited. By coincidence, Mr Brown happened to be travelling in the Midlands at the time that the 'BIC Crystal' was introduced to the public there in August 1958. Upon noticing the apparent initial success of this low-price competitive pen, Mr Brown hurried back to London to assess the overall situation and decide what, if anything, Scripto should do in response to Biro Swan's move.

As soon as it became evident that 20p ball-point pens were going to become tremendously popular in the eyes of the English buying public, Mr Brown decided that Scripto must also introduce a comparable low-price line in order to protect its overall interest in the ball-point pen industry. At the same time, however, Mr Brown felt that the introduction of a 20p Scripto pen should be viewed primarily as a defensive move. In other words, although he felt it essential that Scripto eventually market a pen in the low-priced field, he thought that the company should continue to place primary emphasis on its medium-priced line of pens. Mr Brown felt that there would continue to be a strong market for medium-priced ball-point pens; consequently he thought that the medium-priced line could continue to be the most profitable segment of Scripto's business. He therefore decided that Scripto's strategy should be to "knock the pins out from under the BIC Crystal" by introducing a 20p Scripto pen, while at the same time attempting to keep sales of Scripto's regular line of medium-priced pens at a normal level.

Before Scripto could come out with a 20p ball-point pen, Mr Brown felt it would be necessary to increase the company's production capacity. If demand for a 20p Scripto were high, it might easily surpass the factory's 1958 capacity of 12.5 million pens annually. Therefore, in September, 1958, Mr Brown initiated steps to increase plant capacity by designing and installing a number of new high-speed, special purpose machines that automated various stages of the production process which were previously performed by hand. By early 1959 this programme of expansion through automation had enabled Scripto to cut its factory force from 450 to 400 employees while, at the same time, increasing production capacity from 12.5 million units to 40 million units.

Simultaneously with his programme to increase production capacity, Mr Brown made an effort to "add more value" to Scripto's medium-priced pens. The quality of these pens was improved by increasing the ink supply in each cartridge 50%, installing a new metal tip on one end of the pens, and by introducing more stringent quality control. This programme of increased quality was in line with Mr Brown's desire to continue to place major emphasis on medium-priced pens. By making the above improvements, he felt that Scripto's competitive position in that field would be strengthened.

Finally, Mr Brown embarked on a project to design a new 20p pen. In undertaking this project Mr Brown felt that, if possible, Scripto should come out with a 20p pen which would be superior in quality to the 20p "BIC Crystal" and yet which still could be sold at a satisfactory profit to Scripto. The quality of the first pen that was designed seemed to be equal, but not superior, to the "BIC Crystal". Like the BIC, it was non-refillable and did not have a retractable point. In spite of the fact that this pen had no substantial quality advantages, Mr Brown decided to introduce it to the trade as an interim competitive measure to help arrest the gains being made daily by the "BIC Crystal". Consequently, in April of 1959 Scripto's wholesalers and dealers were offered the opportunity to stock the new 20p pen and sell it as the "SCROLL Longline". Despite the fact that the introduction of the "Longline" was not backed up by any consumer advertising, total sales of the new pen reached the 5 million mark by the beginning of September.

Meanwhile, Mr Brown succeeded in developing a second ball-point pen model which Scripto could profitably sell at retail for 20p and which had the added advantage of a retractable point. Because of this added feature, Mr Brown felt that the new model was just what was needed to compete successfully against the "BIC Crystal".

Accordingly, Mr Brown named the new model the "SCRIPTO BOBBY" and made plans to introduce it to the public. During the beginning of August, Scripto salesmen made a concerted effort to sell advance supplies of the "SCRIPTO BOBBY" to wholesalers and retailers all over England. In selling the new pen, the salesmen emphasised the fact that Scripto had plans to promote its introduction to the public by means of a widespread television and newspaper advertising campaign. Beginning the first of September, Scripto had lined up a five week schedule of frequent spot TV commercials devoted solely to the "BOBBY". Following this period of intensive TV advertising, Mr Brown planned to promote the new pen through a series of advertisements in local newspapers all over England during the remaining months of 1959.

In anticipation of this year-end advertising campaign to introduce the "BOBBY", Mr Brown had conserved on advertising expenditures early in the year. Up until the beginning of September he had spent only about £68,000 of his £300,000 advertising budget. Consequently, he planned to spend about £240,000 on the introductory advertising campaign for the "BOBBY".

Mr Brown had designed the format of this campaign with the idea in mind of directing it almost as much toward wholesalers and retailers as toward the general public. This strategy was in line with Scripto's policy of maintaining strong wholesale and retail relationships. Thus, it was with the feeling that wholesalers and retailers would be favourably impressed by the prestige of TV, that Mr Brown had decided to make such heavy use of this medium.

As a result of the August selling efforts of Scripto's salesmen, about 1,750,000 "BOBBY" pens had been distributed to the trade by the beginning of September. Although Mr Brown did not, as yet, have any specific figures, he thought that these "BOBBY" pens had already begun to move off the retailers shelves at a fairly brisk rate in spite of the fact that the consumer advertising programme had not yet commenced. Meanwhile sales of Scripto's medium-priced ball-point pen lines had continued at what Mr Brown considered to be a "normal" level.

The Situation of August 1959

As of August 1959, Scripto was marketing a full line of ball-point pens with models in every price range. Sales of the 20p line, both in units and in pounds sterling, were still minimal when compared to sales of the company's medium-priced line. However, the company was poised to launch its £240,000 introductory advertising campaign for the "BOBBY" in September.

A list of the company's most important ball-point pen models, along with the price schedule at which each pen was sold, is shown in Exhibit 4.

Biro Swan, meanwhile, was also marketing a full line of ball-point pens; its low-priced line being sold under the "BIC" brand name and its medium

Exhibit 4 *Scripto Pens Ltd Price List as of 15 August 1959*

	Price to Wholesalers (Dozen)	Price to Retailers (Dozen)	Purchase Tax (Dozen)	Retailer's Margin (Dozen)	Retail Price (Each)
SCRIPTO LINE	£	£	£	£	£
Low-price pens					
"Bobby"	1.00	1.33	0.33	0.74	0.20
Medium-price pens					
"250"	2.50	3.33	0.83	1.84	0.50
"450"	4.72	6.30	1.57	3.29	0.93
"T200"	6.50	8.67	2.17	4.40	1.27
High-price pens					
"T650"	7.70	10.27	2.57	5.16	1.50
"Satellite"	17.50	23.33	5.83	11.62	3.40
Refills	1.75	2.33	0.58	1.29	0.35
SCROLL LINE					
Low-price pens					
"Longline"	1.00	1.33	0.33	0.74	0.20
Medium-price pens					
"320"	3.50	4.67	1.17	2.32	0.68
"420"	4.00	5.33	1.33	2.70	0.78
"520"	5.75	7.67	1.92	3.97	1.13
Refills	1.75	2.33	0.58	1.29	0.35

and high-priced lines under the "BIRO" brand name. Biro Swan was currently producing BIC's at the rate of 53 million units per year and BIRO's at the rate of about 7 million units per year. Biro Swan's August 1959 price list is shown in Exhibit 5.

Announcement of Biro Swan's Price Change

On August 26th the management of Biro Swan suddenly announced to the trade that, effective September 1st, big price cuts would be made on all pens and refill cartridges in the medium-priced BIRO line. Pen reductions were to range from 33⅓ % off on the BIRO MINOR (old retail price 60p, new price 40p) to 7½ % off on the BIRO MAGNUM (old retail price £3.80, new price £3.50). Retail prices of refill cartridges were to be cut in half. Prices of the low-priced BIC line were to remain unchanged. Exhibit 6 shows Biro Swan's new price list.

Dealer margins on each unit in the BIRO line were to remain the same from a percentage point of view, but would be reduced in absolute money terms. To compensate for the resulting devaluation of stocks presently in the hands of wholesalers and retailers, Biro Swan proposed a special "bonus" offer (see Exhibit 6). A London Financial Times newspaper article announcing the price change also indicated that Biro Swan had plans to launch a £1 million advertising campaign to introduce the price cuts to the public.

Exhibit 5   *Biro Swan Ltd Price List as of 15 August 1959*

	Price to Wholesalers (dozen)	Price to Retailers (dozen)	Purchase Tax (dozen)	Retailer's Margin (dozen)	Retail Price (each)
BIC LINE	£	£	£	£	£
LOW-PRICE PENS					
Crystal	1.00	1.33	0.33	0.74	0.20
Clic	1.50	2.00	0.50	1.10	0.30
Coronet	1.95	2.60	0.65	1.55	0.40
REFILLS					
(Clic & Coronet only)	0.75	1.00	0.25	0.55	0.15
BIRO LINE					
MEDIUM & HIGH-PRICE PENS					
Minor	2.92	3.90	0.98	2.32	0.60
Citizen	3.80	5.07	1.27	2.66	0.75
Retractable	4.42	5.90	1.47	3.43	0.90
Stylist	5.75	7.67	1.92	4.21	1.15
Deluxe	10.50	14.00	3.50	7.70	2.10
Squire (each)	1.45	1.92	0.48	1.10	3.50
Magnum (each)	1.58	2.12	0.53	1.15	3.80
REFILLS					
Recharge	1.50	2.00	0.50	1.10	0.30
Magnum	1.73	2.30	0.58	1.32	0.35
Insert	1.95	2.60	0.65	1.55	0.40

Exhibit 6 *Biro Swan Ltd Price List as of 1 September 1959*

	Price to Wholesalers (dozen)	Price to Retailers (dozen)	Purchase Tax (dozen)	Retailer's Margin (dozen)	Retail Price (each)
BIC LINE	£	£	£	£	£
LOW-PRICE PENS					
Crystal	1.00	1.33	0.33	0.74	0.20
Clic	1.50	2.00	0.50	1.10	0.30
Coronet	1.95	2.60	0.65	1.55	0.40
REFILLS					
(Clic & Coronet only)	0.75	1.00	0.25	0.55	0.15
BIRO LINE					
MEDIUM & HIGH-PRICE PENS					
Minor	1.95	2.60	0.65	1.55	0.40
Citizen	2.77	3.68	0.92	2.00	0.55
Retractable	3.45	4.60	1.15	2.65	0.70
Stylist	4.73	6.30	1.53	3.57	0.95
Deluxe	7.50	10.00	2.50	5.50	1.50
Squire (each)	1.25	1.68	0.42	0.90	3.00
Magnum (each)	1.45	1.92	0.48	1.10	3.50
REFILLS					
Recharge	0.75	1.00	0.25	0.55	0.15
Magnum	1.00	1.33	0.33	0.74	0.20
Insert	1.00	1.33	0.33	0.74	0.20

Excerpts of the letter which Biro Swan's management sent to the trade to announce the forthcoming price cuts are reproduced in Exhibit 7 overleaf.

Exhibit 7 *Excerpts of Letter from Biro Swan Management to Biro Swan Wholesalers and Retailers*

26th August, 1959

Dear Sirs:

On September 14th, we are announcing to the public the most-important-ever news concerning the genuine Biro range.

All Biro prices will be substantially reduced from 1st September; all pen prices will be down by at least 20p, most refill prices will be slashed by half.

... Advanced techniques backed by new, ultra-modern machinery have enabled us to make significant reductions in our production costs, at the same time as increasing the quality of them.

The new prices will give the Biro range a far wider appeal than ever before. Enormous demand is anticipated, and with it will come greatly increased turn-over, and larger profits for you. Trade margins remain, as they always have been, the most generous in the ball-pen field. The terms on which you buy the Biro range coupled with our Super Discount scheme give you really worthwhile profits on fast-moving merchandise.

We fully appreciate that your existing stocks are devalued by this operation, and we are therefore giving you this advance notice, together with the opportunity to claim a free special bonus during the month of September. All orders received by us between September 1st and September 30th inclusive, for pens and refills in the genuine Biro price range will be invoiced at the new trade price. All orders must be for immediate delivery. The goods will be delivered to you, plus a free bonus of the same goods ordered by you equivalent to the difference between the old and the new retail value of your order. We feel that you will appreciate that this method of adjustment causes you the least effort, and is absolutely straightforward and fair to you and all our customers ...

The National Advertising starts on September 14th and continues until Christmas. We know that it will create enormous demand for the genuine Biro ball-pen, and at the same time ensure repeat business in refills. You can save in this demand simply by stocking up, displaying, and selling the genuine Biro range.

Yours faithfully,

Sales Manager
Biro Swan Limited

This case was prepared by Kenneth Simmonds of the London Business School.
© *Kenneth Simmonds, 1971*

CASE 20

British Electrical Supplies Ltd

Executives of British Electrical Supplies Ltd were divided over the price action to take on their Powerite insulating compound. Some wished to lower the price to £0.50 to counter a decreasing market share, others wished to leave the price at £0.60 because they considered the increased margin more than compensated for the lost volume. As the annual price list was due for circulation, an early decision was being called for by the Sales Office Manager.

Powerite was sold to a wide range of manufacturers for incorporation in electrical motors. BES was not certain of the exact market size, but as near as the Sales Department could estimate, about 5.2 million lbs would have been purchased during the year that was just ending. Of this volume BES sold the largest share, around 45%, and the remainder was produced by two competitors with more or less equal shares of the market. Powerite was stronger than the competing compounds, although they all fulfilled the same function — and many customers preferred it for this reason. Moreover, BES had a high-quality image in the electrical supplies field and some customers claimed that there were fewer imperfections in Powerite shipments and that Powerite would last longer in operation.

In August of each year BES circulated an annual price list to customers and the sales staff followed this up by making supply arrangements with the largest customers. Salesmen were paid on a fixed salary basis and represented BES's full line to their customers; Powerite normally took only a small part of their time.

Up to August, competitors had not announced their prices for the ensuing year and appeared to be waiting for BES before making any price moves. Until the previous year their prices for compounds competing with Powerite had always been the same as the BES price, but when BES had raised the price from £0.50 to £0.60 per lb a year ago neither competitor had followed suit. This had caused BES's market share to decline, as can be seen from the following figures:

	Powerite Price (per lb)	Powerite Sales (million lbs)	Estimated Total Market (million lbs)
Current year	£0.60	2.3	5.2
Last year	£0.50	2.7	4.9
2 years ago	£0.50	2.3	4.4
3 years ago	£0.50	1.7	3.8

Powerite and the competing lines had been introduced as an insulating compound only six years previously and demand had grown rapidly as other insulating materials were replaced. Sales executives felt that future growth would be more moderate and depend largely on the demand pattern for electric motors. There was little likelihood of any technological breakthrough to replace the compound in the next four or five years. In order to get more precise figures for Powerite, they listed the major accounts for the insulating compound and questioned the responsible sales representatives as to the likely growth from each and which buyers might switch volumes to different suppliers as prices changed. From this exercise they estimated that the total market for the ensuing year would be 5.4 million lbs if both BES and competition maintained their current prices, and possibly 5.5 million if BES reduced the Powerite price to meet the competition. The Powerite share they estimated would be 2.1 million lbs or 2.7 million lbs, respectively. If, on the other hand, the competition were to raise price to match Powerite the total sales would be likely to fall to 5.0 million lbs, although Powerite would still sell 2.7 million lbs.

Should Powerite remain above the competition indefinitely, the Sales Manager estimated that there might be a further fall of 15% off the estimate for next year, as the arguments of the competing sales representatives convinced more purchasers to switch. With the current price differentials, though, this would probably be the limit of the BES market share decline, given the premium image held by many customers. The Sales Manager

Exhibit 1   *Powerite Estimated Cost per lb for Varying Volume*

	Volume in million lbs				
	1.8	2.1	2.4	2.7	3.0
	£	£	£	£	£
Direct labour	0.1180	0.1150	0.1120	0.1150	0.1180
Materials	0.0590	0.0590	0.0590	0.0590	0.0590
Scrappage	0.0057	0.0051	0.0047	0.0053	0.0054
Powerite department expense					
Class I[1]	0.0170	0.0170	0.0160	0.0150	0.0150
Class II[2]	0.1055	0.0905	0.0791	0.0704	0.0633
General works expense[3]	0.0393	0.0383	0.0373	0.0383	0.0393
Cost of Manufacture	0.3445	0.3249	0.3081	0.3030	0.3000
Selling & Administration expenses[4]	0.2067	0.1949	0.1849	0.1818	0.1800
Total	0.5512	0.5198	0.4930	0.4848	0.4800

1 Indirect wages, packing, maintenance, supplies etc.
2 Supervision, depreciation, etc.
3 Allocated on direct labour (33.3%)
4 Allocated on works cost (60%)

pointed out that this meant only a 33.3% market share and would lose BES its leadership strength. In the light of such figures he felt BES had no real alternative but to reduce price.

The Factory Manager took the opposite view. Powerite was manufactured in a separate department with its own departmental foreman and its profit figures showed separately in the monthly return covered by the Factory Manager's report. While he naturally preferred to have volume production, the Factory Manager calculated that he would still show a higher profit with the 33.3% market share. Moreover, he was certain that competitors would shortly raise their prices because their current costs with lower volumes were higher than his own and they would currently be recording losses. His arguments were based primarily upon the tabulation of production cost per lb for varying volumes shown in Exhibit 1, prepared by the accounting section at his request.

This case was prepared by Professor Kenneth Simmonds of the London Business School. © Kenneth Simmonds, 1985.

CASE 21

Ampex Videocassette Tapes

Early in 1985, Edwin Pessara, magnetic tape marketing director for Ampex Corporation was considering whether to recommend that Ampex re-enter the United States consumer market for blank videocassette tapes. The USA was a nation of avid TV viewers. Its 85 million homes averaged over 40 hours' viewing per week. Ampex had taken an earlier decision to opt out of the consumer sector because of cut-throat price competition. The take-off in consumer tape demand over the past two years, however, had been extremely rapid and Pessara felt that prices would now stabilise. Furthermore, if Ampex did not take this opportunity to establish its brand at the basic consumer level, he felt that those who did would threaten Ampex's long-established position in sales of videotape for professional uses and even of its magnetic computer tape sales. Ampex had no spare production capacity so it would have to buy in tape or invest in a new plant.

Sales of blank cassettes had jumped to about 100 million units in 1984 from 63 million the year before and 25 million in 1952. The trade press predicted over 120 million in 1985. Behind this growth in demand lay a significant increase in the recording of TV programmes for later viewing. Viewers were using their videocassette recorders (VCRs) much more for this purpose than to view prerecorded tapes which sold only 10 million in 1983 and 20 million in 1984. For every such sale, however, there were about ten rentals of prerecorded tapes. Sales of new VCRs had also increased to 7.6 million units in 1984 and the forecast was for 9 million in 1985. These figures represented a large increase on the 4.2 million units sold in 1983, which itself had doubled the total number of VCRs in use in the USA.

The blank tape industry had become locked in a fierce price war started by 3M's Scotch brand. The average wholesale price of a blank tape had dropped from $11.34 in 1982 to $6.58 in 1984 and was forecast at $6.14 for 1985. Richard G. Mueller, 3M's marketing operations manager for magnetic products, was quoted as saying, "We all see this big carrot and we're all going after it". He had relentlessly courted retailers for shelf space, and had introduced a cash rebate on blank tapes. "Rebates mean the consumer gets the discount but the retailer still makes money", Mueller explained. When competitors followed 3M, Mueller had countered with rebates plus gifts, such as a round-trip ticket on any Republic Airlines' flight for buying 20 of 3M's $10 tapes, or free dinners at Victoria Station restaurants.

John Hollands, President of Sony Tape Sales Co., told reporters: "3M's corporate policy over the past year has been to buy market share at any cost. We felt we had to match their best offer, so it ends up costing us both money." Hollands thought the first firms to drop out would be those that packaged and marketed tape bought in bulk from the six major manufacturers who sold to others as well as marketing their own brands: Sony, TDK, 3M (Scotch), Hitachi (Maxell), Tandy (Memorex) or Fuji. These six firms produced over 80% of all videotape sold in the United States and supplied over sixty other firms.

Those who did not manufacture, however, disagreed that they would be forced out. They pointed to the keen competition between these six manufacturers as well as the possibility of overseas supply. Both Kodak and Polaroid bought in tape and felt that their strong brand identification with consumers would enable them to command a continued price premium. The general manager of marketing in Kodak's consumer electronic division agreed that outside sourcing put pressure on margins but argued that, as they had no significant capital investment in the business, the margin they required was much lower.

TDK supplied Kodak and had led the market before 3M's move. Their director of sales and marketing felt that the worst of the price war was over and that prices would stabilise at $5 or $6 for a standard-grade tape. "Right now demand is increasing", he said, "but nobody is building new facilities. Since a new tape plant is very expensive, we are approaching the point where this industry reaches capacity."

A new tape plant cost around $120 million with a capacity of possibly 20 million tapes per annum. Manufacturing and packaging, allowing for 10% depreciation, cost around $3 per unit, with distribution, promotion and retail mark-ups adding at least $1.50 per unit. On the revenue side, blank tapes in the 120-minute length ran from $37 for 3M's top-of-the-line "HGX Plus" tape all the way down to $4, after discounting and rebates, for standard-grade cassettes. Promotion of higher-grade tapes to build margins, however, was of only limited success. Consumers seemed to have caught on to the fact that there was not much difference technically between $5 tapes and $20 tapes. Over 85% of tape sales were accounted for by standard grades.

There were some really cheap tapes, as low as $3, on super special offers. If substandard, however, these could gum up a VCR's recording heads. There was also a possibility that more very cheap tapes might be introduced by the Koreans and Taiwanese to accompany very inexpensive VCR machines which they were poised to introduce.

This case was prepared by Kenneth Simmonds of the London Business School. © Kenneth Simmonds, 1980.

CASE 22

Albright Ltd

Victor Lonergan seemed to be swimming around in figures. Ever since July when he joined Albright Limited as Personal Assistant to the new Managing Director, Graham Peake, Peake had kept him hard at work analysing historical pricing data. Victor had completed his Bachelor's in Marketing and was prepared for some figure analysis, but he was inclined to think that Peake as an electrical engineer had a bad case of 'compulsive calculosis'. Against his strenuous objection that pricing should be based on an assessment of customers' attitudes to product prices and not on historical cost and price measurements, Peake was now insisting that Victor prepare a written price policy for Albright for the ensuing year, justified in historical terms. "The trouble with business graduates and accountants", said Graham "is that they calculate everything in discrete terms. Somehow, the training doesn't allow for the feedback and system thinking which is the basis of most market processes."

Annual plans for 1981 were due to be submitted by Peake at the end of September to the board of the Beta Group. Albright was a wholly-owned subsidiary. The Chairman had asked Peake to come up with an increased contribution to consolidated profits and he was personally anxious to avoid any slip in the group's earnings per share. A slip might cause an adverse reaction on the stock market just at a time when some were looking for tangible results from his first four years in the chair. As he told Peake "There are only two things the stock analysts care about from a metal components group and those are profits and more profits. And Albright has had an abysmal record so far."

The Beta Group manufactured a wide range of metal and plastic parts, components, sub-assemblies and small products. Albright specialised in standard wall switches and sockets for lights and electrical appliances and was one of the few group subsidiaries with a standard product line. Nevertheless, there was no marketing organisation as such, and the standard group pattern of an engineering trained managing director and a strong financial director was evident. Apparently, Peake had had a disagreement with the Finance Director shortly before Victor's arrival when he complained about the incomprehensibility of the standard cost calculations for the long list of individual items in Albright's range. Peake told Victor he found it impossible to grasp price—volume—cost relationships for individual items from the cost figures because of the large range, fluctuating volumes and dominating percentage of common costs. "There's hardly any difference conceptually between single, double and treble switches, for example, yet we have a set of standards and variations for each — and not one of the costing staff has been able to interpret what it means when every month seven lean variations on standard are gobbled up by seven fat variations. About the only cost figures I can use out of the accounts are the general classification headings and a rough guess as to how they vary." He showed Victor the following breakdown he had developed:

Classification	Percentage of Total Cost	Short Term Variation with Volume	Long Term Variation with Volume
Direct Labour	19	100% Variable	90% Variable
Direct Materials	16	100% Variable	90% Variable
Indirect Expenses	12	100% Variable	90% Variable
Works Expenses	39	50% Variable	90% Variable
Distribution Expenses	3	50% Variable	90% Variable
Selling Expenses	5	Fixed	50% Variable
General and Administrative Expenses	6	Fixed	50% Variable
	100		

The first task Peake gave Victor was to calculate an index of price per average item for each period that followed an adjustment in Albright's price list over the past seven years. Currently Albright's price stood at £1.19 for an average item.

Next, Peake had Victor calculate similar figures for Maynard Switches Ltd, Albright's leading competitor. He asked Victor to calculate an average ratio of Maynard's item prices to Albright's and adjust the Albright average item price by this ratio to give an estimate of Maynard's average item price. This exercise proved to be more straightforward than Victor at first expected. Apparently, Maynard had consistently raised all item prices at the same time by more or less the same percentage. They had also led Albright and the seven or eight smaller competitors with price rises and since April, Maynard's average wholesale price had stood at 12½% above Albright's. Victor's estimates are tabulated in Exhibit 1.

Exhibit 1 *Albright and Maynard: Average Item Prices, Volume and Market Share Estimates — The Historical Pattern*

Period Ruling	Competing Average Item Prices (From Price Lists)			Estimated Market Volume (Exhibit 3 Column 2 Adjusted) M. Items	Albright		Maynard	
	Months No.	Albright Average £	Maynard Average £		Sales (Actual) M. Items	Market Share %	Sales (Est. *) M. Items	Market Share %
May 74—Feb 75	10	.51	.51	35.2	6.9	(19.6)	14.5	(41.2)
Mar 75—Dec 75	10	.56	.56	32.5	6.1	(18.8)	14.2	(43.7)
Jan 76—Jun 76	6	.60	.60	19.5	3.5	(17.9)	9.0	(46.2)
Jul 76—Apr 77	10	.65	.69	27.2	6.1	(22.4)	8.9	(32.7)
May 77—Jun 77	2	.69	.69	6.3	1.4	(22.2)	2.1	(33.3)
Jul 77—Nov 77	5	.80	.80	15.8	3.3	(20.9)	5.9	(37.3)
Dec 77—May 78	6	.87	.87	19.9	4.0	(20.1)	7.9	(39.7)
Jun 78—Mar 79	10	.94	.99	34.1	7.9	(23.1)	10.4	(30.5)
Apr 79—Oct 79	7	1.04	1.05	25.1	5.8	(23.1)	7.7	(30.7)
Nov 79—Mar 80	5	1.19	1.19	18.1	4.0	(22.1)	6.1	(33.7)
Apr 80—Aug 80	5	1.19	1.34	18.3	4.4	(24.0)	5.1	(27.9)

*Maynard Estimate = Market — 3 (Albright Volume)

Peake then asked Victor to analyse the published accounts and other estimates of sales revenue for Maynard and the smaller competitors. Maynard was an independent firm and its 1979 accounts are summarised in Exhibit 2. From the published accounts of the smaller competitors, none held over 10% of the market, and they confirmed the Albright sales staff estimates that these firms together accounted for under 50% of the market. Just as Albright had followed Maynard's price lead in the past, these smaller firms had waited for Albright before they too raised prices. There were a few imports as well, but British building and wiring codes gave some protection. The Sales Manager thought that unless UK suppliers pushed their prices well out of line with cost, no foreign firm would be able to gain enough volume to get costs below Maynard's.

Exhibit 2   *Maynard Switches Ltd: Summary of Accounts*

	1979 £m	1978 £m
Turnover	14.6	13.1
Profit before Taxation	0.4	1.4
Taxation	0.2	0.7
Dividend	0.4	0.4
Current Assets		
Cash	0.4	0.4
Debtors and Pre-payments	2.2	1.8
Stocks	3.3	2.8
	5.9	5.0
Less Current Liabilities		
Bank Overdraft	3.5	2.4
Creditors	1.3	1.6
	4.8	4.0
Net Current Assets	1.1	1.0
Fixed Assets	3.2	3.4
Total	4.3	4.4
Financed by:		
Debentures and Loans	2.7	2.6
Shareholders' Funds	1.6	1.8
	4.3	4.4

From the estimate of total industry revenue, Peake now had Victor calculate industry volume. He first calculated 1979 average item price for Albright from its volume and sales totals, and dividing this into industry revenue gave an estimate of 43 million items for the industry as a whole. On the assumption that industry volume had moved more or less in step with the

Index of Construction Output, Peake then extrapolated backwards to 1974 to get the industry volume estimates shown in Exhibit 3.

Victor had begun by now to disbelieve all of his figures. There were too many estimates, assumptions and averages involved. But Peake was far from finished. He had Victor adjust the estimated market volume from a calendar basis to give volume estimates for the periods over which Albright and Maynard prices had held constant. Victor did obtain fairly reliable figures on the item quantities sold by Albright in each period but Peake had him make the heroic assumptions that any volume change for Albright was directly reflected in Maynard's sales and tripled by similar shifting between Maynard and the other competitors. The resulting market share figures, shown in Exhibit 1, left Victor doubting whether they meant much at all.

Exhibit 3 *Annual Indicators of Volume and Price*

Calendar Year	Index of Construction Output (1970 = 100)	Estimated Industry Volume (1979 = 43m.) (million items)	Wholesale Price Index All Manufactured Output (1980 = 100)
1974	94	43	35
1975	86	39	44
1976	85	39	51
1977	83	38	63
1978	88	40	72
1979	94	43	88
1980 (8 months est.)	95	29	100

Exhibit 4 *Albright Limited: Annual Sales, Item Revenue and Market Share*

Calendar Year	Sales (£m)	Profits Before Tax (losses) (£m)	Volume (million items)	Item Revenue Actual (£)	Item Revenue 1980 Prices (£)	Market Share (%)
1974	4.2	0.4	8.5	0.49	1.40	19.8
1975	4.0	(0.2)	7.3	0.55	1.25	18.7
1976	4.5	(0.3)	7.2	0.63	1.24	18.5
1977	5.8	(0.1)	7.8	0.74	1.17	20.5
1978	8.0	0.4	8.8	0.91	1.26	22.0
1979	10.2	0.2	9.8	1.04	1.18	22.8
1980 (8 mth est.)	8.1	0.3	6.8	1.19	1.19	23.4

Exhibit 5 *Maynard Switches Ltd: Annual Sales, Item Revenue and Market Share*

Calendar Year	Sales (£m)	Annual Report Profits Before Tax (losses) (£m)	Volume (Sales ÷ Item Revenue) (million items)	Item Revenue Actual* (£)	1980 Prices (£)	Market Share (%)
1974	9.1	1.9	18.5	0.49	1.40	43.0
1975	9.2	0.9	16.7	0.55	1.25	42.8
1976	8.9	0.3	14.1	0.63	1.23	36.2
1977	8.5	(0.1)	11.2	0.76	1.21	28.9
1978	13.1	1.4	14.1	0.93	1.29	35.2
1979	14.6	0.4	13.8	1.06	1.21	32.1
1980 (8 mth est.)	11.1	N.A.	8.7	1.28	1.28	29.7

*Exhibit 1 Adjusted to Calendar Year Basis

Finally, Peake thought it would be interesting to see how prices had varied in real terms. Using the wholesale price index for all manufacturing output as a deflator, he had Victor calculate real revenues per item from the Albright and Maynard financial figures as shown in Exhibits 4 and 5.

Now, a week after Peake's meeting with the Chairman, there had been a subtle change in Peake's attitude. All the figures seemed to have become Victor's. He was left with 'his' figures to prepare 'his' price policy.

This case was prepared by Kenneth Simmonds and Shiv Mathur of the London Business School. It was written with the co-operation of Alfa-Laval Management. Facts and figures have been disguised to preserve corporate confidentiality.
© *Kenneth Simmonds, 1980.*

CASE 23
Alfa-Laval Thermal

In November 1975 senior members of Alfa-Laval's Thermal subdivision based in Lund, Sweden, had come together to review the subdivision's strategy. The subdivision was a major international force in the manufacturing and marketing of thermal products. It still held — as it had done over the last two decades — the position of dominant market leader in its chosen product area; but small cracks appearing in its structure and strategy were causing some managerial concern.

Alfa-Laval's International Organisation

Alfa-Laval was in 1975 one of the largest Swedish companies. The original establishment had been founded in 1883 and over the years the company had diversified into a wide range of businesses. A fundamental Alfa-Laval philosophy, however, was its intention to remain in the manufacture and marketing of industrial products.

The company's activities could be divided into three broad categories:

Industrial Equipment — centrifuges, pumps, thermal equipment and installations for the food industry, power production, mechanical engineering industries, shipbuilding, the chemical, pulp and paper industries, as well as for environmental control.

Dairy Processing Equipment — special processes and complete plants for dairies and certain beverage industries.

Farm Equipment — equipment and systems for milking, feeding, manure removal, hygiene and cooling.

In 1975 there were four major company divisions: Farm, Separation, Thermal and Dairy, and Rosenblads. Activities which could not be easily incorporated into one of the four divisions were referred to as "Other Companies and Units". The divisions were profit centres each responsible for a defined range of products and applications, producing for sale to the Group's worldwide marketing network and monitoring and influencing worldwide performance within the scope of their business mission.

Alfa-Laval market companies, as listed in Exhibit 1, provided outlets for the Group's products in many countries of the world. In countries with less demand, Alfa-Laval had distributors and commission agents. Senior management felt the coverage more than adequate for the Group's current needs.

Over the years, many market companies had drifted away from their original role as outlets for Alfa-Laval products. Some had set up manufacturing operations, enabling them to cut down freight costs and reap the advantage of a better local presence. It was, however, neither technologically nor economically justified to move all stages of production to local sites and the more highly capital intensive production tasks remained in Sweden for

Exhibit 1 *Geographical Distribution of Market Companies*

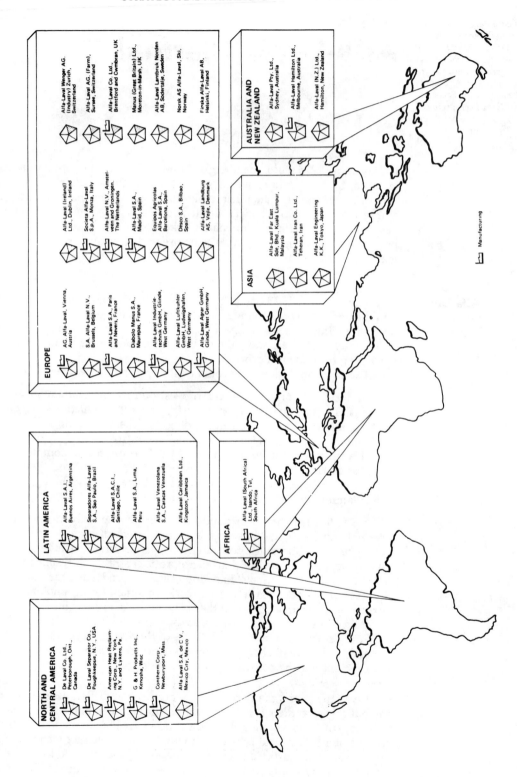

Exhibit 2 *Geographical Distribution of Manufacturing Units*

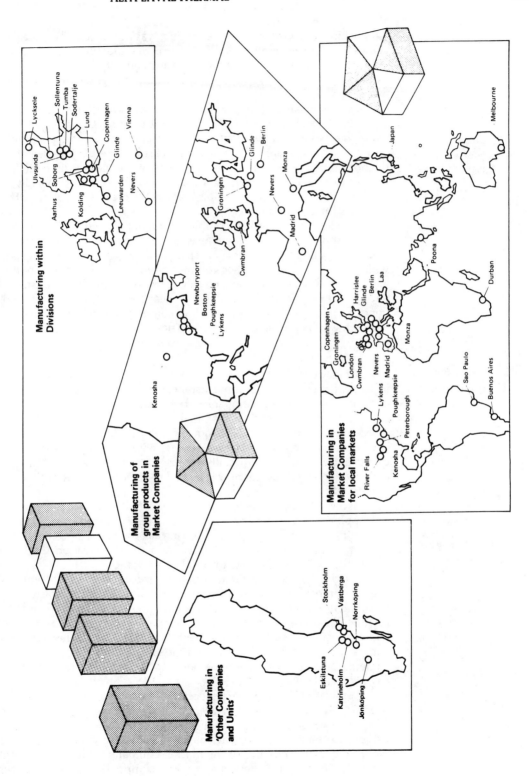

Manufacturing within Divisions

Manufacturing of group products in Market Companies

Manufacturing in Market Companies for local markets

Manufacturing in 'Other Companies and Units'

almost all products. As a consequence, the overseas manufacturing establishment needed for any one product was not large and the local market companies had generally combined local manufacturing for various products and divisions under one roof. These manufacturing activities had often expanded to such an extent that the term "market company" had become a misnomer.

In a few instances the manufacturing activities of market companies had expanded to include production for export to other Group companies. For items that were manufactured by market companies for export within the Group, "Product Centres" at Divisional Headquarters in Sweden attempted to coordinate the manufacturing activities of the various units. Production for local markets, however, was considered the sole responsibility of the domestic market company. Exhibit 2 shows the breakdown of manufacturing activities for the Group.

Though some market companies manufactured both for the local market and the Group, there was a significant difference between the manufacturing activities of market companies and divisions. Production within divisions was in higher volumes, involved larger capital investments and greater R & D, and produced a much more comprehensive range of products. For example, the basic plates for heat exchangers were pressed only in Lund, Sweden, while frames and other components were made in Germany, Spain, the USA and some other countries.

Liaison Between Customer, Market Company and Divisions

The primary contact for either a Scandinavian or overseas customer was the local market company. In some instances, the customer could have a choice of two or more market companies, but such instances were rare and Alfa-Laval attempted to ensure that in any one market there was only one representative for a particular product or service. In many instances the local market company was competent to deal with all aspects of customers' requirements. In others, especially in cases of small market companies and complicated enquiries, there was a need to refer the enquiry to the division concerned.

Just as "Product Centres" within divisions coordinated manufacturing, so "Application Centres" coordinated and assisted market companies with marketing. A market company requiring assistance would get in touch with the appropriate "Application Centre" and the Application Centre would answer the query or arrange for further assistance.

For the less sophisticated products, the local market company was usually competent to deal with customers. For products like Farm and Dairy Equipment, where a complete system had often to be designed and tendered for, the liaison between the market companies and the division concerned had been developed through frequent contact. Over the last few years the company had consciously promoted the sale of complete systems and often tendered bids on a turnkey basis, even to the extent of taking on the civil engineering work.

Application Centres were expected to keep abreast of both market and product development and provide advice to the market companies and the division's senior staff. An Application Centre was headed by a person designated "Sales/Marketing Manager" but did not concern itself with the day-to-day sales activities of the market companies. However, it provided the only formal link between market companies on specific business possibilities. With the growth of system sales, large bids and more and more international customers, coordination was becoming increasingly important. The Application Centres attempted to keep track of major projects in their chosen industrial sector and provide an information service about them to the market companies. Within the Thermal and Dairy Division, however, it was felt that the flow of information was becoming far too one-sided. The Application Centres were providing services and information but receiving little information from the market companies about their general activities and their interest in particular projects.

The Thermal Sub-division

Note: In December 1975 1 Swedish Krona = £0.12 or US $0.22.

The Thermal and Dairy Division of Alfa-Laval had a total 1974 sales figure of Swedish Kronor 312 million*, representing a tenth of the Group's total turnover. The division was in turn divided into four subdivisions. The Thermal Subdivision was responsible for the world-wide sale of thermal products and prided itself on being able to sell anything in its product area, from small individual components to complete processes required for large and complex operations.

The key product in the thermal engineering field was the "heat exchanger". Heat exchangers were used whenever it was necessary to heat or cool any fluid. The conventional tubular heat exchanger, still used most frequently, consisted of a tube pack inside an outer casing with one fluid flowing through the tubes and the other fluid flowing around them at a different temperature and thus exchanging heat. The Alfa-Laval product strategy had been to concentrate on specially compact heat exchangers, based on more sophisticated engineering designs. There were four basic types of heat exchangers in the Alfa-Laval range of which the plate heat exchanger (PHE) was the most versatile and represented the bulk of the sales. The others were: spiral, lamella and closed-tube heat exchangers.

The principle of the plate heat exchanger is fairly simple. As shown in Exhibit 3, it consists essentially of a pile of metallic plates clamped together. Each adjacent pair of plates forms a "flow channel" with the two fluids at different temperatures flowing in alternate channels. Gaskets separate each plate from the others, thus preventing the mixing of the two fluids. Though the basic concept is comparatively straightforward, it is essential that the material used for the plates, the corrugations on them, and the material for the gaskets, be chosen to fit the particular task in hand. Thus a corrosive fluid of high viscosity at a high temperature and pressure necessitates an entirely different solution from another under different operating conditions.

Alfa-Laval prided itself on its lead in the design of the most efficient engineering solutions for various operating conditions. The choices of plates, material, size, corrugations and gaskets were carefully examined to provide a tailor-made match for a customer's thermal requirements. Often it would be necessary to include other types of heat exchangers and ancillary equipment, such as cooling towers and air coolers, to meet the complete requirements of a client. The Thermal Subdivision had gradually expanded and diversified its activities in these fields to meet the market. In fact, this emphasis on technical competence and coverage had been explicitly recognised by the Subdivision in 1968 in its "Business Mission and Policy" statements:

> We are in the "heat transfer" market and should act and become known as "thermal engineering specialists". Our goal is to develop, produce and market on a

worldwide level, thermal engineering equipment and processes of a high technical standard and to get a growing share of the world market.

It is our aim to obtain a reputation among engineering customers as the most reliable supplier in our range and also to maintain our reputation as the biggest and most advanced supplier of heat exchangers, including software services.

With the growing software needs, the Application Centre at Lund expanded to take on a number of qualified thermal engineers capable of designing complicated systems and of consultation on a wide variety of design problems. There was also a gradual shift in the development section at Lund towards the development of large PHE's and those made of special materials for difficult operating conditions. Emphasis on the manufacture of large units and complete systems gave Alfa-Laval a competitive edge in the

Exhibit 3 *Plate Heat Exchangers*

Plate heat exchanger (PHE)

Alfa-Laval plate heat exchangers are assembled on the construction kit principle from individual standard channel plates that can be arranged according to the needs of the specific duty.

The plates are assembled in packs and clamped in a frame, each adjacent pair of plates forming a flow channel with the two media flowing in alternate channels. Different channel groupings can be chosen to give the desired pressure-drop characteristics and flow pattern. Two or more independent sections, separated by special connection plates, can be housed in the same frame. The gaskets separating the plates — which may be made of different materials according to the nature of the medium — prevent any mixing of the two media in the unit.

Flexible construction system

The construction system used for Alfa-Laval plate heat exchangers makes it possible to tailor them exactly to the requirements of varying working conditions throughout their wide range of applications. A plate unit is easily opened for inspection and cleaning of the plates and gaskets, but it can also be cleaned in place by detergent circulation, in which case it need not be dismantled at all.

The special corrugations of the channel plates generate an intensely turbulent thin-layer flow. They also stiffen the plates so that extremely thin-gauge material can be used. This improves the heat transfer coefficient and at the same time makes it economically feasible to use such expensive materials as titanium.

Typical applications

Plate heat exchangers are maids of all work. Their handiness, high thermal efficiency and flexibility make them far and away the most economical choice in a host of applications, subject only to the pressure and temperature limits of the type.

This is true above all in the food industry with special reference to pasteurisation and sterilisation of cheap food and beverage products, where heating costs must be kept to a minimum and regular cleaning of the equipment is an essential feature of the high standard of hygiene demanded today.

Other suitable fields are general heating and cooling duties. Dissipating the heat from engine and machinery coolants — for example on shipboard and in stationary power plants — is a field in which plate heat exchangers have proved their worth many times over. Another natural application for the plate type of unit is heat recovery in cases where a small difference in temperature between the media means that only a really efficient heat exchanger can do the job economically.

Plate heat exchanger type A 20

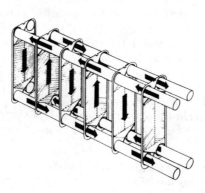

Flow pattern in a plate heat exchanger

more advanced uses. The quality of Alfa-Laval products had always been good, but with steady attention to quality, it had become difficult by 1975 for company officials and customers to recall an example of outright failure of an Alfa-Laval component. After-sale service was mainly limited to replacing plates and gaskets which had succumbed to wear and tear.

By 1975 the Thermal Subdivision had five Application Centres in its Marketing Department at Lund (Exhibit 4). Market companies requiring assistance on an enquiry were free to get in touch with the relevant Application Centre, but were under no compulsion to do so. Market companies were given direct access to the comprehensive computer programmes that had been written to calculate specific heat exchanger requirements, and a back-up service assisted with technical drawings and after-sale service. The Marketing Department also offered training for marketing personnel in the technical aspects of the heat exchanger business. For all these services there was little or no direct charge, as Lund believed that these services more than paid for themselves through increased sales and better customer liaison; and gave the company the very advantage that it was eager to retain in a market that was becoming increasingly competitive.

Exhibit 4   *Thermal Subdivision — Organisation 1975*

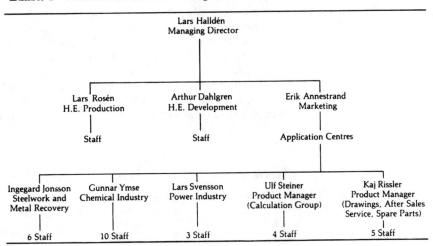

Thermal know-how was particularly important in the chemical, steel, power and mining industries. These market segments were distinguished by large orders and large HE units, often involving international contracting. Thermal management saw a great opportunity here for expansion in sales. While few products from other Alfa-Laval divisions were sold along with HE's to these industries, Thermal could draw on its strength of a complete thermal line and use its extensive application know-how to effect. In 1975 the Subdivision's "Business Mission" was amended to read:

> We shall also promote marketing of complete functions for the large and fast-growing central cooling market. That can be done by selling complete installations for seawater or cooling towers or by selling installation software with our heat exchangers.

We shall have the largest resources, the best know-how with superior products and a reliable delivery capacity.

On large bids, or on business that might involve international contracting or be of continuing importance to the Group, market companies could if they wished approach the Application Centre for an advantageous transfer price on centrally produced components to enable them to make a more competitive quote. Frequently, a market company would ask for assistance to get Alfa-Laval products specified at the design stage for a major contract; but in keeping with the company's policy of autonomy for its market units, the rule was quite clear — assistance was given by invitation, rather than any Head Office imposition.

Competitive Position   The greater part of Alfa-Laval's heat exchanger orders (about 75%) were accounted for by plate heat exchangers, which competed with conventional tubular heat exchangers and PHE's of other makes. The tubular HE was by far the most widely used HE for industrial application and had a surprisingly strong hold on the American market. Acceptance of the PHE as a suitable replacement, however, was growing. For application in the marine, dairy and other fields, where compactness and hygienic or environmental effects of heat exchangers were major considerations, the competition was all between different makes of PHE's. In marine and dairy industries, moreover, Alfa-Laval's other subdivisions had strong process know-how. Exhibit 5 shows a breakdown of Thermal PHE sales by industry of application.

Through conscious choice Alfa-Laval had not involved itself in the market for conventional tubular HE's which were fabricated in a large number of countries by many small, highly competitive but technically less advanced companies. In the view of Alfa-Laval management this market, though many times larger than that for PHE's, was generally more suited to

Exhibit 5   *Thermal Division Plate Heat Exchanger Sales by Industry of Application*

	1970 %	1972 %	1974 %
Power	2	3	2
Factory	5	4	4
Mining	1	1	1
Steel	12	15	18
Chemical, Organic	14	13	12
Chemical, Inorganic	18	15	15
Marine	18	20	21
Brewing, Fermentation	7	7	7
Dairy Plant	12	12	10
Other	11	10	10
	100	100	100
Index of Invoice Value Adjusted to 1974 Prices	83	78	100

small local manufacture and was not one where a company like Alfa-Laval could compete effectively.

The mix of small, medium and large PHE's sold from Lund had altered over the years as shown in Exhibit 6. Exhibit 7 also indicates the increase in size of orders serviced from Lund. Thermal Subdivision sales were shifting towards larger units and larger customers. This shift was not altogether an unwelcome change. The percentage of profit contribution from small PHE's for 1974 was not very significant and the segment was coming under increasing fire from small national competitors. They had cut prices in order to break into a stronghold where Alfa-Laval had earlier had great market and technical superiority.

In 1975 there were about twenty PHE manufacturers in the world. Of these, about seven were of any significance. The more important competitors were:

1. APV — UK   4. Vicarb — France
2. Schmidt — West Germany   5. Ahlborn — West Germany
3. Hisaka — Japan   6. DDMM — Denmark

Exhibit 6   *Thermal Division Plate Heat Exchanger Sales and Profitability by Size*

	% of Total Thermal Subdivision Sales		% of Total Thermal Profit Contribution
	1974	(1975) (Est.)	1974
Small PHE	13	(10)	4
Medium PHE	51	(48)	40
Large PHE	12	(19)	35

There were very significant variations in the market share of these main competitors. Alfa-Laval now held perhaps 50% of the world market for PHE's, as against 60% in 1970. APV was the leading contender, with Schmidt and Hisaka following to take much of the remaining volume. Even more noticeable, however, was the different level of technical services provided. Competition was largely confined to small and medium PHE segments. The bigger specialised products and systems that Lund was putting on the market faced little or no competition. Alfa-Laval's advanced designs, protected by patents, had given the company substantial cost advantages which the smaller companies found difficult to match. For applications in which the competition for plant construction was international, then, Alfa-Laval held a very high percentage of the market share.

The international distribution outlets for the leading competitors as estimated by Alfa-Laval staff are listed in Exhibit 8. Not all could be thought of as competitors in the international PHE market. Some could more adequately be described as national companies with export activities.

Of the really international competitors, APV of the UK was the closest, with a broad range of activities in thermal engineering and a wide distribution and marketing system. APV had fifteen affiliated companies in the principal industrialised countries and numerous agents across the globe. In a manner similar to Alfa-Laval, APV had developed a wide variety of technical information and computer programmes to promote its products. APV was particularly strong in the chemical, food and dairy industries.

Competition from the remaining companies had been largely confined to domestic markets and even then often in specialised segments of the market. But the competition, when faced, could be very real indeed and

Exhibit 7   *Thermal Division Plate Heat Exchanger Sales by Size of Order and Model*

Size of Order in Swedish Krona	% of Total Number of Orders	
	1972	1975
Below 50,000	92	80
50 — 500,000	7	18
Above 500,000	1	2
	100	100

	% of Total Unit Sales	
	1972	1975
Small	48	34
Medium	52	56
Large	—	10
	100	100

Exhibit 8   *Alfa-Laval and Competitors' Distribution Systems*

	Affiliated or Associated Companies	Licensees	Agents
APV	15 in principal industrialised countries	—	Numerous globally
Schmidt	Austria	—	10–15
Hisaka	—	1 in UK 1 in USA	Australia, India, Korea, Taiwan, Netherlands
Vicarb	—	—	10
Ahlborn	—	—	10–15 Several agents in same country
DDMM	—	—	5–10

there were increasing instances of prices and quotations undercutting Alfa-Laval by as much as 15% or 20%, and these companies seemed to be gradually looking further afield for business.

In spite of its great strength and momentum, Alfa-Laval was receiving small bits of information from various market companies that were causing concern. The Japanese company, Hisaka, for instance, had captured about 85% of the Japanese market and was looking enviously at the European and North American markets. There were rumours that Hisaka, DDMM and the French company, Vicarb, were about to expand plate pressing capacity and might extend the size-range of PHE's they manufactured. DDMM and the French had been having some success in getting into the coveted marine market. Exhibits 9 and 10 summarise Alfa-Laval's information about competition in various industrial sectors and indicate the changes taking place.

Exhibit 9 *Penetration of Market Segments*

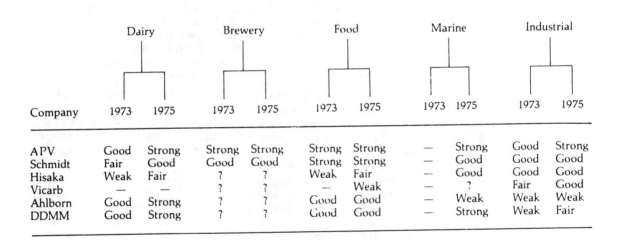

INDUSTRIAL SECTOR

Company	Dairy 1973	Dairy 1975	Brewery 1973	Brewery 1975	Food 1973	Food 1975	Marine 1973	Marine 1975	Industrial 1973	Industrial 1975
APV	Good	Strong	Strong	Strong	Strong	Strong	—	Strong	Good	Strong
Schmidt	Fair	Good	Good	Good	Strong	Strong	—	Good	Good	Good
Hisaka	Weak	Fair	?	?	Weak	Fair	—	Good	Fair	Good
Vicarb	—	—	?	?	—	Weak	—	?	Weak	Weak
Ahlborn	Good	Strong	?	?	Good	Good	—	Weak	Weak	Weak
DDMM	Good	Strong	?	?	Good	Good	—	Strong	Weak	Fair

Exhibit 10 *New PHE Models Introduced 1965–1975*

Company	Number of PHEs Introduced 1965–73	Number of PHEs Introduced 1973–75	Expected Introduction
Alfa-Laval	8	1	
APV	3		1
Schmidt	12		1
Hisaka		3	1
Vicarb	4		1
Ahlborn	3 (2 withdrawn)	1	
DDMM		4	

Product Development Philosophy

Product Development in the Alfa-Laval group of companies continued to build on the very impressive technological lead that the company had established. There had been a steady expansion of the range of thermal equipment offered and the company had most recently ventured into central cooling systems. Instead of providing individual HE's for the many local requirements in various parts of a factory, these developments made it possible to provide a single central cooling system. Such systems meant a substantial change not only in the hardware sold by the company, but also in the software service provided. Some Thermal managers believed that the emphasis should be to educate the market on the economic and technical benefits of single large PHE's and associated complete systems, and to explain that these benefits far outweighed the disadvantages. Smaller but parallel systems could provide a built-in back-up facility in the event of technical failure of single large units. Alfa-Laval management pointed to the absence of technical failure to emphasise the very low probability of such an event.

The philosophy of the development department at Lund, as shown in the following extract, was to retain Alfa-Laval leadership through creative new products:

> A brief historical sketch of the 1950's and 60's shows clearly that the key concepts for successful companies have been production and marketing. The company that realised the importance of building up an efficient, rational, production apparatus in the 50's and learnt to do so, was able to compete most successfully. In the 60's, which can be characterised as the decade of marketing, it was the companies who concentrated on developing their marketing capability that laid the best foundation for favourable development.

> In the future, production engineering and marketing are unlikely to have the same decisive importance as in the past. They are, of course, still two important components of a company's operations, but their importance from the point of view of competition is declining. Most companies know how to run their production and marketing operations, so standards in these respects have now become more uniform.

> It is research and development that will be the big thing in the future. Although product development has always played an important part in corporate strategic planning, the constantly changing external demands on both our company and our products means that in the future it will not be enough to concentrate only on the traditional engineering aspects. We shall have to broaden the base of product development in future and integrate it into the corporate strategic planning process in a more concrete manner.

> An ambition to lead the market demands products of a very high standard and, by the same token, product development of a very high standard. It is not enough for our products to satisfy the demands of the market; they must also be technically superior to those of our competitors.

The Thermal marketing group, however, believed that the development of new products and systems should follow an increase in the application know-how within the company, including:

1. The search, within known and established processes, for areas of application:
    where heat exchangers have not previously been used;
    where compact heat exchangers have not previously been used, but where other types such as tubular heat exchangers are already used;
    where it is possible to deliver a high degree of process know-how.

2. The search for applications of the company's product mix in new processes.

Only a small part of the company's application resources had been directed in the past towards these objectives. The division's Application Centres had been more occupied in providing technical and commercial support to the field organisation within established markets. This past orientation was partly an outcome of the technical superiority of Alfa-Laval's products which had created their own markets in areas where the competition was not troublesome. There had been, however, a gradual change in the attitude of Lund's marketing personnel, who now felt that with the increase in competitive activity and pressure on Alfa-Laval's profits and margins, the Application Centres should adopt a more aggressive stance. Marketing personnel felt that they should be informed as a matter of course of all important activity, especially large projects in their respective industrial sectors, and not have to sit and hope that the marketing companies would have the goodness to get in touch with them. To face the growing competition, the Marketing Department saw the remedy in aggressive central marketing activity.

There was another school of thought, however, that argued for decentralisation of product development rather than centralisation of marketing. Frequent discussions had taken place as to whether it would be preferable to retain the relatively large development group working internationally with the national market companies or build small engineering groups in each of the major national companies. Until now the primary responsibility for product development had rested with the division, but it had been found practical to keep some development activities close to production and sales in market companies. Thus most of the development work for cooling towers had been done in Spain, where the relevant production unit was located.

Pricing Policy The Thermal Subdivision administered a complicated pricing policy. Despite a general acceptance that this policy was unsatisfactory, it had not been changed because the various alternative suggestions were either too cumbersome to implement or did not accomplish what the Subdivision considered to be the central purpose of its pricing strategy — that is, to maintain divisional autonomy and, at the same time, provide the required incentive to maximise total company performance. Management's attitude had been to accept the 'devil you know'.

A company catalogue laid down the internal sales prices for products calculated as shown in Table 1; note that these are disguised percentages but should be taken as actual for the purpose of this case:

Interdivision sales took place at the manufacturing price, and in about 80% of the cases the market companies paid the catalogue price less a discount varying according to the country of destination. The size of the discount was determined through negotiation between the management of the Thermal Subdivision and the respective market company, though occasionally Group management was involved. The discount for a particular market company, however, remained constant unless there were very special reasons. The aim of this market discount was to allow for the different competition, and hence price levels, that had grown up in the different country markets. In Germany, for example, Alfa-Laval held a leading market share; but Germany was a large, price-conscious market and under continual competitive pressure.

Table 1   Calculation of Internal Sales Prices

Standard Variable Production Costs, Stock Holding Charges etc.
Work's Overheads, Specially Installed Equipment
Product Division's Charge for Development and Coordination (Approx. 30% on MP)
Product Division's Profit Charge (Approx. 20% on MP)
Market Company Cost Charge (Average 40% on MP)
Market Company Profit (Average 10% on MP)

Production Cost

Manufacturing Price (MP)

Internal Sales Price (Catalogue)

Customer Sales Price (CSP)

Where it was felt that a particular order was of such importance to the Group that a particularly low price should be quoted, it was possible to request a special discount. This happened for under 10% of the business, but the assessment of whether an order justified a specially preferential price had become one of the major concerns of the Application Centres at Lund.

A number of dysfunctions of the pricing system had been recognised. These statements are taken from internal subdivision papers:

> It appears that the subsidiary is treated as an external customer. Since the easiest way for a subsidiary to improve its profitability is to obtain extra discounts from the product division, attention is drawn to the wrong quarter. But, on the other hand, the price system does not guarantee that the subsidiary gets enough freedom of action, e.g. in external pricing. The information transferred to the subsidiaries via the price system does not correspond to the actual position for the current decision.

> A subsidiary company can show good profits at the expense of a product division in Sweden.

> Each fixed internal pricing system has effects on resource allocation. To use a price system with a resource allocating purpose without either informing the units involved or drawing out the consequences must be condemned. The relation between different product divisions (e.g. competition for the favours of the subsidiary) or between different subsidiaries (e.g. competition for the same international buyer) can be serious.

> The structure of the internal pricing system provides the subsidiary with little incentive to increase its volume. There is a tendency to "skim" the market.

> The Internal Sales Price is determined by a pre-calculated standard catalogue price. A preliminary calculation such as this is always based on a number of assumptions about volume, distribution of joint costs, depreciation and interest on fixed assets. Each estimation of these costs is more or less arbitrary and, in turn, is based on a number of more or less unspoken assumptions. With

the present system for internal sales price calculation, it is hard to relate the cost calculation to the actual decisions.

As the Thermal Subdivision found itself dealing more and more with large international customers, problems were becoming evident on large bids with regard to division of profits, differences of price levels, and differences in technical solutions suggested by various Market Companies. For the Thermal Conference of 1975, a partially fictitious case had been written to open the discussion as to how the marketing approach, particularly pricing, should be amended:

The Case of a Major Opportunity

Alfa-Laval has market companies (MkA, MkB, etc.) in 6 countries: A, B, C, D, E and F. There are 3 contractors competing to obtain the main contract:

Contractor 1B has its head office in country B and subsidiaries in countries C and D.
Contractor 2E has its head office in E.
Contractor 3F has its head office in F and a subsidiary in B.

The ultimate customer, an end-user, is located in country A and local regulations require 20% of the equipment to be manufactured in A. Alfa-Laval's MkA in A has local assembly facilities for some types in the product range, but not the types specified in the quotations.

Step 1   MkA informs Thermal about the project, stating which contractors are bidding.

Step 2   Thermal forwards information to MkB, MkE and MkF where the 3 contractors have their head offices. Since the project is at a very early state, none can obtain material for a quotation but must wait.

Step 3   Contractors start work in project design and MkC, which has previously collaborated with Contractor 1B's subsidiary in C on other projects, receives an enquiry without knowing which project it refers to.

Step 4   MkB, MkD, MkE and MkF now also receive enquiries from Contractor 3F's subsidiary in B. All enquiries except the one to MkF are forwarded to Thermal for coordination. MkA receives an enquiry direct from the end-user.

Step 5   MkC, which has its own manufacturing facilities for some products, makes its own technical solution and its own price quote to Contractor 1B's subsidiary in C, still unaware of which project is involved.

Step 6   Thermal makes its calculations and prepares quotations with a recommended technical solution and bid price, which are then forwarded to our MkA, MkB, MkD, MkE and MkF.

Step 7   The reaction to Thermal's proposal from the various Mk's are:
A: Our MkA accepts and quotes the price proposed by Thermal direct to the end-user and persuades him to specify plate heat exchangers.
B: Relations with Contractor 1B have previously been good and MkB has virtually a fixed price level for this customer. Contractor

1B is committed to a particular technical solution for this kind of application and MkB will, therefore, not accept the Thermal proposal.

D: MkD has generally been able to maintain a very high price level and, therefore, does not approve the level recommended by Thermal. The technical solution is acceptable.

E: The quotation is accepted and passed on to Contractor 2E.

F: It is discovered that MkF has already submitted its own quotation to Contractor 3F, with almost the same technical solution but at a higher price than the one recommended by Thermal.

Step 8   Thermal advises that its technical solution and price level should be used regardless.

Step 9   Contractor 1B gets the order.

Step 10 What happens now to relations between Alfa-Laval and the Contractors?

Contractor 1B is irritated because Alfa-Laval has also quoted direct to the end-user and takes the line that Alfa-Laval is competing with its own customer. Discovers that Alfa-Laval has different price levels in different countries and will in future ask for quotations from several Alfa-Laval offices. Is annoyed that we argue for different technical solutions for the same application, depending on the country in which the discussion takes place. We can, however, counter this by pointing to a different operational experience in different countries.

Contractor 2E has no problem.

Contractor 3F has also discovered that Alfa-Laval has different price levels in different countries, and having previously done business with MkF on other projects now suspects that he has been overcharged on previous occasions. Will not give Alfa-Laval another chance.

Step 11 Contractor 1B places the order with MkB.

Step 12 What efforts have the Alfa-Laval market companies made and what permanent changes have resulted?

A: Has persuaded the end-user to specify PHE's. Has passed on Thermal's quotation. Gets the after-sales service.

B: Has passed on Thermal's quotation. Has carried on technical and economic discussions with the customer to explain away the differences in price and technical solution. Has secured the order. Has lost some of its goodwill in its relations with Contractor 1B. Has lost a customer — Contractor 3F's subsidiary in B.

C: Has worked out its own technical solution. Has written its own quotations.

D: Has passed on Thermal's quotation. Has had its price level cut.

E: Has passed on Thermal's quotation.

Subjects for Discussion

How should we modify our organisation and methods to ensure:

closer contacts and coordination with main contractors;
involvement at an earlier stage;
a correct price policy;
optimum technical solutions?

How can we keep the question of division of profits out of the quotation work and ensure that a fair division is made *after* the order has been secured?

Who should be responsible for:

the technical solution;
the price level;
making the quotation?

The Way Ahead

Though "The Case of a Major Opportunity" was fictitious, it was sufficiently accurate to characterise the sort of problems that the Thermal Subdivision was facing in the international marketplace. The discussion brought home to all participants that fairly fundamental changes were called for, both in terms of distribution strategy and cross-country sales. Management was keen to decide what a future Thermal Subdivision should be like, what it should do, how it should control, and how such an organisation should be reached given the constraints of a hundred years of organisational tradition. Some managers felt that the well-established organisational culture was going to be a major stumbling block, that changes should be moderate and gradual. Others disagreed.

This case was prepared by Kenneth Simmonds of the London Business School. © Kenneth Simmonds, 1974.

CASE 24

Phipps and Company

Geoffrey Fanshaw, principal consultant with a small London consulting firm specialising in marketing management, had been asked for advice by Arthur Stanford of Phipps and Co in the first week of 1974. Early 1974 was a particularly worrying period for British managements who were faced with the world oil crisis, protracted union problems, and a government reduction of public sector investment in an attempt to stem inflation. Economic forecasters were predicting from zero to five percent reduction in gross national product during 1974. As building contractors dependent on continued investment, Phipps and Co could be severely affected. Stanford, Phipps' Managing Director, therefore asked Fanshaw for a rapid indication as to how much Phipps' prices should be lowered, as well as a general marketing assessment. The current supply shortage might lead to further cost increases for a period, but Stanford felt Phipps could cover itself adequately against supply shortages and further cost escalation.

Several days' investigation by Geoffrey Fanshaw confirmed that the marketing data available from Phipps was very sketchy. Phipps operated throughout the Southeast of England engaged mainly on apartment blocks, office buildings and small industrial plants. No market figures, however, were available for the area covered. Even within Phipps no usable records were kept of the volume of invitations received. Simon Grange, Phipps' Commercial Director, told Fanshaw that collecting market data would be a waste of money. He claimed that Phipps represented only one per cent or so of the total capacity in the area and although the firm went ahead with bids or negotiations on only two-thirds of the enquiries, it would not be difficult to get Phipps onto many more bidding lists.

From the firm's accounting records and Grange's records of bids submitted, Fanshaw was able to compile the comparative sales summary shown in Exhibit 1. Around one quarter of all orders were at negotiated prices some 2% above markups on orders obtained through bidding. For 1973 Phipps general and administrative overheads ran at £420,000, leaving a profit before tax of £286,000. Orders in hand were at a high level with sufficient work to stretch the work force through April. After that the loading fell off quite steeply at about 10% per month — but work from current bids could be commenced by April.

Phipps' prices were set at a weekly bidding meeting attended by Stanford, Grange, the chief estimator and the financial director. Stanford, a solicitor aged 60 who represented a significant shareholding and had been appointed from outside three years previously, was very conservative in his pricing. He did not readily accept the more radical pricing recommendations advanced by Simon Grange. Grange had worked for the firm for nearly thirty years since leaving school at 17 and started as a trainee estimator. He held very definite views about the market and competition and he argued these

Exhibit 1   *Comparative Sales Summary*

		1971	1972	1973 12 mths	1973 Jan—Jun	Jul—Dec
Sales Invoiced	£m	9.7	10.7	11.1	5.3	5.8
Gross Margin	£00,000	650	740	706	316	390
Negotiated Work	£m	2.6	2.8	2.9	1.4	1.5
Average Markup on Cost	%	(9.8)	(8.4)	(9.7)	(8.3)	(11.1)
Bids Submitted	£m	47.0	44.0	49.0	20.0	29.0
Successful Bids	£m	8.9	7.7	9.7	3.6	6.1
Average Markup on Cost	%	(7.7)	(7.7)	(7.8)	(6.2)	(8.9)
Total Orders Obtained	£m	11.5	10.5	12.6	5.0	7.6
Average Markup on Cost	%	(8.2)	(7.9)	(8.3)	(6.7)	(9.3)

forcefully. In the last six months of 1973, for example, Grange had argued that markups should be raised well above the 10% norm because conditions were good. He was currently arguing for a reduction to 5% in advance of the bad times.

Fanshaw had great difficulty in finding any competitor data on which to base his own pricing recommendations. After a lot of searching, however, he uncovered 13 bids made during 1973 for which competitor prices were available — five dating from before the summer and eight made more recently. The competitor prices recorded are shown in Exhibit 2. As far as Fanshaw could ascertain, these bids were a representative sample of the total in size, type of work and competition, although Phipps was successful on none.

Exhibit 2   *Bid Prices Available*

Bid No.	Date	Bids Submitted (£'00,000's) (* indicated Phipps' bid)								Phipps' Contribution on Cost
										%
703	Jan. 16	9.3	9.9*	10.1	10.1	10.2				5
709	Feb. 27	8.9	9.2	10.2	10.5	11.0	11.2	11.5*	13.6	5
715	Apr. 3	3.3	4.0*	4.1	4.1					10
716	Apr. 8	11.0	11.6	11.8*	12.0	12.6	13.0			6
723	May 19	8.8	8.9	9.0	9.6	10.2*				8
730	Aug. 20	1.5	1.6	1.6	1.8*					17
731	Sep. 3	6.8	7.1*	7.8						11
733	Sep. 11	6.2	6.4	6.8	6.9	6.9*	7.1	7.4	7.7	16
738	Sep. 19	10.4	11.7*							14
745	Oct. 23	18.2	19.1	19.4*	19.9					14
746	Oct. 25	6.4	6.4*	6.6	6.7	7.3				5
754	Nov. 8	26.5	29.3	30.0*	31.5	32.3	33.8	35.7	36.7 40.4	12
758	Nov. 30	7.5	7.8	8.2*	9.5	10.3				10

This case was prepared by Professor Adrian B. Ryans as a basis for class discussion rather than to illustrate either effective or ineffective handling of an administrative situation.
© The School of Business Administration, The University of Western Ontario, 1982.

CASE 25

Northern Telecom (A)

In early 1975 a three-person task force, with representatives from Northern Telecom Limited, Bell—Northern Research Limited and Bell Canada, was asked to develop a strategy for Northern Telecom in the central office switching market. Central office switching equipment is the telephone exchange equipment owned by telephone companies that connects a user with the telephone at the number he/she has dialled. This equipment includes both local telephone exchanges and toll or long-distance exchanges that connect all the local exchanges together. The decisions about Northern Telecom's central office switching strategy were viewed as crucial ones, since revenues of hundreds of millions of dollars were at stake.

Northern Telecom's major entry in the central office switching market, the SP-1, was experiencing rapid growth, but competitors were agressively introducing new products which threatened to cut into future sales of the SP-1.

The task force was faced with two major alternatives:

1. Introduce all or part of a new digital central office switching line as soon as possible, with the first major elements of the product line being available in 1979. The technical and business risks associated with such a strategy were viewed as being very large. Furthermore, the announcement of a digital switching product might have an adverse effect on sales of the SP-1 product line.

2. Delay the introduction of the digital switching line until 1981 or later. This would alleviate Northern Telecom's short-run cash flow problems, and would probably extend the product life cycle of the SP-1 switch. Since the SP-1 switch was under increasing competitive pressure, one possibility was to introduce an updated enhanced version of the SP-1 switch (perhaps called the SP-2). Depending on the number and type of enhancements selected, this upgraded switch could be announced within a few months and could be available to customers by 1977.

The Company Prior to 1956, Northern Electric Company Limited (as Northern Telecom was formerly called) was 40% owned by Western Electric, the manufacturing arm of American Telephone and Telegraph (AT&T). Its prime mandate was to manufacture Western Electric products for Bell Canada. During this period Northern Electric had only a very small R&D staff. In 1956, as the result of a consent decree with the US Department of Justice, Western Electric relinquished ownership of Northern Electric, and Northern Electric became a wholly-owned subsidiary of Bell Canada. Northern Electric continued to manufacture certain Western Electric products under licence.

*The Development of
a Central Office
Switching Product
Line*

In 1958 Northern Electric Laboratories was established and its priority task was the acquisition of expertise in switching and transmission, and the development of a product line that would meet Canadian needs. By the early 1960s, it had become apparent to Northern Electric management that the next generation of switching products would make extensive use of electronics to replace electro-mechanical components. Bell Canada had continued to have a working relationship with AT&T through a service contract. Before this relationship ended, Bell Canada was anxious to get access to the latest technology AT&T had to offer. AT&T had announced an electronic central office switch (the #1 ESS) in the early 1960s. Bell Canada was able to negotiate an arrangement whereby Northern Electric would manufacture under licence a #1 ESS switch for the World's Fair in Montreal (Expo '67). This contract resulted in Northern Electric becoming involved both with Bell Laboratories (the R&D arm of AT&T) and Western Electric as part of the development team. Ultimately, a total of 11 of these #1 ESS switches were built by Northern Electric under licence from Western Electric for Bell Canada. The switch was a large local switch able to handle from 10,000–60,000 lines. The product, which was expensive to manufacture on Northern Electric's scale, was phased out of the Northern Electric product line in the early 1970s.

Northern Electric's experience with the #1 ESS switch reinforced management's desire to develop a product line attuned to the needs of the Canadian market — particularly products that would be economical at low line sizes and would continue to be economical over a wide range of line sizes. By 1964, the basic architecture of such a product had been outlined. In 1965 a commitment was made to proceed with the SP-1 (Stored Program 1st System), and the product development team grew from half a dozen people in 1965 to well over a hundred by the end of the decade. The first trial office (a switch installed in a telephone company exchange) was installed near Ottawa in November 1969, and the first commercial office was placed in service in November 1971.

Exhibit 1 *Sales History and Sales Forecasts for SP-1 Central Office Switches ($m.)*

Year	Canada	United States	Other Exports	Total
1971	6	0	0	6
1972	15	0	0	15
1973	33	2	0	35
1974	76	26	0	102
1975 (estimated)	148	27	0	175
1976 forecast	137	12[a]	0	149
1977 forecast	171	8[a]	8	186
1978 forecast	183	9[a]	7	198
1979 forecast	192	10[a]	12	214
1980 forecast	202	12[a]	15	229

[a] Northern Telecom was to begin manufacturing some SP-1 switches in the United States beginning in 1976. These forecasts only include exports from Canada to the United States. Forecasts of shipments from the US plant were not available.
Source: Company Records.

By 1975, versions of the SP-1 switch were available that could handle local exchanges from about 3,000 to 25,000 telephone lines, medium-sized toll exchanges, and a combination of both. Every major telephone company in Canada had bought the switch and the SP-1 had achieved about a 90% market share of the addressed segments of the switching market in Canada. Sales through 1975 were much higher than expected, with 25% of 1974 sales being made in the United States, and the SP-1 was viewed by non-AT&T companies in North America as the premium stored program switch. The sales history and some sales forecasts for the product are shown in Exhibit 1. The expected flattening of sales in 1975 in the United States was due largely to the 1974—75 recession, which was having a significant impact on capital expenditure programmes in the telephone industry.

Bell—Northern Research By 1970, Northern Electric Laboratories had become a major research and development organisation, employing about 2,000 people. At that time the decision was made to incorporate it as a separate entity. On 1 January 1971, Bell—Northern Research Limited (BNR) came into being and the employees of Northern Electric Laboratories became employees of the "new" company. BNR did research and development work for both Northern Telecom and Bell Canada.

The Telephone Industry At the end of 1974, 357 million telephones were in service around the world, and that number had been growing by about 8% per year. About 44% of the world's telephones were located in the United States and Canada, with a further 27% and 12% in Western Europe and Japan, respectively. Construction expenditures by telephone companies in North America, which included expenditures on switching equipment, had grown (in nominal dollars) at over 15% per year in Canada and 9.5% per year in the United States during the period 1965 to 1975. Expenditure growth rates were even higher outside North America.

Canada Bell Canada, its subsidiaries and its affiliated companies provided most of the telephone services in Ontario, Quebec, the Atlantic Provinces, and the Northwest Territories. Together, these companies operated about 8.4 million telephones and were expected to spend approximately $225 million on central office switching equipment in 1975. There were four major non-Bell telephone companies operating in Canada. British Columbia Telephone Company had about 1.5 million telephones in service, and Alberta Government Telephones, Saskatchewan Telecommunications and Manitoba Telephone System together had about another 2.0 million telephones in service. Several hundred smaller telephone companies served about 300,000 telephones. Between them, the non-Bell companies were expected to spend about $150 million on central office switching products.

All the major Canadian telephone companies were members of the Trans-Canada Telephone System (TCTS), which co-ordinated trans-continental telephone service, data communications, and television network facilities. In 1973, TCTS members had put into operation the world's first commercial national digital data transmission facility called Dataroute, demonstrating the Canadian telephone companies' leadership in, and belief in, digital technology.

United States About 144 million telephones were in service in the United States in early 1975. AT&T (Bell System) provided service to about 82% of the telephones in the United States. Western Electric was wholly owned by AT&T and, as a matter of policy after the 1956 consent decree with the US Justice Department, with very few exceptions sold its products exclusively to Bell System operating companies and to the US government. AT&T was expected to spend $1,650 million on switching equipment in 1975.

The remaining 18% of the telephones in the United States were served by about 1,600 independent telephone companies. While many of these companies were tiny, some were very large companies. General Telephone and Electronics (GTE) serviced about 45% of all telephones served by the independent telephone companies and had telephone-related revenues of almost $2 billion. The major independent telephone companies, the number of telephones they served and their estimated 1975 expenditures on switching equipment, are shown in Exhibit 2. The large independent telephone companies provided a full range of telephone services. Smaller independent telephone companies typically relied on others, particularly AT&T Long Lines, for the provision of toll services. The two largest of the independent telephone companies, GTE and United Telecommunications, had their own major manufacturing companies, GTE Automatic Electric and North Electric respectively, which supplied much of the central office switching equipment to their owners.

Exhibit 2 *Major US Independent Telephone Companies in 1975*

Company	No. of Telephones Served (000s)	Estimated Expenditure on Central Office Switches in 1975 ($m.)
General Telephone Company	11,800	218
United Telecommunications	3,236	70
Continental Telephone	2,246	
Central Telephone	1,222	240
Other Independent Telephone Companies	7,500	

The independent telephone companies generally served the more rural areas of the United States, not the major concentrations of population (although a GTE operating company did serve much of Los Angeles). This resulted in a higher proportion of their central offices being in the smaller line sizes relative to the Bell System. The Bell System, through AT&T Long Lines, serviced the long-distance and international markets which required a large number of large toll central offices. In fact, while only 23% of AT&T's central offices had less than 1,000 lines, 64% of the independents' central offices were this size. Conversely, 43% of AT&T's central offices had over 5,000 lines, whereas only 8% of the independents' central offices were this large.

Europe The European market for central office switching equipment was growing rapidly, with total expenditures on central office switching equipment in

1974 amounting to $3 billion. The European market was more fragmented than the North American market, since each country had its own government postal telegraph and telephone company (PTT). Most of the PTTs had restrictive technical standards and took other steps to protect their domestic telecommunications equipment manufacturers. Furthermore, Europe had quite different technical standards for telephone switching equipment than North America and Japan, which meant that a manufacturer had to modify his switching equipment extensively if he wanted to sell in both markets. The development cost of these general modifications for the overseas market was estimated by Northern Telecom to be up to $20 million for a particular type of central office switch, with at least an additional $1 million to meet the idiosyncrasies of each individual PTT. Nevertheless, despite these barriers, the European market was an attractive market with a lot of future potential. Telephone service penetration was typically only one-third to one-half of the US penetration of 60 telephones per 100 people. Much of the European telephone plant and equipment was obsolete and was ripe for replacement. In much of the rest of the world the situation was similar, except that telephone penetration levels were usually lower.

Northern Telecom's View of the 1975 Market

Northern Telecom executives generally viewed their North American customers as falling into three major segments: (1) Bell Canada, its subsidiaries and affiliated companies; (2) system telephone companies (the other telephone companies in TCTS, the Bell System operating companies in the US, and the major independent telephone companies in the US); and (3) the smaller independent telephone companies in the United States and Canada.

Northern Telecom's close relationship with Bell Canada gave it access to operating company information which was very useful in setting product specifications and planning production. These two companies also shared the same knowledge base with Bell—Northern Research. Many executives viewed this close working relationship as providing a major advantage to both corporations. Bell typically identified its approximate requirements for switching equipment from Northern Telecom about two to three years in advance and provided detailed specifications of its needs about one year in advance. Northern Telecom provided firm price quotations at this point and such prices were required to be as low or lower than those provided to any other customer.

Alberta Government Telephones (AGT), Manitoba Telephone, and Saskatchewan Telecommunications used a more competitive buying procedure, with AGT being the most extreme on this dimension. AGT typically developed tender documents with a detailed set of specifications, and Northern Telecom and other interested manufacturers would be asked to submit bids. B.C. Telephone and Quebec Telephone were special cases in the Canadian market, reflecting their status as subsidiaries of GTE. Since GTE had its own manufacturing subsidiary, GTE Automatic Electric, B.C. Telephone and, to a lesser extent, Quebec Telephone bought most of their switching equipment from GTE Automatic Electric. B.C. Telephone only bought switching equipment from Northern Telecom when Automatic Electric did not manufacture the required type of switch, or when Automatic Electric could not meet its delivery requirements.

In the United States, the major independent telephone companies, except the GTE and United Telecommunications operating companies, generally used competitive tenders to buy equipment. This resulted in about 8% of the US market being awarded on a competitive tender basis. Their needs and buying criteria were generally similar to the major Canadian telephone companies and, hence, they were usually seeking similar benefits from the switching products. These customers typically bought switching equipment from more than one supplier.

Many of the smaller independent telephone companies used low-interest loans from the Rural Electrification Authority (REA) to buy switching equipment. The REA set specifications for switching equipment, and telephone companies using REA money to purchase switches had to use a competitive tender against specifications, with the business being awarded to the lowest bidder. In total in the United States, about 80% of Northern Telecom's switching equipment sales were the result of competitive tenders, with the remainder being directed orders.

The Bell System operating companies and the GTE operating companies generally bought almost all their central office switching equipment from Western Electric and GTE Automatic Electric respectively. Only in rare circumstances, when these manufacturing subsidiaries were unable to supply required equipment in a timely manner, did they go to outside vendors.

In dealing with all segments of the market, Northern Telecom executives believed customers preferred to deal with a supplier who could offer a full line of switching equipment to meet their needs. For large telephone companies, this would include everything from small local exchanges to large local and toll exchanges.

The sales of central office switching systems were comprised of two parts: the sale of the initial switch, and the extension sales which allowed the basic switch to be expanded to meet the growth in the market served by the exchange. In the case of the SP-1 switch, the average initial installation was approximately 8,000 lines, and the average ultimate capacity of each exchange sold was expected to be 20,000 lines. In other words, for every $1.00 spent on an SP-1 initial office, another $1.50 or more in extension sales would occur in subsequent years. Once a customer purchased an initial office from Northern Telecom or another vendor, he was committed to purchasing the extension equipment from the same vendor. Thus, the product life-cycle for a central office switch such as the SP-1 was made up of two sub-cycles, the first being initial sales and the second being extension sales. With respect to the SP-1 sales in Canada, shown in Exhibit 1, 100% of the sales in the period 1970 to 1973 had been initial sales, with this percentage declining to 90 and 82 in 1974 and 1975 respectively. The importance of extension sales to the customer also made it difficult for new suppliers, particularly foreign suppliers without local manufacturing and support facilities, to break into the central office switching market. Telephone companies had to be convinced that a supplier was in the market for the long term so that the telephone companies would be able to expand their switches and obtain spare parts many years into the future.

Central Office Switching Systems Technology

A central office switching system is the equipment that connects a telephone user's telephone with the telephone number dialled. Sometimes, as in the case of a long-distance call, connections might have to be made through several central offices (local or toll exchanges) before the two telephones are connected (see Exhibit 3a). Essentially, a central office switching system has

Exhibit 3　*Digital Technology*

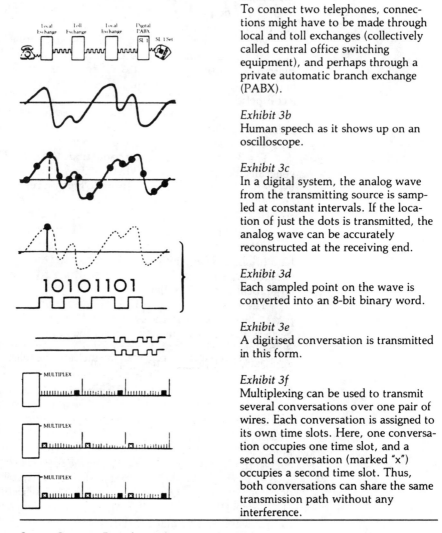

Exhibit 3a
To connect two telephones, connections might have to be made through local and toll exchanges (collectively called central office switching equipment), and perhaps through a private automatic branch exchange (PABX).

Exhibit 3b
Human speech as it shows up on an oscilloscope.

Exhibit 3c
In a digital system, the analog wave from the transmitting source is sampled at constant intervals. If the location of just the dots is transmitted, the analog wave can be accurately reconstructed at the receiving end.

Exhibit 3d
Each sampled point on the wave is converted into an 8-bit binary word.

Exhibit 3e
A digitised conversation is transmitted in this form.

Exhibit 3f
Multiplexing can be used to transmit several conversations over one pair of wires. Each conversation is assigned to its own time slots. Here, one conversation occupies one time slot, and a second conversation (marked "x") occupies a second time slot. Thus, both conversations can share the same transmission path without any interference.

Source: Company Records

two major components: the switching network and the central control system. The switching network is the electromechanical or electronic equipment that connects two telephone lines together and provides the dial tone, ringing, and busy signals. The control system activates the switching functions.

Digital Transmission of Speech and Data

Human speech shows up on an oscilloscope as an analog wave (see Exhibit 3b). The height of the wave is directly proportional to the level of the signal transmitted. The number of waves in a given time period is a representation of the pitch or frequency of the signal. Thus, the analog wave is a direct electrical representation of the sound waves used to generate it, and is readily converted back to sound waves at the earpiece of the receiving handset.

In a digital system, the analog wave from the transmitting source is sampled at constant intervals, represented by the dots on the wave in Exhibit 3c. A digital signal is then generated to describe the position of the dot on the wave. The digital signal takes the form of a binary word of eight bits (which can describe 256 different positions of the dot). A sample signal is shown in Exhibit 3d. In order to get an accurate representation of the original analog wave, it must be sampled several thousand times every second by a codec (*co*der and *dec*oder) — a specialised electronic circuit. Technically, this process is called pulse code modulation (PCM).

After a conversation has been digitised, it looks like Exhibit 3e, with one path for transmission in each direction. Multiplexing can then be used to interleave several conversations on a single communication path (2 wires). A sample is taken from the first conversation, then one from the second conversation, and so on, forming a frame of a predetermined number of samples. Each succeeding frame contains samples of the same conversations in the same sequence. At the receiving end, the samples are removed from the frames by a demultiplexer and the multiple analog signals reconstructed by a codec. Thus, all the conversations share the same two-wire transmission path, but are separated by time (see Exhibit 4f). Technically, this approach to signal transmission was called time division multiplexing (TDM).

Switching Systems   Space division switching (SDM), with different conversations being transmitted over separate wires, was the method the telephone industry had used prior to the mid-1970s to switch its analog signals. The earliest SDM switches were electromechanical step-by-step systems (S X S systems). While these systems were cheap and had large line capacity, they required large amounts of space, had few features, had high labour and maintenance costs, and were "noisy", making them unsatisfactory for data communication. The next generation of SDM switches were electromechanical crossbar switches. These crossbar switches had several advantages over S X S switches, including more features, a more compact size, and lower labour and maintenance costs. A major advance in switching was the development of electronic switches, the first commercial model of which was the #1 ESS switch developed by AT&T and introduced commercially in 1965. The #1 ESS switch again used SDM signal path technology.

Modern exchanges, such as the SP-1 switch, used stored-program-control systems. Here, the software program controlling the system is stored in memory. This allows changes in the control system to be readily made. The availability of stored-program-control systems meant that a switch could be given a variety of features by making changes in the software. The computer could be readily programmed to handle maintenance, traffic analysis, and a host of other tasks that have to be done by a telephone company.

Northern Telecom and other industry executives believed that a successful all-digital system would provide significant benefits to users and telephone companies beyond those of state-of-the-art stored-program-control analog systems. Being able to move many times as many signals over one transmission line would lead to better utilisation of communication lines. Being digital, the information sent was always uniform; that is, it was a bit of information, either a pulse or no pulse (again, see Exhibit 3e). When a signal of this type became degraded through line loss etc., it could readily be regenerated to its original shape through the use of a digital repeater. This was particularly important when transmitting data. Northern Telecom first made use of the TDM—PCM technology in the T1 carrier which was commercially demonstrated in 1963. The T1 carrier was used for inter-exchange transmission of signals, but it was expensive to manufacture and was only economically practical on heavily used portions of a telephone company's network.

By 1972, the first laboratory samples of large-scale integrated (LSI) circuits were becoming available. These allowed very complex circuits of hundreds or thousands of individual components to be put on a tiny electronic chip. By 1975, Northern Telecom had been able, with the assistance of LSI technology, to incorporate time division multiplexing, pulse code modulation, and stored-program-control into a private automatic branch exchange (PABX), the SL-1. A PABX is essentially a small switching system that controls the private telephone system within an organisation. Northern Telecom executives and engineers could envision fully digital switching and transmission systems in the future with digital switches, transmission systems, and digital PABXs all linked together.

Competition

The market for central office switching products was intensely competitive, with North American, European, and Japanese companies competing for shares of it. The major manufacturers and their estimated sales of telecommunications equipment (including central office switching equipment) are shown in Exhibit 4.

Western Electric was the largest manufacturer of central office switching equipment in the world. As a result of the 1956 consent decree, it was not generally a factor in non-AT&T markets. A high proportion of its 1975 switching equipment sales were stored-program-control ESS switches of different sizes (#1 ESS, #2 ESS and #3 ESS). In the mid-1970s, AT&T had announced a very large digital toll switch, the #4 ESS, which was for sale to non-AT&T companies in the US and Canada. This was a specialised toll switch for use in the largest metropolitan areas and had a fairly limited market. The product was expected to be available in 1976 or 1977.

Both GTE Automatic Electric and North Electric (the United Telecommunications manufacturing subsidiary) also had large captive markets in their own companies. GTE Automatic Electric's sales of its #1 EAX stored-program-control analog switch were growing, even though Northern Telecom executives believed that the SP-1 switch had better architecture and features that allowed it to be used in a wider range of applications. The announced #2 EAX switch, which was expected to be commercially available in 1978, was expected to be a very formidable competitor to the SP-1. Automatic Electric had also announced a digital medium-size toll switch, the #3 EAX. This switch was scheduled for introduction in late 1978. It was expected to have some impact on sales of the SP-1 in toll applications. In many ways, the most serious competition for the SP-1 in 1973 and 1974 had been provided by North Electric's NX-1E stored-program-control analog switch.

Exhibit 4   *Major Manufacturers of Telecommunications Equipment and Worldwide 1974 Sales and Net Incomes ($m.)*

Company	Sales	Net Income
Western Electric (USA)	7,400	311
ITT (USA) — Telecommunications Equipment Only	3,000	176
Siemens A.G. (West Germany) — Telecommunications Equipment Only	1,600	—[a]
L.M. Ericsson (Sweden)	1,500	79
Nippon Electric Company (Japan)	1,500	18
Northern Electric (Canada)	958	54
GTE Automatic Electric (USA)	700	42
Canadian Subsidiary	117	6
North Electric (USA) — Subsidiary of United Telecommunications	290	7
Stromberg—Carlson (USA) — Subsidiary of General Dynamics	234	10

[a] Income on total sales of $6,600 million was $92 million.
Source: Telecommunications Market: Operating Telephone Company and Manufacturers Statistics, Northern Electric Company Ltd, 1975.

International Telephone & Telegraph (ITT) was the largest European-based supplier of telephone equipment. In 1974, ITT had introduced its Metaconta-L line of stored-program-control analog switches into the North American market, and this line was beginning to provide new competition for Northern Telecom. Ericsson was also developing and promoting its AXE stored-program-control analog switch in Europe, and some industry observers believed that this product's architecture had benefited from knowledge of the strengths and weaknesses of the SP-1 architecture, and was superior to it. Ericsson was believed to be developing digital switches that would be integrated into the AXE line.

NEC America, a subsidiary of Nippon Electric Company, manufactured a stored-program-control analog switch, the D-10. In 1974 and early 1975, NEC had been very aggressive in its pricing on some bids in North America.

A brief description of the major competitive stored-program-control analog switches that were available or had been announced for the North American market is included in Exhibit 5. These switches generally cost between $150 and $300 per line depending on the size of the switches, their features, etc. Exhibit 6 contains the particular switches Northern Telecom executives viewed as being most competitive in each of the major market segments. They did not view the SP-1 as being competitive in really large local and toll applications due to its maximum line size capacity. Furthermore, Stromberg-Carlson had a stranglehold on the small switch segment of the independent market with their old technology X-Y step-by-step equipment. SP-1 and other stored-program-control switches could not compete at the smaller line sizes with the X-Y system.

Exhibit 5 *Competitive Stored-Program-Control Analog Switches — Available and Announced*

Company	Product	Nominal Size Range (in lines)	Comments
Northern Telecom	SP-1	3,000–25,000	
GTE Automatic Electric	#1 EAX	4,000–40,000	Competitive with SP-1 in large line sizes. Northern Telecom felt architecture inferior to SP-1. Does not have all the features of SP-1.
	#2 EAX	4,000–40,000	Introduction expected in 1978. Viewed as a very serious threat to SP-1.
ITT (Europe)	Metaconta-L	5,000–60,000	Introduced in 1974. Active bidding for orders in the US and Canadian markets.
North Electric	NX-1E	1,000–20,000	Significant sales to US independents.
Stromberg–Carlson	ESC-1	2,000–20,000	Significant sales to US independents.
Siemens (West Germany)	ESK	500– 3,000	Field trial under way in North America.
Philips (Netherlands)	PRX	5,000–25,000	No sales to date in North America.
Nippon Electric	D-10	2,000–40,000	Introduced in Japan in 1971. First North American installation expected in early 1977.

Source: Company Records.

Exhibit 6 *Competition — By Size and Type of Exchange and Market Segment — Available and Announced*

	Small	Medium	Large — Local	Large — Toll
Bell Canada and Subsidiaries and Affiliates	None[a]	None	None	Auto. Electric 3-EAX[b] Western Electric 4-ESS[c]
Other Canada	Auto. Electric 1-EAX	Auto. Electric 1-EAX Auto. Electric 2-EAX	Auto. Electric 1-EAX ITT Metaconta-L	Auto. Electric 3-EAX[b]
United States	Auto. Electric 2-EAX North Electric NX1E Stromberg–Carlson ESC1	Auto. Electric 2-EAX Auto. Electric 1-EAX North Electric NX1E ITT Metaconta-L		

[a] Bell Canada would likely buy only Northern Telecom products in these sizes and types of switches.

[b] The Automatic Electric 3-EAX was an announced digital toll switch and was expected to be able to handle 10,000–20,000 trunks

[c] The Western Electric 4-ESS was a huge digital toll switch which could handle 25,000–100,000 trunks (i.e. it was only suitable for very large metropolitan areas such as Toronto, Montreal, Vancouver, and major US cities). Western Electric had begun to market this product to non-AT&T companies in Canada.

Source: Company Records

Digital Switch Development Efforts at Northern Telecom

Prior to 1969 digital switching had been regarded by the telecommunications industry as possible, but too expensive to be practical. The rapid advances in electronics in the late 1960s led Bell—Northern Research (BNR) Systems Engineering to re-examine the status of digital switching in 1968. In early 1969, they reported:

> The (technical) feasibility of integrated (TDM—PCM) switching has been demonstrated in many countries ... Digital switching in the present situation can hardly compete with conventional switching systems. ... However, the near availability of large-scale integrated circuits will probably change the competitive position in favour of digital switching within 5 years, and definitely within 10 years. In addition, the development of the pulse code modulation transmission system, which is now well underway in most industrialized countries, will eliminate the need for interface equipment, and, therefore, will give integrated switching a decisive advantage over conventional systems, both from economic and technical viewpoints.

They recommended that Northern Electric consider very seriously the development of an integrated digital switching system to be available for domestic sales within 7 to 10 years. The report and its recommendations were not accepted by all managers in Bell Canada and Northern Electric. A great deal of money and manpower was then being used to bring the SP-1 stored-program-control analog switch to market. Since it incorporated the latest technology, many managers were convinced that this switch would meet the telephone companies' switching needs for the next 15 years and they were not convinced that there was a need to spend money on the exploratory development of a digital switch.

In early 1971 Bell Northern's Systems Engineering Group notified selected individuals in Bell Canada, BNR and Northern Electric that technological advances in memories, logic, crosspoints, etc. now convinced them that the SP-1 system would be obsolete for new local and toll installations by 1980. In late 1971 work began at BNR to build a laboratory "test bed" to demonstrate the technical feasibility of digital switching and to demonstrate solid-state digital switching and circuit design techniques. In 1972 an initial budget for digital research was proposed by the switching division to the Board of Northern Electric calling for expenditures of $22 million over 7 years, with $1.5 million firm for 1974.

In 1972 BNR demonstrated a Large Scale Integration (LSI) codec that would be a key element in any digital switching product. This codec was a key element in the SL-1 PABX, which was to be available by late 1975. By 1973 BNR concluded that its exploratory development programme had successfully demonstrated the technical feasibility of digital switching, and that the SP-1 programme was providing a solid base of experience in stored-program-control techniques, much of which would be applicable to a digital switch. A detailed economic analysis of the impact of using digital switching in Bell Canada's Montreal switching network suggested by projection that Bell Canada might be able to reduce its capital expenditures in the metropolitan areas in its service area by $100 million in the period 1982—92 if it moved to digital switching.

In November 1974 the Digital Switching Division was formed in Northern Telecom Canada to begin developing a product plan for the digital line. In December 1974 the realisation began to spread that development of a line of digital switches was going to require huge expenditures on research and development (much more than the $22 million envisioned in 1972), and

Exhibit 7   *Northern Telecom Limited, Selected Financial Data 1971—74 ($m.)*

Earnings and Related Data

	1974	1973	1972	1971
Revenues	957.7	608.1	531.3	573.8
Revenues of company manufactured products	799.8	512.9	448.5	473.4
Research and development expenses	44.0	32.7	28.0	29.7
Provision for income taxes	49.6	30.5	21.0	14.5
Net earnings	53.8	32.0	20.1	12.6

Financial Position at 31 December

	1974	1973	1972	1971
Assets				
Cash and Equivalent	14.1	69.4	52.3	27.4
Accounts Receivable	144.9	100.1	85.5	104.5
Inventories	255.0	177.3	112.5	112.2
Current Assets	433.7	360.1	260.1	253.6
Gross Plant	278.2	261.5	237.5	230.0
Accumulated Depreciation	158.2	142.5	128.4	124.4
Net Plant	120.0	119.0	109.1	105.7
Investments in Affiliates	9.0	6.5	5.5	5.0
Other Assets	5.1	6.7	1.7	1.3
TOTAL ASSETS	567.8	492.3	376.4	365.6
Liabilities				
Current Liabilities	150.6	149.7	84.9	83.3
Long-term Debt	104.5	69.6	73.5	77.1
Owner Liabilities	27.5	28.0	25.9	21.4
Shareholders' Equity	285.2	245.0	192.1	183.8
TOTAL LIABILITIES	567.8	492.3	376.4	365.6

Source: Company Records

that these expenditures might have a major negative impact on Northern Telecom's earnings. Some executives pointed out that delaying development of the digital switches for two or three years would relieve Northern Telecom's tightening cash flow situation. Selected financial data for Northern Telecom are shown in Exhibit 7. These financial concerns precipitated a major review of Northern Telecom's whole digital switching strategy. Three people were appointed to develop a marketing strategy for central office switches. A presentation was to be made to the Tricorporate Policy Coordinating Committee (which includes top executives from BNR, Northern Telecom and Bell Canada). The task force was composed of Dr Donald Chisholm from BNR, Mr Lloyd Webster from product line management at Northern Telecom, and Mr Bill Anderson from Engineering at Bell Canada.

The Situation in March 1975   While the telephone industry was still strongly feeling the effects of the 1974—75 recession, economists were beginning to forecast robust growth in the Canadian and US economies in 1976 and 1977. Most Northern Telecom executives, in early 1975, believed that the degree of competition in the central office switching market would increase markedly during this same period of time. GTE's #2 EAX, and other similar second-generation stored-program-control analog switches, as well as late market entrants such as ITT's Metaconta-L, were expected to have a negative impact on new initial orders for the SP-1. Executives also believed that one or more of several competitors might introduce digital switches in North America in the 1978–82 time frame. Stromberg-Carlson, IBM, North Electric, Philips, ITT, Ericsson, and Nippon Electric Company were all believed to be doing some development work on digital switches and might be able to introduce such a product in the North American market by 1980. Something had to be done to maintain and improve Northern Telecom's position in the central office switching market. Two major alternatives were open to Northern Telecom.

Alternative 1: Delay Introduction of the Digital Switching Line

Make no firm commitment to a major research and development effort on a digital switching line yet, and merely continue with exploratory research on digital switching. Given the increasing competitive pressure on SP-1, the SP-1 could be upgraded or enhanced to make it more competitive with the second-generation stored-program-control analog switches that were becoming increasingly available. Development costs for an enhanced version of the SP-1 (perhaps called the SP-2) might vary from $5 million to $20 million, or even more, depending on the particular enhancements incorporated. The risks associated with this alternative would depend on the particular enhancements selected, but were in all cases significantly less than those associated with a digital product line, since no major new advances in technology or manufacturing capability were required to bring it to market.

Alternative 2: Move Rapidly to Introduce the Digital Switching Line

Commit immediately to a heavy research and development programme to introduce some or all of the digital switching products as rapidly as possible. As of March 1975, exploratory or development work was either being considered or was under way on five separate digital products:

1. D256 — a digital switcher-concentrator which would be used in a small community to switch calls in that community and to concentrate the outgoing/incoming calls for digital transmission to/from the central office serving the community. The product was designed to serve from 24 to 256 lines. The earliest this product could be available was 1976.
2. SL-1 — development work was well advanced on Northern Telecom's SL-1 PABX, which was to be available to customers in late 1975. It was considered possible to develop a small central office switch from this product by 1979.
3. DMS (no number assigned) — another digital switch designed to serve small local offices with 1,500+ lines. It could be available in 1979.
4. DMS (no number assigned) — a large digital toll switch handling up to 50,000 trunks. It could be available in 1980.
5. DMS (no number assigned) — a large digital local switch with the capacity to handle up to 100,000 lines. It could be available in 1981.

The work to date on the last three of these products had only been very exploratory and no firm commitment to develop them in any time frame had been made.

Executives expected this digital line to provide major benefits to telephone companies in terms of low space requirements, substantial reductions in outside plant, particularly cable (given that many digital signals could be handled on one transmission line), and lower maintenance and operating costs. The proposed digital line could accommodate growth from a very small number of lines to very large line sizes, would allow telephone companies to service small communities cost-effectively through the satellite switchers-concentrators and, in general, would provide the customer with a very flexible system.

While most observers of the telephone industry expected that the industry would eventually move to all-digital systems, the conventional wisdom was that such a change would not really begin to occur until the early to mid-1980s. Bell Laboratories and AT&T executives, who met frequently with the executives of independent telephone companies to set equipment standards, etc., regularly voiced this view. AT&T was heavily committed to stored-program-control analog switches (and was installing almost one #1 ESS office every working day). Since digital transmission of signals between exchanges was increasingly prevalent in North America, Bell Labs and Western Electric people claimed that the logical point of entry for digital switches was in large toll switches, since the digital machines could be directly tied into the digital transmission network without the need for any analog to digital interfacing. This was where Western Electric's #4 ESS and Automatic Electric's #3 EAX switches would fit.

Within Northern Telecom's digital alternative there were options. Work on parts of the line could be accelerated by increasing expenditures on R&D, or cash could be conserved in the period 1975—78 by initially focusing development on the small local offices (products 1 to 3). Two of the possible plans under consideration were:

Plan A Focus major development efforts on the small local office switch only. With this option, R&D expenditures on the digital line would be $32 million. The small local office would be available in 1979.

Plan B Develop the architectural concepts for the total line initially with a phased introduction of the digital line (small local office in 1979, large toll office in 1980, and a large local office in 1981). Under this plan, R&D expenditures were expected to total $66 million.

Some managers were also concerned that a major acceleration of the digital line could have a negative impact on its future competitiveness. In one internal memorandum to members of the task force, it was pointed out that "the timing of the digital switch affects the technology/manufacturing plateau on which the design will be based — too soon may result in noncompetitive costs after initial introduction. Too advanced a technology base may result in a high risk design, delays, and subsequent field problems." In the same memorandum, the Vice-President of Marketing pointed out that the full potential of a digital switch would only be realised in a digital transmission environment. The greater the amount of digital transmission equipment in place, the less interfacing needed between analog and digital switches, and the more economical the digital switch would be. However, the Vice-President of Marketing stated that he felt that even in early 1975 the mix of digital/analog transmission circuits was such as to make the cost savings significant for most telephone companies.

If the decision were made to proceed rapidly with the digital switching line, top management realised that an integral part of its decision would be when and how to time announcements of the various products. Sales of the SP-1 were growing rapidly, and management wanted to sell as many initial offices as possible in order to generate the largest volume of subsequent extension business. This extension business was captive business and was typically more profitable than the initial orders, since competitive pressures were less and costs were lower. Furthermore, announcement of a digital switch competitive with the SP-1 would probably have a negative impact on the sales of this product and its product life-cycle.

Preparing for the Presentation

As the members of this task force began putting together their presentation for the Tricorporate Policy Coordinating Committee meeting on 6 March 1975, they realised that this was perhaps the most critical decision Northern Telecom would make in the 1970s. The R&D costs involved in developing the digital switching line were very large compared to other projects Northern Telecom had been involved in in the past. The technological problems associated with the digital switches were huge — one executive, who was familiar with the technical problems involved, suggested that the development of the digital toll switch alone was about eight times as complex as the problems of developing the SP-1. But the market potential for central office switches was huge. One study done by Northern Telecom market researchers suggested that the market available to Northern Telecom in North America alone would be about $1.5 billion between 1980 and 1984 (see Exhibit 8). This excluded any extension sales and possible sales to the telephone operating companies of AT&T, GTE (including B.C. Telephone in Canada), and United Telecommunications. In one confidential internal memorandum that the task force had just received from a member of its staff, the manager stated:

> Can Northern afford the program? Central office switching is the real strength of the industry. It is the most difficult to get into because of the high investment needed and the depth of experience to reduce (customer risk). It also represents essentially a captive long-term business once the initial offices are sold. *Northern Telecom cannot really afford not to be in digital switching* — it is a matter of minimizing investment and selecting the right time. If it comes to a choice of priorities, there are many other product investments that should be cancelled before Northern's position in the central office switching business is jeopardized.

The week before the 6 March meeting, Mr Lloyd Webster, the Northern Telecom representative on the task force, was to meet with the top management group of Northern Telecom to hammer out its position with respect to digital switching for the Policy Coordinating Committee meeting. As he reviewed all the inputs provided by a large number of Northern Telecom managers, he wondered what position he should take in the meeting with Northern Telecom top management. As he thought about the decision, he kept coming back to the risks involved for Northern Telecom: "Are we sure we can build a digital line? Are we right that this is the time to go digital, when Bell Laboratories and others think it is premature? Are we willing to bet $70 million of Northern Telecom's money that this is the right time to go digital? What is the probability, if we do choose a digital option, that all we shall do is kill a successful profitable product line?"

Exhibit 8   *Estimated Size of Available North American Market ($m.)*

	Canada[a]		USA[b]			Number of Equivalent
Year	Local	Toll	Local	Toll	Total	Lines (000s)[c]
1980	73	17	86	4	180	630
1981	82	18	196	5	300	1,100
1982	93	19	205	5	322	1,240
1983	105	20	210	5	340	1,290
1984	112	21	220	5	358	1,365
Total	465	95	917	23	1,500	5,625

[a] Canadian available market excludes B.C. Telephone requirement, SP-1 extension sales, and all crossbar and step-by-step extension sales.

[b] US available market excludes AT&T, GTE, and United Telecommunications markets, and the SP-1 extension market. The toll market includes only the one US independent telephone company that had previously bought a medium-sized toll switch from Northern Telecom. This was believed to be a conservative estimate of the available toll market in the US.

[c] Equivalent lines were calculated by adding the number of local lines to five times the number of toll trunks.

Source: Company Records.

Organising and Implementing the Marketing Effort

This case was prepared by Professor Kenneth Simmonds and Dr Jules Goddard of the London Business School. © Kenneth Simmonds, 1986.

CASE 26

Nystrom Office Systems

Early in 1985 Dr Brian Beckett was appointed general manager of Nystrom Office Systems, a fully-owned United Kingdom distribution subsidiary of Nystrom Electronics. Dr Beckett's appointment had been made by Mr Klaus Hartmann who, as Vice-President International of Nystrom, was responsible to the board of directors for all foreign subsidiaries. The previous general manager had retired early for health reasons and Hartmann had persuaded Beckett to transfer to the office systems division from the scientific instruments division where he had held the position of assistant to the managing director.

Hartmann pointed out to Beckett that the past results of NOS were poor and that the board did not want to see the company continuing with lines which were below the company minimum target return on assets of 10% after tax.

NOS was organised into four product lines, as shown in Exhibit 1. Low-end systems covered electronic typewriters, dictation equipment, small

Exhibit 1 *NOS Organisation Chart*

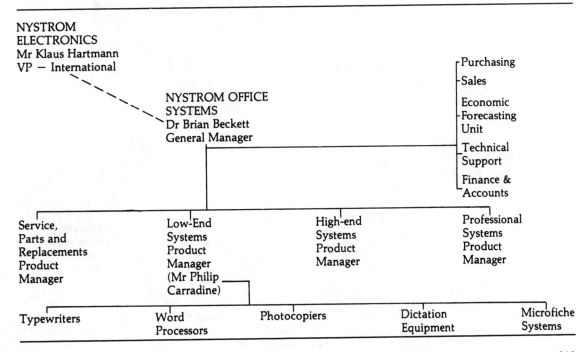

photocopy machines, microfiche systems, and stand-alone word processors. High-end systems covered a wide range of computers, from personal computers to minis and financial terminal systems. The professional line was sold to universities and research laboratories and included applications-dedicated systems which were larger and more expensive than those sold to commercial users. However, it was the smallest line, with only 12% of Nystrom's sales revenue. Finally, the service department was also considered a product line. It handled service, parts and replacements for the other three lines.

The sales staff were responsible directly to the sales manager, not to the four product line managers, and worked through distributors, dealers and software houses or, in the case of professional systems and some of the high-end products, direct with the end user. Each salesman had a specific territory to cover.

Beckett began his appointment by asking the product line managers to prepare a full-scale report on their product lines and their plans for the future. Three weeks later Mr Philip Carradine, the manager of the low-end line, presented the report set out in Exhibit 2. The low-end line had been showing the lowest return of the four lines.

Mr Carradine had by now received the Nystrom planning guide announcing the 10% minimum return on assets target for each line of activity. In commenting on his report he said that Dr Beckett should be careful in interpreting the figures because they tended to make his line look worse than it really was. This is the argument that Carradine put forward:

> Most of the expenses in my profit and loss are allocated rather than direct costs. Except for sales and technical support, the accounting practice has been simply to allocate all the expenses for the company — advertising, promotion, rent, heat, light, warehousing, provisions for bad debts and inventory losses, allocated corporate overhead, and so on — on the basis of the product line sales budgets. The way the accounts are set up, it is impossible to find out what the low-end line is actually spending. It also seems to me that allocating the costs among product lines on the basis of sales budgets is wrong. If a manager has budgeted low and has a good year, this method makes him look doubly good because he is charged with less than his proper share of expenses. Likewise, if he has been too optimistic with his sales projections, he looks doubly bad because he's carrying more than his load of costs.
>
> Another problem concerns debtors. The accounting practice has been to report debtors for the firm as a whole, by customer and by type of account — such as special terms account, regular open account, instalment contract account, and so on. For purposes of calculating the return on assets of the various product lines, the accountants first compute the ratio that total debtors bear to total sales. They then apply this ratio to the sales of each product line and come up with an allocated debtors figure for each. The same sort of formula has been used to allocate cash and fixed assets to the product lines, although these items aren't quite as large as debtors and therefore not as important. I would say that the actual overall debtors figure for the low end does not exceed 120 days' sales and is probably closer to 90 days' sales. Yet my allocated debtors are reflecting the experience of the other product lines. Also, some of the products within the line are doing much better than others on asset return. Some may be doing 10% or more. But because I can't get exact or detailed debtors figures, the whole product line is made to look bad.

Beckett decided that he should discuss these issues with other executives before he decided what to do about Carradine's report. He discovered that a number of these executives had strong reservations about the validity or

Exhibit 2 *NOS Internal Memorandum*

TO: Beckett
FROM: Carradine
SUBJECT: Low-End Line Plan

Analysis of the sales volumes, gross margins and operating figures shown in Table 1 (overleaf) points up the following facts:

1. The decrease in sales has been most noticeable since the peak year 1983. In 1983 gross margins were cut and longer credit terms were extended to distributors and dealers. In addition, many of them bought more goods during this period than they were able to move and consequently went into 1984 with large overstocks.

   Other factors hindering sales in 1984 were higher prices and shortened credit terms. These moves were taken with a view to restoring gross margins, reducing receivables, and thereby increasing profits.

   Despite the lower sales, figures show that this move was successful.

2. Sales of dictation equipment reached a peak in 1983, but the market is becoming saturated.

3. Our range of word processors has lost volume, mainly because of increased competition from US producers and personal computer inroads.

4. Sales of photocopiers were hurt critically because poor products were shipped in 1983–1984. With this problem now out of the way, there should be no difficulty in making up lost ground.

5. Typewriter volume has increased since 1982 and has remained fairly constant. There has been some hesitancy to purchase because of the novelty value of word processors. However, orders are coming in now and we may even exceed last year's figures.

6. Microfiche products are being withdrawn from the market, since a recent Nystrom policy statement has argued that they have no part in a business selling "office systems".

7. Total gross margins are improving and will continue upward. Low grosses were taken in 1983. Since then they have improved measurably, despite sizeable markdowns and write-offs due to defective photocopiers.

8. Expenses have been cut appreciably: where there were seventeen people engaged in the marketing function a year ago, we now have only seven. Mechanisation of order handling has also helped cut expenses.

9. Net profit — we broke even in 1984 and will be well in the black in 1985 despite lower volume. With the expenses further pared down, lower inventories, and the write-offs on photocopiers behind us, we can expect a greatly improved net profit in 1986.

10. Total assets peaked in 1983 due to large debtors and high levels of inventory. Here again good progress has been made and the assets will be brought down to a point more consistent with volume and profit potential.

11. Next year we're determined to get our sundry debtors into line. By shortening our terms we should be able to reduce debtors by 40%. But there still remains a problem so far as overdue debts are concerned. An estimated £2 million will be difficult to collect.

12. Return on assets will show great improvement this year and the 3.0% return is conservative, as we see a good possibility of 7.3% for 1986. With continued progress on inventories, gross margins, expenses and receivables, we should, within the next few years, realise 10% return on assets.

Table 1 *Low-End Systems: Sales, Gross Margins and Operating Figures (£m.)*

		1982	1983	1984	Budget 1985	Budget 1986
Stand-alone	Sales	11.6	14.8	7.9	5.8	5.4
Word Processors	GM(%)	(14.3)	(14.8)	(14.6)	(14.0)	(13.6)
Dictation	Sales	4.3	10.5	6.1	5.8	6.0
Equipment	GM(%)	(15.9)	(14.3)	(18.2)	(18.4)	(18.8)
Electronic	Sales	2.9	5.8	4.8	4.6	4.7
Typewriters	GM(%)	(15.1)	(14.3)	(17.6)	(23.8)	(26.8)
Desk-top	Sales	2.4	3.1	1.9	2.0	2.5
Photocopiers	GM(%)	(16.2)	(16.4)	(16.2)	(16.8)	(19.8)
Microfiche	Sales	2.2	2.6	1.8	0.3	0.2
Systems	GM(%)	(15.3)	(13.8)	(15.0)	(20.0)	(24.8)
Total Sales		23.4	36.8	22.5	18.5	18.8
Total Gross Margins		3.51	5.39	3.68	3.37	3.67
(% to Sales)		(15.0)	(14.6)	(16.4)	(18.2)	(19.5)
Expenses		3.28	4.74	3.68	2.53	2.18
(% to Sales)		(14.0)	(12.9)	(16.4)	(14.0)	(11.8)
Net Profit						
(after 50% Tax)		0.12	0.33	0	0.39	0.72
Average Inventories		4.5	9.1	6.8	3.1	2.2
Sundry Debtors		8.8	15.2	13.1	9.3	7.1
Total Assets		13.8	24.6	20.5	12.9	9.8
Current Liabilities		6.5	9.3	5.8	4.6	4.2
Return on Assets (%)		0.8	1.3	0	3.0	7.3

usefulness of the product line reports, particularly about return on assets as a measure of a product line's performance. One product line manager said:

> We're merchandisers, not accountants. You can't tell just from looking at figures what makes a good product mix, and you certainly cannot expect every product to yield the same profit. What about loss leaders? They're as old as the history of merchandise. I'm not saying we should carry a line that shows a steady loss, but neither do I think we should consider dropping it just because its profit doesn't come up to some arbitrarily established level. The low-end line helps us to sell other lines, we should regard our most popular office products as the calling cards of our business. They're a way of getting the Nystrom name known and respected so that later, when we try to sell specialist lines and bigger systems, people will know who we are.

When asked what value he thought carried over from his line to the others, Carradine observed that, while it was difficult for him to assess the role that the low end played in cultivating markets for other Nystrom lines, he had found that a given product frequently helped generate interest in and preference for other products in his own line. He pointed to the relation between typewriters and word processors as a case in point. In areas where Nystrom typewriters enjoyed popularity, they had paved the way for the introduction of Nystrom word processors. He added that possessing a full line of office products was important in establishing and maintaining Nystrom's position with distributors and dealers.

Another of the product line managers, who had been with NOS for many years, told Beckett that within the firm the level of gross margins had traditionally been the measure of the value of a product line and that, in his opinion, gross margins were still the soundest index. He thought this was particularly true since gross margins were based entirely on actual figures, completely avoiding the question of allocated costs of assets. He pointed out that the average gross margin on low-end systems had risen from 14% in 1983 to 16.4% in 1984 and that it would probably exceed 18% in 1985.

Yet another product line manager expressed the view that, while return on assets might be a valid measure of a product line's performance in some business organisations, it was not a valid measure at NOS because product line managers did not have complete control of either the assets for which they were responsible or of certain cost elements which affected profits. He pointed out, for example, that the purchasing function was not under the direction of the product line manager:

> I have no complaint against our purchasing people and I know that they make purchases only on orders from the product line managers. But anyone knows that a purchasing agent who's got his heart in it can save a lot of money and help keep inventory levels down. The problem is that the purchasing people aren't on the product manager's team; they aren't under the manager's control; I don't see how he can be held responsible for asset management.

> More important, though, is the fact that the sales operation isn't under the product line manager's control. While sales aren't as removed from the product managers as purchasing, still the sales people don't share the product manager's profit-and-loss responsibility, with the result that they may not try as hard on a sale, or press for terms, as they might if they were on the marketing team. This matter of credit terms also affects the manager's performance in asset management. We all know that the product manager has the right of final approval on variations from established credit terms, but he has to rely largely on the sales organisation's appraisal of what terms it's going to take to close a deal. If a salesman is a little too liberal in his estimate, the product managers get tied down to higher debtors which, of course, reduces return on assets. I think if the salesmen were on the product manager's team and shared his profit responsibility, they'd be more hard-headed about credit terms. Finally, the fact that sales aren't under the product manager's control means he may not have the sales force he would like to have representing his line, or that the sales force isn't administered in the way he thinks best.

> These are all factors that affect a product line's return on assets, and they're outside the manager's control. So I don't see how you can consider return on assets an accurate measure of a product line's performance.

NOS's controller expressed the view that return on assets, though a useful financial yardstick in determining the effectiveness of a given product line, was not the only measure to be considered.

> I think that before you drop a line you have to take into account how much it contributes to the total sales volume and how much overhead it may be carrying, especially if you don't have any other product to replace it. Low-end products provide the second largest sales volume among NOS's product lines and accounted for 35% of 1984 sales. At this level, the low end absorbs significant amounts of NOS's own overheads, of head office expenses, and of the manufacturing division's factory overhead and product engineering expenses. If one were to estimate these figures, which is perfectly possible, it would be seen that the low-end line is making an important corporate-wide contribution

to fixed expenses. If the line were dropped, these expenses would continue and would simply have to be reallocated, thus jeopardising the profitability of other lines.

Since this argument called for estimates of overhead that would not be eliminated if the product line were dropped, Beckett asked the controller to obtain for him the appropriate figures for 1984 to 1986. These estimates are shown in Exhibit 3.

Exhibit 3 *Controller's Estimate of Overhead That Would Not Be Eliminated by Dropping the Low-end Line (£m.)* *

	1984	1985	1986
Included in Cost of Sales: Manufacturing Divisions' Fixed Overheads Including Depreciation and Amortisation of Product Engineering Expenses	4.9	3.9	3.9
Included in Product Line Expenses: Nystrom Electronics' Allocated Corporate Expense	0.20	0.16	0.16
NOS's Fixed Administrative Expenses	0.62	0.46	0.38
	0.82	0.62	0.54

* Based on actual 1984 volume and budgeted 1985 and 1986 volumes.

This case was prepared by Professor Kenneth Simmonds of the London Business School. © Kenneth Simmonds, 1986.

CASE 27

Hits Marketing

In mid-1984, the United Kingdom record industry was reeling from declining unit sales (see Exhibit 1). Behind the decline lay the increased incidence of home taping which was estimated to have cost the industry £260 million in 1983 — not far off the value of total record sales. Increased use of video cassette recorders was also having some effect.

In an effort to hold their sales, record companies had responded by increasing their marketing budgets, aiming at the youth audience and at increasing the Gallup chart position of their new singles. Industry advertising had risen from 1% of sales in 1971 to 16% in 1983. Spending on trade promotion to radio, television, press and retailers had gone up steeply. Promotional videos had become more sophisticated and expensive. So had packaging. Four-colour picture sleeves, pull-outs, badges and double packs were all now commonplace. One record company even issued a single for the Thompson Twins in three different jig-saw shapes that fitted together to form a picture of the group.

The philosophy had emerged of investing in losses on singles in order to make profits on albums. As the chart manager for Gallup said, 'The album charts *show* what's happening, but the singles' charts actually *affect* what's happening. They dictate what's on radio and TV and what the record shops order.'

Executives in the record business were beginning to question how far this strategy should go. Everyone had heard the story of the single sold shrink-wrapped with a free promotional video. It went right into the charts — but the artist did not make it to album status. In any case, should each record company attempt to push every single up the charts? How far up was success?

Aware of the growing concern in the industry, Jules Goddard, who was a consultant with The Planners Collaborative, a London-based consulting group specialising in strategic market planning, had gained an opportunity to make a presentation for business to the top management of one of the leading record companies. He immediately set to work collecting data about how records were currently marketed. He first telephoned for appointments with managers in marketing functions within a wide selection of record companies. He told them he was researching the marketing of records and had little difficulty in getting anyone to talk about the problems.

An advanced specialisation in individual marketing functions had evolved within the industry. There was separate specialisation in artist relations, product management, promotion, selling, distribution, advertising, public relations and market research. Goddard interviewed several managers in each function. Firms in the industry appeared to be managed along fairly similar lines. In fact, managers' allegiance to the industry and their function within it tended to surmount allegiance to their firm.

STRATEGY AND MARKETING

Numerous managers had worked with other record companies but almost none had recent experience outside the industry ... all seemed to have joined the industry initially because of an interest in music. Jules encountered no-one with formal training in marketing.

Exhibit 1   *The United Kingdom Music Market*

		1979	1980	1981	1982	1983	1984*
Population		55.820	55.770	55.720	55.680	55.640	55.600
Households		19.985	20.125	20.265	20.405	20.545	20.685
Consumer Expenditure	Current Prices	117.070	135.740	151.040	165.600	176.500	188.300
Inflation Factor (%)	Consumer Prices	13.4	18.0	11.9	8.6	4.6	5.1
Ownership	Record Playing Equipment	17.126	17.388	17.809	18.015	18.026	17.991
	Tape (Cass/8TR) Equipment	24.885	28.331	31.452	34.432	39.528	44.662
	Compact Disc Equipment	0.000	0.000	0.000	0.000	0.013	0.044
Penetration	Record Playing Equipment	85.7	86.4	87.9	88.3	87.7	87.0
	Tape (Cass/8TR) Equipment	124.5	140.8	155.2	168.7	192.4	215.9
	Compact Disc Equipment	0.0	0.0	0.0	0.0	0.1	0.2
TOTAL MUSIC MARKET							
Quantities (× 1000)	SP Rec. inc. 12"	89.085	77.800	77.330	78.640	74.000	71.500
	LP Records	74.536	67.400	64.000	57.840	54.250	51.000
	Tapes	23.530	25.235	28.720	31.480	35.780	35.800
	Compact Discs	0.000	0.000	0.000	0.000	0.320	0.970
Actual Retail Price	SP Records	0.90	1.01	1.12	1.27	1.40	1.43
	LP Records	3.36	3.53	3.75	4.07	4.30	4.32
	Tapes	3.33	3.33	3.57	3.81	3.97	4.22
	Compact Discs	0.00	0.00	0.00	0.00	9.53	9.33
Actual Retail Value	SP Rec. inc. 12"	80.400	78.200	86.300	99.500	103.890	102.250
	LP Records	250.400	237.600	239.900	235.200	233.110	220.100
	Tapes	78.300	84.100	102.500	120.000	141.950	151.000
	Compact Discs	0.000	0.000	0.000	0.000	3.050	9.050
	TOTAL MUSIC	409.100	399.900	428.700	454.700	482.000	482.400
Classical Records/CDs		19.450	18.300	17.900	16.100	16.300	18.600
Classical Tapes		6.250	6.500	7.200	8.640	8.800	9.100
Growth % Total Market	LP-Units	−7.9	−6.4	−0.1	−3.0	0.4	−2.9
	Retail Value	7.8	−2.2	7.2	6.1	6.0	0.1
Music as % of Consumer Expenditure		0.349	0.295	0.284	0.275	0.273	0.256
LP-Units/Equipment	Records	5.22	4.62	4.32	3.94	3.69	3.50
	Tapes	0.97	0.91	0.93	0.93	0.92	0.82
	Compact Discs	0.00	0.00	0.00	0.00	24.62	22.05
% of Total Market	Records	81.0	79.0	76.0	74.0	71.0	69.0
	Tapes	19.0	21.0	24.0	26.0	29.0	31.0
	National Pop	46.0	56.8	59.9	63.6	64.8	65.3
	Internat. Pop	47.7	36.0	33.2	31.0	30.0	29.0
	Classical	6.3	6.2	5.9	5.4	5.2	5.7

* Projected

Artists and Repertoire The development of acts was the first step in the marketing process. This function was usually the responsibility of the Artists & Repertoire staff. One A & R manager described A & R men as "Talent spotters. But 90% of their work is after the act has been signed. The A & R man is responsible for the act and what records it makes. He is in charge of all aspects of song writing, recording and producing the actual music. He has final judgement over the record. He forms a bridge between the rest of the company and the act itself. Fundamentally, the industry is A & R led. A company is only as good as the records its artists make. But the relationship A & R has with the rest of the company is one of conflict — often breaking out in the form of a confrontation between A & R and Marketing, A & R and Promotion, and so on." Each A & R man watched over some 10 to 12 acts, usually of widely different age and market positioning, and generally stayed with them over their performing lifetime.

A particularly difficult part of their job as seen by A & R managers was moving an act's record buyers from its primary, "cult" market into secondary and tertiary markets: "The problem is that as the act moves into the secondary and tertiary market, it drops out of the primary market — and it is usually this market that has given the group its chart success; thus one gets into a double-bind situation."

Product Management The responsibility for marketing an act's music usually rested with a product manager. Each product manager might look after some 10 to 12 acts which could vary considerably in music and style. Product managers emphasised their more business-oriented approach:

> What is important here is that success should be judged in the longer term on the basis of business performance — efficiency and profit. Success should not depend upon chart hits — one miss and you are out! Long-term profitability is what should count.
>
> It is pretty important that an act is sold to the people who have to work on it. If the people who work on it are not sold on it, then it is difficult for them to market it. The first thing then is to get some feel and understanding of the act and to catch up on the reason why the A & R man signed it up. We must understand basically what it is we have captured so that what we then put into it in terms of packaging and presentation is congruent with it, as well as the act being comfortable with what we add and capable of filling the expectation. The relationship with A & R is particularly important at this stage because everything flows from that. Unless I have an understanding of the artist's particular quality, I find it very difficult to sell. Once we are clear on the positioning, a recording plan is then set up and some sort of discussion follows about how we proceed: release pattern, live work, etc. When this is done, we involve PR and start talking about packaging.
>
> We try to prepare the market to minimise the risk by getting the record out to the retailers. The overriding factor, however, is merchandising to the media. Nothing is more important than media exposure — radio and TV. The music press is important, but it is difficult to disassociate the media opinion from prior market impact. If an act has potential for the 14—24 age group, the only real way to prove it is to get on TV once.
>
> Albums are more expensive and tend to be a more considered purchase; therefore, for very many acts, pre-exposure via a single is very important. Album selling, in the main, is led by single selling. It is also very difficult to get media exposure for an album because of the format of radio in this country.

There is very little album air play. It is possible that the 14—24 age group might never know that an album exists. One would then have to rely on the attraction of a couple of singles on the album.

With most significant acts we also advertise. The effect of the advertising with a known act is to make a known market aware that a new product is released. In the case of a group with a very small following, it would be mainly to demonstrate commitment to the media, as much as to anyone else.

We advertise on the Channel 4 programme "The Tube", which gets a high level of 17—24-year-old viewers, because I want to get at this segment and because I believe aiming at the mass market is wasteful. But we need to know why they watch that. We simply make an assumption that the 17—24 age bracket is a big market, in gross terms, and this ducks the issue.

The close relationship between A & R and product manager continues over time. The A & R role is a continuous one of carrying a torch for that act and as the act evolves, we must adjust. We use feedback about acts from the music press and radio. But there are no aesthetics in pop — no rules.

We do carry out some research. I have had one piece of qualitative research done on an act and it told me quite a bit about the act's market. But generally we do very little. Probably because first guesses are usually fairly accurate. In terms of selling a record, you are very much in a particular area of the market. In terms of consumer research, I would really like to know why they think a record they buy is better than other records. But market research is tough, the universe is so huge. It would be better to resarch in more general terms to find out how music fits into leisure purchases.

Jules Goddard gained the impression that although product managers talked about profitability, it was chart success that mainly concerned them. They worked hard for initial chart positions and again for album chart position. With a single product manager handling 10 to 12 groups, however, this could mean as much as 30 releases a year for which one manager was responsible. The sheer complexity of accounting for a mixture of new and old releases at any point in time made it very difficult. How would unsold inventory be valued? How much advertising should be written off?

Promotion   The manager in charge of promotion in one record company described his job as follows: "I have to try and get product exposed on radio and TV. In addition to getting artists heard on radio and seen on TV, there are other greyer areas. The difference between someone good and someone bad in promotions is the amount of imagination and flair that is applied to fill in those greyer areas. What we do with radio is get advance play. The trick is to get play before the record hits the shops. This way the dealer hears it and the punter hears it and perhaps drifts into the shop and enquires about it. As the sales guys come in, there is already interest — a kind of warming-the-ground. After that, the task is to sustain radio plays as long as possible. In London, we do that by taking records around by hand. Radio 1 is the biggest, most formidable and most influential station in the country. It has got to be done on a personal basis. Promotion is to the producers, not the jockeys. The producers usually have most influence on what records are played. Apart from Radio 1, the local commercial radios have been a disappointment. Radio play is really dominated by the charts. Whenever the music business hits a lull, like now, radio gravitates back towards a chart orientation."

Sales

Sales management described its function as having three major tasks. The first was to sell into the trade pre-release. Sales staff endeavoured to load up retail outlets with singles and albums prior to release to ensure sufficient stocks when the record was launched. Singles chart success depended on high initial sales. To achieve high retail stocks, the sales force would often discount heavily to the trade. This encouraged stocking, which created pressure on the retailer to promote the record to the customer in his shop.

Woolworths, W.H. Smith and record retail chains were usually dealt with at a key discount level. Sometimes, though, head offices of these organisations only produced purchase lists and left the final decision to branches. The product still had to be 'sold-in' at branch level. Selling-in was usually a fairly straightforward task when the artist was established and the album contained a number of already successful singles. However, the task was more difficult if the artist was unknown or the album contained no previous singles' hits.

The second sales task was to support products after release. Sometimes this was met by a separate sales staff who supplied retailers from stock they carried in the boots of their cars. They would carry out stock checks on the retailers' premises and attempt to push records whenever an opportunity arose. They also carried point-of-sale promotion material. Such sales staff offered little or no discounts after launch, except for key account agreements. This policy, however, had encouraged retailers to de-stock existing products in favour of discounted pre-release material. Retailer effort was directed towards the launch period and less to the decline period, thus accentuating any decline.

Lastly, sales staff were responsible for meeting orders received by telephone from retail outlets. Staff operating from a central sales desk were expected to encourage sales through their telephone contact.

Market Research

Most record companies maintained some central data gathering capability. Staff were usually responsible for collection of statistical market data and for central market research services. There was a strong emphasis on analysing comparative sales and chart data against both total market performance and individual competitors. One market research executive interviewed had created a 'Fact Book' updated monthly, containing some 80 statistical tables of volumes and prices of UK sales of singles, LPs and tapes plus a computerised data base of Gallup chart data. Market research executives did not feel that regular high-quality information could be obtained from surveys of individual customers. The sample would need to be so large and the survey so complex and slow that it would be uneconomic.

Life-Cycle Marketing

In the course of his interviews, Jules Goddard encountered many suggestions that the ideal way to market records was to follow an act's original fans — a life-cycle marketing approach. This approach is described well in the following extract from a paper in *Music and Video Week* (19 March 1983), under the title of 'Facts and Fashion':

> In music what is fashionable today becomes the catalogue of tomorrow, and the mid- and budget-price item of the day after. A company which consistently gets this fashion market right is securing its future catalogue.

Taking the fashion market as that product bought by 15—24-year-olds gives us a good starting point. This group buys a much greater proportion of pre-recorded music than one would expect from its representation in the population. However, this group is not homogeneous. People at the younger end are very different to those at the older end, and this appreciation is key to my rationale.

If this market is split in two — the teenagers (15—19) and the young twenties (20—24) — and we develop two archetypes describing their music-related behaviour, then we have an interesting tool with which to analyse changes within the fashion market.

Teenagers have a tremendous amount of leisure time (they are in full-time education, at the early stages of their working lives, or — in increasing numbers today — unemployed) and they favour music-related activities such as clubs, discos, concerts and visiting friends to play records.

Whatever their source of income, a high proportion of it is kept for discretionary spending. Total income may be low, but they are probably still living at home paying a nominal amount on bed and board, and spending the rest as they wish. Much is spent on records, tapes, disco/concert tickets and hi-fi.

Central to my approach is the understanding that teenagers have no loyalty to established acts. These acts did not pay their dues to the teenager; they do not play venues that are easily accessible and/or cheap. To the young kid in Sheffield the rock star living in LA or Montserrat, producing an LP every two years, and doing a six-nighter at Earls Court just about as often is hardly someone with whom he can empathise. He and his like-minded friends will find and follow their own new musical heroes.

What is more, teenagers form the rump of the consumer music press readership. *Sounds, Record Mirror, Smash Hits, The Face,* NME and MM all major on new acts, and keep the teenager informed (if a little confused). So, the teenage archetype has the time, the money, the inclination and the information to pick up on new acts.

Compare and contrast this group with the young twenties archetype.

Leisure time is much less a feature of their lives. Most are out of full-time education and developing their careers. Music suffers more competition for what leisure time remains after the development of new responsibilities, hobbies and activities is taken care of.

Many young twenties have moved away from home, perhaps married, and the consequent pressure on their income means that they have less — proportionately if not absolutely — discretionary income than teenagers. Time is committed to career, home and family activities. Music related activities as part of leisure are downgraded in importance. Established acts — the acts they grew up with — find favour with this group. This hardening of the taste arteries is encouraged by information they receive on music — as they move away from the pop press and towards reliance on radio, TV and music columns in the national press (all of which focus on the "star system" for good copy).

One implication that several record executives drew from this type of argument was that marketing responsibility should be regrouped around customer age groups — perhaps with managers of the same age as the customers themselves. In this way, they would not have to handle acts that were at different stages in their life-cycles.

This proposal, however, seemed to ignore the need for a real success to build fame through the entire market. And it also overlooked the potential outside the United Kingdom. An act developed successfully in the United Kingdom could bring the record company royalties and fees from worldwide publishing. It was the general custom, however, to measure United Kingdom A & R managers and product managers on the basis of UK sales. The feeling

Exhibit 2 *Nationwide Music Ownership Survey*

Percentage of Segment Who Own a Recording of:

	Base No. In Sample	Rod Stewart				Duran Duran				Dire Straits				Siouxsie & the Banshees				Jean Michel Jarre			
		Any At All	Single	LP	Tape	Any At All	Single	LP	Tape	Any At All	Single	LP	Tape	Any At All	Single	LP	Tape	Any At All	Single	LP	Tape
Total	599	50	27	29	16	38	24	17	14	32	12	15	15	25	18	10	6	22	5	12	8
Male	292	47	23	27	15	40	27	18	13	37	15	19	16	31	20	14	7	29	5	18	11
Female	307	52	31	30	17	36	22	15	14	27	9	10	13	20	16	6	4	14	4	6	6
Age:																					
Total 15–17	123	35	20	15	8	49	34	27	20	20	7	8	11	37	29	11	11	15	3	7	7
18–19	116	42	31	16	12	44	31	17	15	33	12	13	14	23	18	11	5	22	5	11	9
20–21	116	50	28	33	22	33	28	13	7	37	17	18	19	35	28	13	6	24	5	17	7
22–24	122	57	35	34	17	35	20	14	11	39	13	18	16	18	8	9	3	25	6	12	7
25–29	122	63	23	45	21	30	7	12	15	31	4	16	15	12	8	5	3	24	2	14	12
Male 15–19	119	32	20	14	7	47	34	24	15	29	14	13	13	38	28	14	11	26	5	14	11
20–24	116	51	28	31	21	37	30	15	10	47	20	26	20	32	21	16	5	34	6	22	11
25–29	57	68	23	47	19	30	4	14	16	37	7	18	16	16	7	7	4	28	2	21	11
Female 15–19	120	45	32	16	12	46	31	20	19	23	13	8	11	23	19	8	5	10	3	3	5
20–24	122	57	35	36	19	31	18	12	8	30	10	11	8	21	15	6	4	16	5	8	2
25–29	65	58	24	43	23	29	9	11	14	26	2	15	14	9	9	3	2	20	3	8	14
Class ABC1	272	46	19	31	19	34	21	17	13	39	13	18	19	24	16	12	6	24	4	14	10
C2DE	327	52	33	27	13	41	26	17	14	26	11	12	12	26	21	8	5	20	5	11	7
Purchased Any Singles	394	51	32	27	27	44	33	19	13	31	14	14	13	31	25	12	6	21	5	12	8
Last Year Any Albums	534	55	27	28	16	39	24	18	12	33	12	16	15	26	19	10	6	22	4	13	8
Regularly NME/MM/Sounds	183	45	26	26	16	38	26	18	15	42	16	21	20	42	31	21	7	33	5	21	11
Read Smash Hits/No. 1	161	50	37	20	15	53	41	24	22	22	13	6	10	35	25	12	11	17	7	9	5
Regularly Top of the Pops	382	52	31	27	16	42	28	18	15	31	13	15	14	25	19	9	5	22	6	12	8
Watch The Tube	171	46	29	25	12	44	31	22	18	37	13	16	16	41	21	19	8	22	6	16	5

seemed to be that if acts could not make profit in the UK market they would, with few exceptions, be poor performers internationally. Conversely, if they were successful internationally, that would reflect back on the UK market demand.

Individual Acts

There was ample data available describing individual acts' releases of singles and albums and the chart positions and sales they had achieved. Jules Goddard was also able to obtain from one market research company a copy of a Nationwide Music Survey among 599 United Kingdom respondents. Exhibit 2 is extracted from this study and shows particulars of record ownership for five acts in descending order of total ownership:

> Rod Stewart
> Duran Duran
> Dire Straits
> Siouxsie and the Banshees
> Jean Michel Jarre

Extracts from the acts' "biographies" are included in the Appendix with a notation of their important LPs and those of their singles which reached the British Singles Charts.

APPENDIX
Rod Stewart

Born 10 January 1945, London.

Gritty-voiced singer Rod Stewart was the son of a Scottish shopkeeper, born and raised in London. By the time he left secondary school, he longed to be a professional soccer player. After a year of bench-warming and odd jobs, Stewart took up with English bohemian folksinger Wizz Jones. Jones supposedly taught Stewart guitar and banjo, and the two performed on Continental street corners until they were arrested for vagrancy in Spain and deported to England in 1963.

In London, Stewart began hanging out at the R & B clubs. He played harmonica with the Five Dimensions, and the following year he joined the Hoochie Coochie Men. That group lasted a year, during which time Stewart moonlighted as a session musician and recorded a single, **Good Morning Little Schoolgirl**. He then sang with Steampacket. **Rod Stewart and Steampacket**, compiling various obscure recordings, was later released on Springboard. Stewart left the group in 1966 and joined Shotgun Express, but this too broke up within a year.

In 1967, Jeff Beck enlisted Stewart as lead vocalist for the Jeff Beck Group. Two albums, **Truth** (1968) and **Beck-Ola** (1969), established Stewart as a vocal stylist, and his tenure with Beck taught him to phrase his sandpaper voice around the lead instrument.

In 1969, while still with Beck, Stewart signed a solo contract with Mercury Records. His solo debut was **The Rod Stewart Album**. Stewart's solo material was a grab-bag of gentle folk songs, bawdy drinking songs, a taste of soul and a couple of barrelhouse rockers. The album sold modestly — Jeff Beck Group fans considered it too subdued — but critics were impressed by Stewart's five original songs. Stewart now joined the Faces. He spent the next seven years dividing his time between that group and his solo career.

In 1970, the Faces recorded **The First Step**, Stewart recorded **Gasoline Alley**, and together they toured the United States twice. When **Every Picture Tells a Story** came out in June 1971, the response was swift and strong. In October, the album was simultaneously No. 1 in America and Britain, the first record to do so. The first single from the album, **Maggie May**, a Stewart—Quittenton song, was the second record to do the same. Before **Maggie May** had faded, Stewart followed up with a gritty version of the Temptations' hit (I Know) I'm Losing You. Never a Dull Moment, with "You Wear It Well", was also a hit album.

With two gold albums, Stewart's role in the Faces became strained. Legal battles were waged between Mercury and Warners (with whom Stewart had signed a solo contract) over control of the Faces. While court proceedings kept him out of the studio, Mercury released a greatest-hits compilation, Sing It Again, Rod. The next year, the disputing companies jointly issued Coast to Coast Overture and Beginnings, a live album billed under "The Faces/Rod Stewart". Late in 1974, Mercury released Smiler, Stewart's last album for the label.

Stewart hired veteran American producer Tom Dowd to record his Warner Brothers debut Atlantic Crossing. In 1975, he moved to Los Angeles to escape British taxes. His romance with Swedish movie starlet Britt Ekland (which ended in 1979) made him a gossip column staple.

Stewart retained Dowd and the American studio musicians for A Night on the Town and came up with an even better-selling album than Every Picture, largely on the strength of the biggest single of 1976, "Tonight's the Night", which topped the US chart for eight weeks. Two other singles, Cat Stevens' "The First Cut is the Deepest" and "The Killing of Georgie", a song about a homosexual friend's murder, rode the charts through 1977 and made Stewart a star in the previously indifferent international market.

Stewart now formed a new, American touring band. The hits kept coming — raunchy rockers like "Hot Legs", romantic ballads like "You're in My Heart" and even a No. 1 pop hit with "Da Ya Think I'm Sexy?" (1979). Stewart even recaptured the critics with 1981's Tonight I'm Yours and the worldwide tour that followed. He had a hit with "Young Turks" in 1982, and Body Wishes included the hit "Baby Jane".

Important Albums	
1969	The Rod Stewart Album (Mercury)
1970	Gasoline Alley
1971	Every Picture Tells a Story
1972	Never a Dull Moment
1973	Sing It Again, Rod
1974	Smiler
1975	Atlantic Crossing (Warner Bros)
1976	A Night on the Town
1977	Best of Rod Stewart, Volume I (Mercury)
	Best of Rod Stewart, Volume II
	Foot Loose and Fancy Free (Warner Bros)
1978	Blondes Have More Fun
1979	Greatest Hits, Volume I
1980	Foolish Behaviour
1981	Tonight I'm Yours
1982	Absolutely Live
1983	Body Wishes

Singles in the British Charts

Released		Highest Chart Position	Weeks in Charts
4 Sep 71	REASON TO BELIEVE	19	2
18 Sep 71	MAGGIE MAY	1	19
12 Aug 72	YOU WEAR IT WELL	1	12
18 Nov 72	ANGEL/WHAT MADE MILWAUKEE FAMOUS (HAS MADE A LOSER OUT OF ME)	4	11
8 Sep 73	OH NO NOT MY BABY	6	9
5 Oct 74	FAREWELL/BRING IT ON HOME TO ME/YOU SEND ME	7	7

Released		Highest Chart Position	Weeks in Charts
16 Aug 75	SAILING	1	11
15 Nov 75	THIS OLD HEART OF MINE	4	9
5 Jun 76	TONIGHT'S THE NIGHT	5	9
21 Aug 76	THE KILLING OF GEORGIE	2	10
4 Sep 76	SAILING (re-issue)	3	20
20 Nov 76	GET BACK	11	9
4 Dec 76	MAGGIE MAY (re-issue)	31	7
23 Apr 77	I DON'T WANT TO TALK ABOUT IT/FIRST CUT IS THE DEEPEST	1	13
15 Oct 77	YOU'RE IN MY HEART	3	10
28 Jan 78	HOTLEGS/I WAS ONLY JOKING	5	8
27 May 78	OLE OLA (MUHLER BRASILEIRA)	4	6
18 Nov 78	DA YA THINK I'M SEXY?	1	13
3 Feb 79	AIN'T LOVE A BITCH	11	8
5 May 79	BLONDES (HAVE MORE FUN)	63	3
31 May 80	IF LOVING YOU IS WRONG (I DON'T WANT TO BE RIGHT)	23	9
8 Nov 80	PASSION	17	10
20 Dec 80	MY GIRL	32	7
17 Oct 81	TONIGHT I'M YOURS (DON'T HURT ME)	8	13
12 Dec 81	YOUNG TURKS	11	9
27 Feb 82	HOW LONG	41	4
4 Jun 83	BABY JANE	1	14
27 Aug 83	WHAT AM I GONNA DO	3	8
10 Dec 83	SWEET SURRENDER	23	9
26 May 84	INFATUATION	27	7
28 Jul 84	SOME GUYS HAVE ALL THE LUCK	15	10

Duran Duran   Formed 1978, Birmingham, England.

Simon LeBon (b. 1958), voc.; Andy Taylor (b. 1961), gtr., synth.; Nick Rhodes (b. 1962), kybds.; John Taylor (b. 1960), bass; Roger Taylor (b. 1960), drums.

Duran Duran were one of several British New Romantic bands — that being a fashion-conscious merger of new wave and disco. Duran Duran began as Nick Rhodes and John Taylor. Andy Taylor, answering an ad in *Melody Maker*, joined later. Simon LeBon met the group through a friend of his who worked at the Rum Runner, a club the group frequented and at which Rhodes had been a DJ. They had hit singles in Europe in 1981 with 'Planet Earth' and in the US in 1982 with 'Hungry Like the Wolf'. Lead singer Simon LeBon became a popular pin-up boy among British teens, and the group achieved some notoriety for its videos, particularly 'Girls on Film', which featured female models in various stages of undress and was banned by BBC-TV and, in the US, by MTV.

Important Albums   1981 — Duran Duran (Harvest)
1982 — Rio
— Carnival (EP)

Singles in the British Charts	*Released*		*Highest Chart Position*	*Weeks in Charts*
	21 Feb 81	PLANET EARTH	12	11
	9 May 81	CARELESS MEMORIES	37	7
	25 Jul 81	GIRLS ON FILM	5	11
	28 Nov 81	MY OWN WAY	14	11
	15 May 82	HUNGRY LIKE THE WOLF	5	12
	21 Aug 82	SAVE A PRAYER	2	9
	13 Nov 82	RIO	9	11
	26 Mar 83	IS THERE SOMETHING I SHOULD KNOW	1	9
	29 Oct 83	UNION OF THE SNAKE	3	7
	24 Dec 83	UNION OF THE SNAKE (re-issue)	66	4
	4 Feb 84	NEW MOON ON MONDAY	9	7
	28 Apr 84	THE REFLEX	1	14

Dire Straits Formed 1977, London.

Mark Knopfler (b. 1949), gtr., voc.; David Knopfler, gtr.; John Illsley, bass; Pick Withers, drums.

British songwriter/vocalist/guitarist Mark Knopfler led Dire Straits to international success in the late seventies. Their debut album introduced Knopfler's minor-key Dylanesque songs and his limpid mixture of J.J. Cale's and Albert King's guitar styles; the Dire Straits trademark is a dialogue between Knopfler's vocals and guitar lines.

Mark and David Knopfler, sons of an architect, both learned guitar in their teens. By early 1977, Mark was teaching literature part-time and jamming with David (then a social worker) and David's roommate, John Illsley, a timber broker who was working on a sociology degree at the University of London. In July 1977, after rehearsing with studio drummer Pick Withers, the group made a 5-track demo tape that included "Sultans of Swing". Critic and DJ Charlie Gillett played "Sultans" on his BBC radio show, *Honky Tonkin'*, and listeners and record companies responded.

After opening for Talking Heads on a 1978 European tour, the group spent 12 days and about $25,000 to record **Dire Straits**, which eventually sold over a million copies worldwide as "Sultans of Swing" became a hit (No. 4, 1979). Jerry Wexler and Barry Beckett produced the three-million-selling **Communique**.

During sessions for **Making Movies** in July 1980, David Knopfler left, and pianist Roy Bittan sat in. For the ensuing tour, Dire Straits added Lindes and Alan Clark to play the longer selections from **Making Movies**, which also went platinum. Later, Withers departed and was replaced by drummer Terry Williams. Tommy Mandel also joined. **Love over Gold**, with no singles-length cuts, sold over two million copies in six weeks.

Important Albums 1978 — Dire Straits (Warner Bros)
1979 — Communique
1980 — Making Movies
1982 — Love over Gold
1983 — Twisting by the Pool (EP)

Singles in the British Charts

Released		Highest Chart Position	Weeks in Charts
10 Mar 79	SULTANS OF SWING	8	11
28 Jul 79	LADY WRITER	51	6
17 Jan 81	ROMEO AND JULIET	8	11
4 Apr 81	SKATEAWAY	37	5
10 Oct 81	TUNNEL OF LOVE	54	3
4 Sep 82	PRIVATE INVESTIGATIONS	2	8
22 Jan 83	TWISTING BY THE POOL	14	7
18 Feb 84	LOVE OVER GOLD (Live)/SOLID ROCK (Live)	50	3

Siouxsie and the Banshees

Formed 1976, London.

Siouxsie Sioux, voc.; Sid Vicious, drums; Steve Havoc, bass; Marco Pirroni, gtr.; −Vicious; +Kenny Morris, drums; −Pirroni; +John McKay, gtr.

Siouxsie and the Banshees began as Sex Pistols' fans; shortly after their formation, original member Sid Vicious became a Pistol himself. In the end, the Banshees outlived their fandom and the Pistols, going on to spend a few years in the avantpunk forefront of British rock.

Of the founding four, only Siouxsie Sioux and Steve Severin were still around when their debut single, "Hong Kong Garden", and the LP **The Scream** came out. The two records set standards the Banshees found difficult to live up to with their next album, **Join Hands**. Unlike its predecessor, it never received an American release, and the group dissolved back to its two leaders, replacements coming in the form of ex-Magazine guitarist John McGeoch and Budgie, formerly of Big in Japan and the Slits. The new group was more focused and more tuneful, as attested by their British hits "Christine" and "Happy House".

Important Albums

1978 − The Scream (Polydor)
1981 − Kaleidoscope (PVC)
    − Juju

Singles in the British Charts

Released		Highest Chart Position	Weeks in Charts
26 Aug 78	HONG KONG GARDEN	7	10
31 Mar 79	THE STAIRCASE (MYSTERY)	24	8
7 Jul 79	PLAYGROUND TWIST	28	6
29 Sep 79	MITTAGEISEN (METAL POSTCARD)	47	3
15 Mar 80	HAPPY HOUSE	17	8
7 Jun 80	CHRISTINE	24	8
6 Dec 80	ISRAEL	41	8
30 May 81	SPELLBOUND	22	8
1 Aug 81	ARABIAN KNIGHTS	32	7
28 May 82	FIRE WORKS	22	6
9 Oct 82	SLOWDIVE	41	4
4 Dec 82	MELT/IL EST NE LE DIVIN ENFANT	49	5
1 Oct 83	DEAR PRUDENCE	3	8
24 Mar 84	SWIMMING HORSES	28	4
2 Jun 84	DAZZLE	33	3
27 Oct 84	THE THORN	47	3

Jean Michel Jarre   Born 24th August 1948, Lyon, France.

Jean Michel began piano lessons at the age of five, and by secondary school age was taking classes at the Paris Conservatory in harmony, counterpoint and fugue. He also played electric guitar for a number of rock groups. He completed a degree in literature and in 1968 joined the Musical Research Group in Paris. Here he began to think of music not only in terms of notes but also in terms of sounds. He wrote a thesis on non-European music and then left the group to pursue a less intellectual appeal to the popular music market — building on the synthesizer as the basic instrument.

By 1971, he was the youngest composer to have performed at the Paris Opera — introducing electronic music. He moved on to novel-sounding music for films, TV, ballet, department stores and airports.

In 1976, he recorded his first work for public release, **Oxygene**, and was chosen Personality of the Year by *People* magazine in the USA. This album sold six million copies around the world. He released **Equinoxe** in 1979, **Magnetic Fields** in 1981 and **The Essential Jean Michel Jarre** in 1983 — all albums. In 1984, he released **Zoolook** on LP with vocal effects as rhythm tracks.

Singles in the British Charts	Released		Highest Chart Position	Weeks in Charts
	27 Aug 77	OXYGENE PART IV	4	9
	20 Jan 79	EQUINOXE PART V	45	5

This case was prepared by Kenneth Simmonds of the London Business School. © Kenneth Simmonds, 1979.

CASE 28

Crestlight Paper Company

The speed of David Farrel's management changes had surprised everyone. Aged 33, David was the first of the firm's graduate MBA recruits to reach the divisional general management level. He always seemed quiet and reserved, but interested in and understanding of others' viewpoints and his promotion from Assistant Manager in the Forms division to General Manager of the Education division had been a popular one. Three weeks after he took over from the retiring general manager, however, the Education division had a new personnel manager, a replacement for the accountant and two entirely new posts advertised for product managers. Now Farrel was calmly asking Andrew Smythe to take over as Divisional Sales Manager. "Wesley McFarlane expressed his interest in early retirement," said Farrel, "and we agreed that there would be little purpose in a drawn-out handover period. He will formally retire from Crestlight at the end of March, but hand over the reins of the sales force to you as from Friday week, 24th February. Unfortunately, I shall be away at the Group Conference all next week, but we can go over the situation in detail as soon as I am back — let's say the afternoon of Monday, 27th February."

Farrel's approach was so unexpected and his manner so direct, that in five minutes Andrew found he had accepted the promotion, agreed to clean up his outstanding commitments at Group Head Office within two days and to spend the next week, Wesley McFarlane's last, learning all he could from Wesley. As he walked back to his office, Andrew was elated with his new appointment; but he had a strange feeling of his future vanishing into a vacuum. Farrel had somehow stopped him asking about where he, Farrel, wished to lead the Education division and had avoided any discussion at all about Wesley McFarlane's sales achievements. Had Wesley been good, bad or indifferent? Whatever the answer, this was the sort of opportunity Andrew had been waiting for. In fact, it was beyond his immediate expectations. He had believed his image in Crestlight to be that of a future "comer" who would be given a year or two to prove himself in some assistant sales management post before he would be offered a senior divisional appointment. Farrel had certainly picked Andrew up and put him on the escalator.

Andrew Smythe

Andrew Smythe had joined Crestlight eighteen months ago, on completing his Master of Business Administration degree at Manchester Business School. He had been based at the Group Head Office as assistant to the Group Marketing Director and given a succession of non-repetitive problems to sort out — mainly concerned with matching supply and forecasts for Crestlight lines. Off and on over the past six months he had also participated as a member of a team sorting out a new group acquisition. But at 28 he was becoming restless in a staff position. He felt that he should get into some operating post. Operations seemed the only way to the top at Crestlight. At Business School he had positioned himself as a finance specialist, but then became disillusioned with capital asset pricing theory and rather low finance grades and, anyway, marketing had seemed from outside the function of the future in Crestlight. From within, he was not so sure. He had come to regard the Marketing Director as little more than the Group's senior sales person, with the added concern for investigating major foreign orders and new agency possibilities.

Prior to his two years at Business School, Andrew had been a sales management trainee with a branded food company. There, too, the position had been a misnomer — probably titled to attract graduates. The post had amounted to two and a half years as a field representative, calling on supermarket buyers and store managers and arranging special promotions. He supposed it was good experience, but he had not really enjoyed the job and he could see that his Bachelor's degree in Economics from Nottingham was not going to move him along in any way at all — he needed an MBA for that.

Andrew shared a flat in London with two other Business School graduates and led an active social life. He still played rugby, turning out for a team in Esher on Sundays, and for the last two years he had taken winter skiing holidays. He had no plans for marriage and the idea of settling into a Wates house in Croydon, as one of his friends had done, did not appeal to him; although he had toyed with the idea of buying a house in order to build up some equity.

Crestlight Education Division

Crestlight had grown from a small beginning in the late 1940s, based on a license from the US to manufacture and distribute throughout the UK a coated paper used in industrial drawing offices. Over the years the firm had added a whole range of photographic and reproduction papers and supplies, together with a line of equipment for reproduction of large size drawings. Then in 1964 Crestlight had moved onto the acquisition trail and added a speciality paper merchant and a major form printing house. A divisional organisation pattern had emerged almost without planning. There were now five principal divisions — Equipment, Supplies, Paper, Education and Forms — and four non-integrated subsidiaries.

The Education division had been formed in 1970 to give specialist attention to the increasing demand from the education sector for special paper and reproduction supplies and equipment. Nine years later the division carried a range of 1,000 items and sold directly to Local Education Authorities (LEA's), Central Supplies Departments (who usually supplied several authorities), universities, polytechnics and some large schools. Several education wholesalers were also supplied. Some of these carried a much broader line of education supplies than Crestlight — including, for example, scientific apparatus — and had very active salesforces calling on similar direct customers.

Profit margins differed from order to order. The standard gross margin for direct supply to Local Education Authorities and individual establishments was 40% of total sales value, while on sales to wholesalers and central purchasing stores the average margin was only 26%.

Learning from Wesley McFarlane

Wesley McFarlane was friendly and relaxed when Andrew moved in with him the following Monday. Tall and well-dressed, he reminded Andrew of a trained athlete as he seemed to flow around the office without effort. Although he was only 52, he seemed to have welcomed the early retirement and gave no hint at all that he felt he had been moved out. Andrew rather gauchely tried to sound him out about the internal politics behind the move by asking him whether he minded moving at this stage in his career. Wesley came back without any hesitation, "Should have done it years ago. Sales management will never get you anywhere against the engineers and accountants, and a safe middle-of-the-road salary is a living death in Britain today." He then went on to outline to Andrew his plans for a partnership with his brother in a caravan sales agency south of London. Now that his three children were safely through school and launched on their own careers, he could turn his sales skills to his own advantage without family demands requiring him to draw too much out of the business at the wrong times. Wesley was so convincing with the detail of his own plans that he spent an hour explaining to Andrew the 'ins' and 'outs' of the caravan business. Andrew couldn't help but feel it more fascinating than selling school supplies.

Wesley finally brought Andrew back to earth by starting on a comprehensive survey of the Education division salesforce. As Wesley talked, Andrew took his own brief notes and asked for photocopies of the annual sales figures and salesforce and territory details that Wesley showed him. Exhibit 1 shows the divisional sales figures and Exhibits 2 to 6 the territory and salesforce details and performance. Exhibit 7 sets out the notes on individual salesmen as Wesley pictured them — but, as Wesley said, Andrew would get a better picture by meeting them himself. He had, accordingly, arranged the next sales meeting for Wednesday, so that he could introduce the salesforce to Andrew before he formally took over.

The remainder of Monday vanished rapidly as Wesley outlined his overall sales philosophy to Andrew:

> Last year's sales of one and a half million were just above a 20% increase over 1977. Most of this represented price increases rather than volume and by my guess market penetration has gone up slightly from 19.5%. When I say "guess" I am basing this on my estimates of market size for the three product lines. These have been asked for each year for the annual plans and what I do is to identify all the competitors and place a sales figure against each. One or other of the

Exhibit 1 *Crestlight Paper Company: Education Division Market and Sales by Product* (£'000s)

| | Market Estimates | | Sales | |
	1978	1977	1978	1977
Special Paper	3,600	3,050	696	560
Reproduction Supplies	2,200	1,850	401	337
Reproduction Equipment	1,300	1,100	363	311
Total	7,100	6,000	1,460	1,208

Exhibit 2   *Map of Sales Territories*

salesmen is bound to have heard something about a competitor's sales levels, and I do some questioning around outside as well and check the competitors' annual reports and published estimates of educational purchasing. There are too many customers to build a figure up from their estimated annual order potential and industry figures don't coincide with our narrow line definitions.

Exhibit 3 *Sales Territory Details*

	Territory	Salesman	Area ('000s sq km)	Secondary and Higher-Level Pupils 1978 (millions)	Estimated Potential Accounts	Home Base
1.	Greater London	HALBERT	1.6	1,60	570	Twickenham
2.	South East	JENNINGS	25.6	2.27	1,060	Bromley
3.	South West & Wales	BINDON	44.6	1.55	934	Cardiff
4.	Midlands East	VEREKER	28.2	1.18	653	Leicester
5.	West Midlands	PRINCE	13.0	1.24	566	Solihull
6.	North West	ANDERSON	7.3	1.65	699	Liverpool
7.	Humberside	RANDALL	15.4	1.16	531	Bradford
8.	North	THOMPSON	15.4	.83	423	Newcastle
9.	Scotland	CAMPBELL	78.8	1.32	529	Glasgow
	Total		229.9	12.80	5,965	

Exhibit 4 *Sales Force Details*

	Salesman	Age	Year Joined Crestlight	Qualifications	Previous Experience	
1.	HALBERT, Russell	54	1965	—	Textile Salesman Accounts Clerk	(10 years) (7 years)
2.	JENNINGS, Frederick	42	1973	H.N.C.	Post Office Teleprinter Salesman Equipment Maintenance	 (4 years) (16 years)
3.	BINDON, Harold V.	33	1971	B.A. (Geography)	Joined as Sales Trainee	
4.	VEREKER, John	29	1975	—	Head Storeman Despatch Clerk	(3 years) (3 years)
5.	PRINCE, Alan	57	1976	—	Salesman, etc.	(35 years)
6.	ANDERSON, Graham	37	1969	B. Tech.	Production Scheduling	(5 years)
7.	RANDALL, John	48	1951	—	Joined as Clerk in original Crestlight unit. Appointed Salesman 1964	
8.	THOMPSON, Herbert	33	1975	B.Sc. (Metallurgy)	Wallpaper Sales Rep. Research Technician	(4 years) (2 years)
9.	CAMPBELL, Ian	43	1971	B.A. (English)	Teacher	(12 years)

Exhibit 5   *Sales Force Performance*

| | 1978 | | | | 1977 | | | |
	Sales £('000s)	Accounts Sold	Gross Margin £('000s)	Calls Made	Sales £('000s)	Accounts Sold	Gross Margin £('000s)	Calls Made
HALBERT	258	239	75	1,230	217	279	69	1,260
JENNINGS	239	509	79	1,168	198	539	69	1,194
BINDON	156	476	59	1,051	129	503	48	1,018
VEREKER	112	353	41	1,409	98	356	36	1,290
PRINCE	154	413	55	1,196	123	382	43	1,185
ANDERSON	112	398	39	1,450	97	412	34	1,410
RANDALL	142	202	50	1,171	125	198	42	1,293
THOMPSON	123	364	47	1,220	101	323	39	1,163
CAMPBELL	143	317	53	1,135	123	326	46	1,088
	£1,439		£498		£1,211		£426	

Exhibit 6   *Remuneration and Expenses, 1978 Education Division Sales Force (£)*

Name	Salary 31.12.78	Commissions 1978	Total Remuneration	Expenses 1978
HALBERT	5,800	3,870	9,670	1,980
JENNINGS	4,800	3,585	8,385	2,810
BINDON	4,200	2,340	6,540	5,010
VEREKER	3,800	1,680	5,480	3,820
PRINCE	4,900	2,310	7,210	2,600
ANDERSON	5,100	1,680	6,780	1,940
RANDALL	5,200	2,130	7,330	3,400
THOMPSON	4,000	1,845	5,845	3,200
CAMPBELL	5,000	2,145	7,145	3,300
	42,800	21,585	64,385	28,060

They are all good men. There is not a bad egg among the nine and they work willingly if you don't push them too hard. Of course there are differences in sales performance, but these occur in all sales teams. Besides, you have to bear in mind the travel times some of them need to reach quite small accounts as well as the amount of work that has been done in the past to build up our accounts in a territory.

These same factors have to be taken into account in territory sizes. I think we have them about right now. As you can see from the territory variation in numbers of secondary and higher level pupils, the range between smallest and largest is only a factor of two — which is, in fact, very small. But each salesman has plenty of potential to uncover, no matter what his territory size.

Exhibit 7 *Wesley McFarlane's Comments on Salesmen*

RUSSELL HALBERT	Our star salesman. Very experienced. Knows central area. Reacts well to new ideas and well liked by customers. Has a smooth, competent air about him.
FREDERICK JENNINGS	Very sound man, systematic and conscientious and well dressed. Moved across from equipment side, so knows the technical aspects. Had some marital problems last year but apparently straightened them out.
HAROLD BINDON	Very large area but really gets round it. Presents himself well. Sales coming along nicely. Could go a long way in the company.
JOHN VEREKER	Sales not really very high. Young man with a lot to learn. Probably as a young man about town is taking time off for other things.
ALAN PRINCE	Grandad of the team. An old sales lag. Joined only 3 years ago. Will not readily adopt new approaches, but you cannot teach an old dog new tricks. Will not be around for more than five years. No really formal education, so unlikely to make general impact on buyers in the education area. Nevertheless, doing quite acceptably.
GRAHAM ANDERSON	Has a degree, but very disappointing sales results. Technically competent and extremely conscientious in covering his territory. A good worker and a rather engaging personality.
JOHN RANDALL	Bright and attractive personality. Good salesman type. Always thinking up new ideas. A bit of a troublemaker. Fairly lazy and sales below what they might be. A good pep talk should move him along.
HERBERT THOMPSON	Only been with us a few years, but keen to perform. Will take time to develop the polish of the true salesman, but the material is there. Needs guidance from sales manager about sales technique.
IAN CAMPBELL	Very solid and unexciting. Always quiet at sales meetings. Suspect he will never make an outstanding salesman. Knows the Scottish educational buying scene very well. A chess player at competition level as a hobby.

The basic salaries can't be adjusted very much. You have to keep the basic high enough to attract new reps, who might not make much commission for a while, and yet not so high that they have an easy time. Actually, I had been thinking about raising the commission rates. I think the carrot works a lot better than any pseudo-analytical target that tries to push from behind. Commission rates are only 1½% and if we raised them a further 1% instead of a salary increase this year, I think we would get five times as much back in gross margin.

Expenses are pretty much under control; I get the daily call reports and I know who they are entertaining and where they are travelling. Harold Bindon spends more time away from home than any of the others and his entertainment goes up as a result, but if life were too dreary we would have problems with that territory.

Tuesday rushed quickly past as Wesley and Andrew waded through the files for each of the product groups in the Crestlight Education range. Eighty per cent of the sales came from internal production in the other divisions but the remaining twenty per cent included a very long list of products. In some of these cases, Wesley had been required as part of the agency agreement to provide quite detailed reports on the sales efforts and results.

The Sales Meeting The Wednesday meeting got underway in the conference room with a great deal of joking and laughter. As Andrew came in, Wesley was called away to the telephone, but the salesmen knew all about the management change and introduced themselves in ones and twos before drifting towards the table with coffee cups in hand. Wesley took the seat at the head of the long table and Andrew drew up a chair towards the other end, between John Randall and Ian Campbell.

Andrew could feel that Wesley was genuinely well liked and respected. He admired the way Wesley led the group smoothly through the agenda, starting with a discussion of the January sales figures and the effects that anticipation of a change in political party had had on educational spending. One foreign manufacturer of educational forms had been threatening to withdraw his line from Crestlight and this provoked a comparison of current buyers with those who had rejected the line. Wesley also had a spate of announcements concerning new items and replacements in the line. Under 'Other Business' a long discussion boiled up around order procedure problems that had stemmed from some abstruse ruling in the Department of Education.

As the meeting was drawing to a close, John Randall stood up and on behalf of the salesmen made a short farewell speech thanking Wesley for his years of leadership. Wesley acknowledged the round of applause, thanked them warmly and then everybody headed for the 'Three Feathers' where Wesley had booked a table for lunch.

The lunch went on rather a long time with numerous rounds of drinks and a series of wild sales stories directed at Wesley. John Randall and John Vereker were the most vociferous. Randall elaborated at great length about a female purchasing officer from a Local Education Authority who had him take her out until 3 a.m. every night for a week before placing an order for a gross of protractors — while Vereker seemed the authority on landladies' daughters. At one point, Andrew ventured a story about clam digging that had been told with much hilarity at the Rugby Club. It went reasonably well, but was quickly lost in the stream of wisecracks and competing comments.

Finally, about 2.30 p.m., Wesley looked at his watch and the group began to break up. Andrew and Wesley were separated by the salesmen as they said their farewells. What struck Andrew as strange was that although each salesman used his own words, their message was the same: 'If I can be of any help in showing you the ropes, don't hesitate to ask.'

This case was prepared by Professor Kenneth Simmonds and Shiv Mathur of The London Business School. © Kenneth Simmonds, 1984.

CASE 29

Philips Industries – Viewdata

In early 1979 senior executives of Philips Industries UK, a wholly-owned subsidiary of N.V. Philips Gloeilampenfabrieken of The Netherlands, were debating how to react to the introduction of a public Viewdata service in the UK. Opinions about the future of Viewdata differed widely — some experts argued that it would have limited public impact, while others felt that it was the biggest development in the UK since North Sea Oil. Not only had these uncertainties to be taken into account in forming Philips Industries' national product strategy, but there was also a widespread belief within the larger Philips organisation that Viewdata heralded the first of a new class of products that would seriously question the traditional organisation boundaries within Philips. The UK was becoming a testing ground on which the Dutch multinational's response to a new generation of electronic goods would have significant repercussions for its longer-term strategy and structure.

How Viewdata Operated

Viewdata was, in concept, closely related to Teletext. Teletext was a system by which pages of printed words and numbers could be sent from a broadcasting centre and displayed on a domestic TV terminal. Teletext had been primarily developed to aid TV "watching" by deaf people through subtitling the spoken word on the screen. From this start, Teletext grew into an extensive service via BBC's "Ceefax" and ITV's "Oracle" using spare capacity on existing channels for topical information such as news headlines, football results and weather forecasts. This information was transmitted at a fairly low cost and the only cost to the viewer was the one-off purchase of a Teletext adaptor or a new set with Teletext capability. Spare capacity on existing TV channels limited the number of pages available for Teletext to a maximum of a couple of hundred. Any further increase in the number of pages, however, would soon make the average waiting time for a required page to appear on the screen completely unacceptable. While further channels solely for Teletext might extend the service, Teletext was further limited because it was a one-way service. Information could be transmitted only from centre to receiver, and not vice versa.

Viewdata was to change all this. Though there was little technologically new about Viewdata, its novelty lay in linking domestic television receivers to existing telephone handsets. Viewdata permitted two-way communication from centre to subscriber and back, and from subscriber to subscriber. It shared with Teletext the circuitry for generating characters on the receiving screen and a new industry standard ensured that a set receiving the more complex Viewdata system could also receive Teletext, although not vice versa.

The British Viewdata service had been developed by the Post Office under the name of Prestel. Information stored on computers in digital form was converted into an analogue form so that it would be sent down a telephone. At the receiving end, a "modem" reconverted the analogue into digital form and a character generator then presented the information on a screen. The procedure was reversed for two-way communication. By pressing a few buttons on a hand-held control or integrated keyboard, the user could get the set to dial the Post Office computer which flashed an index page onto the screen. Selection of one item led the user to a more detailed index under that heading and the process was then repeated until the user reached the information desired.

Worldwide, there were many competing viewdata systems in 1979. A French system called Teletel used a similar television/telephone link, but with a more sophisticated character display unit, to produce fairly similar results. The Canadians had their own system loosely based on Prestel. The Germans and Scandinavians had been more true to the Prestel prototype. Various sophisticated versions of the same system existed — some had more extensive memories built into the receiving terminals so that information could be dumped and the set then disconnected. Two-way cables had been used in some countries to serve as a communication channel in preference to telephone lines. Another Canadian system used a memory that could reconstruct characters from basic dots instead of the traditional character generator. It was argued that this approach would be more versatile in the long run. Other sophistications existed. The Japanese, for example, had overcome Prestel's limitations of being able to transmit only alphanumerics and graphics by incorporating electronic repeaters, at great expense, to enable photograph transmission.

Prestel was, in one important way, different from the other systems. It was in early 1979 an operating public service. The others were not. A trial service with a few hundred subscribers had just been launched in London and enthusiastically received.

Experts argued the advantages of one system against another. The French, for example, not uncharacteristically felt that their "Teletel" was far superior to Prestel, and the British predictably disagreed. On one aspect there was agreement and that was that internationalisation of any particular system would bring rich rewards to its promoters. German and Scandinavian decisions to design their own systems based on Prestel, and the British Post Office action in setting up a US subsidiary to spread the Prestel gospel in the most important of all markets, augured well for Prestel. Prestel, the promoters argued, was cheap, reliable and available. Others pointed out that these should not be reasons for its adoption because in the electronic field even the most sophisticated and complex systems were eventually only marginally more expensive than the basic versions. Pioneers in the electronic field were often those who lay face downwards in the dirt with arrows in their back, and Prestel was already in the process of being overtaken, if not overrun.

Viewdata as a Revenue Source   Prestel required two categories of hardware — the data-base computer and associated paraphernalia at the transmitting station and, secondly, the modem and specially adapted TV receiver at the receiving end. To complete the system, the information to be transmitted had to be provided. The system thus offered revenue potential for three supplier groups: the British Post Office (PO) which arranged for the computer and peripherals, the TV set manufacturers who produced the adapted TV set complete with modems, and the Information Providers (IPs).

The economics of the system at first appeared a bit complex. The information providers paid for the privilege of buying a number of data pages on the Post Office computer. A lump sum, as well as annual rental, was charged. The information provider who did not wish to purchase pages in bulk could sub-lease from umbrella information providers who also provided a complete data maintenance service. The Prestel user paid for a page of information in three ways. Firstly, the user paid for a telephone call; secondly, for Post Office computer time; and thirdly, a charge levied by the information provider, which could vary from 0 to 10p per page depending on the type of information requested. A fairly routine one-page enquiry at peak time could cost between 15 and 20p. Some economy, however, might be achieved by recording messages that were required for more than instant viewing, either as audio (after the signal came over the telephone but before decoding) or video (off the television screen). The charges to the user came in one neat bill from the PO which in turn passed on to the information providers their part of the revenue after deducting a 5% service fee.

The Post Office and the information providers were thus rewarded on a continuing basis for the service provided by them. They hoped that Prestel would open a vast new market for them and encourage the use of an under-utilised, if dated, telephone network. The set manufacturers would not participate in this continuing inflow of money but would benefit from the sale of new Prestel sets at a time when the industry's capacity to produce TV sets was far above the demand.

Prestel Markets   In theory, anyone who had or could acquire a telephone set and TV receiver was a prospective customer. But the market was constrained by the type of information that could be communicated profitably via Prestel. It was important for operating reasons that the information be relatively stable, in the sense that it need not be updated more than two or three times a day. Yet for the system to retain an advantage over less frequently updated sources such as catalogues, the customer must acquire relatively current data. Volatile information like stock prices would probably require alternate channels. Further, the PO would have a limited number of computer ports and must not be deluged with queries. Items like football scores would thus be more adequately handled by Teletext.

Prestel could also provide a service to Closed User Groups (CUGs). Firms with their own computers could relay data over the Prestel network with the help of suitable interfaces. Firms without their own computers could buy capacity on a Prestel computer and larger businesses could use Viewdata to augment in-house data transmission. Companies such as GKN and Whitbread were already using Prestel compatible computer systems as part of their management information network. There had been enquiries from groups such as estate and travel agents about setting up CUGs using the Prestel network. To such customers the central attraction was the availability of a dedicated and economical nationwide hardware capability that permitted the relay of "control" and "operational" information rather than the "general" information provided by IPs.

A vast domestic market also existed that could use Prestel to satisfy many information needs. Exchange rates, price-lists and timetables would become instantly available without the endlessly engaged tones resulting from overworked enquiry staffs. Home shopping might even be carried out by punching a credit card number on a two-way system. If the pundits were to be believed, a whole host of middlemen and services would be phased out as Prestel developed.

Prestel's Take-Off Problems

All three supplier groups — the Post Office, information providers and set manufacturers — would need to target on the same segment for the full benefits of any promotional work to be realised. A divergence of opinion, however, was apparent in early 1979. The Post Office was conditioned to planning years ahead and was keen on the introduction of a public service that emphasised the domestic consumer. The computer capacity reserved by the Post Office for the business sector was limited and the intention was to provide parallel computers and information centres in all major towns in the UK rather than extending capacity in selected locations to accommodate more business users. Many set manufacturers and potential information providers, on the other hand, believed in a strategy that concentrated initially on the business user because of that customer's greater ability to pay. All agreed that the domestic market was where the dominant demand would finally lie; the disagreement was on how to get there. There were one or two indications, though, that the Post Office was at least thinking of changing direction. For example, the Post Office subsidiary in the US was making a concentrated effort to get the business sector interested.

Some take-off problems were already beginning to emerge for Prestel. The enthusiastic public launch in early 1979 had come before adapted sets were generally available. Information providers were disappointed at the rate of information use, particularly as their economic resources were more limited than for the other two parties. Some felt that if the market did not move into a positive cycle of increased use and decreased cost, it might slip into a negative cycle instead. There was also some concern about the PO's lack of control over the information providers. Providers operated individually, using tree structures to index information that made cross references between their data bases very difficult. Some trees even referred a user to an outside on-line system rather than to another Prestel data base. Moreover, 20% of the users were getting lost in the branches of the tree structure that had been designed to be "child's play". Directories which permitted cross-referral and direct access to a particular page were clearly needed.

The problems were even more complex for the UK set manufacturers (Thorn, Philips, Rank, ITT and others). Who would be the first one to make the investment in plant and equipment to raise the volume of adapted sets beyond the hand-crafted prototype levels? Even if one manufacturer did get the ball rolling, there was no guarantee that other UK manufacturers would not reap the benefits with production geared to even more novel technology. And, further, if all moved together, it was possible that all they would accomplish would be to split production so that none achieved a critical volume and the sole beneficiaries would be the Japanese companies who haunted the dreams of patriotic and inefficient British set manufacturers.

Patriotic concern about British industry had drawn the attention of government bodies to the plight of Teletext and, to an extent, Prestel.

Teletext had sat firmly on the bottom of any take-off curve since its launch
five years earlier, with total ownership still measured in the thousands instead
of the projected millions. The special section set up in the Department of
Industry (DOI) to propagate the use of microprocessors was particularly
concerned to stimulate the pace of market adoption as these sets would use
large numbers of microprocessors. In early 1979, the Department appeared
willing to offer assistance of about £2 to £3 million to set manufacturers to
get Teletext off the ground. The Department felt that this contribution could
help to get 300,000 sets to the market over a period of 18 months. Set
manufacturers were of the opinion that the assistance required would have
to be of the order of £25 per set to make any impression on the market. It was
widely acknowledged that Prestel development was also of national importance and would have fundamental technological and international trade implications for the UK; and its success or failure would have many indirect
effects — for example, in the competitive field of electronic telephone
exchanges. Exactly what role Government should play in the development of
Prestel, however, was still unclear.

What Was the Product?

The most fundamental unit of the Prestel set was what was commonly
known as a TV screen but could be described more generically as a Visual
Display Unit (VDU). With a suitable electronic memory and data processing
capability, the VDU could be turned into a personal computer (though there
existed computers without VDUs). Add a slow printer and it became a computer with basic ancillary features to which software on audio cassettes and
the newly developed "floppy disc" memories could be added. If more
memory and software were added along with a fast printer, the resulting
assembly could be more accurately described as a word processor or again as
an editing terminal for a mini or mainframe computer. Word processors
with modems for telephone connection, moreover, would form the basis of
an electronic mail system. The lines of demarcation between a Prestel set,
with its basic one-page memory, a personal computer, a word processor/
editing terminal and a basic electronic mail capability were thus very hazy.

Some applications would develop along the personal computer
pathway. A TV set with basic intelligence could be used to play TV games
and more by plugging in local software. If the intelligence were extended, it
was quite feasible to send software down the telephone line, capture it locally
and turn the hardware into a personal computer with access to mainframe
backup. The receiving subscriber might calculate personal tax liabilities or
mortgage repayments and enlist electronic help for the children's homework.
Or to get away from it all, he need only press more buttons to check timetables, communicate with his banker and book an airline ticket to Marakesh.

This was just one type of application. With intelligent VDUs connected
to telephone lines, it was simple to visualise situations in which a mainframe
computer would send messages to and receive instructions from terminals all
over the country. Terminals could "talk" to each other and transfer between
them data stored on the new "floppy discs". With word processing software,
"letters" could be transmitted from one VDU to another, edited at a distance
and copies retained in local electronic memory files or typed with the help of
a fast printer. A fully-fledged electronic mail service could get underway just
as soon as terminals could economically transmit graphics in addition to
words and numbers. Experts were forecasting a steep decline in costs and a

five-fold increase in electronic mail over the following 7 to 8 years to make it a $2–$3 billion business worldwide. If the consumer reacted as enthusiastically as the experts, postage stamps would become finally and truly a collector's item.

Prestel sets were the harbinger of whatever one wanted to choose from the already large and constantly growing list of possible uses. The labels that could be put on the fundamental concept were many. "Enhanced TV Sets", "Viewdata", "Remote Copiers", "Personal Computers", "Word Processors", and "Electronic Mail" were just some of them. For each label there was a market, and for each market there were companies in closely related disciplines who were interested. In which direction would the production finally take off, and in what volume? Any real market research was so limited as to be virtually nonexistent. One thing, however, was certain — there would be no prizes for guessing incorrectly. Growth in one direction would almost certainly mean lower growth in another.

Viewdata Within Philips

The development of Prestel technology clearly was of major concern to a wide range of industries. This breadth of concern was mirrored within Philips Industries as commercial and technical management for several Philips divisions attempted to visualise the impact of Prestel-like services on its own businesses. Philips had its fingers in many electronic pies and to cope with this diversity of interest, related products were grouped into fourteen divisions as described in the Appendix.

In the UK, the less-than-total integration of the Pye Group of Companies, which was now wholly-owned by Philips, added another dimension of complexity and it sometimes happened that a particular product was manufactured and marketed both by Philips and by a Pye subsidiary. At the very least, the following divisions and companies within the UK Philips group would have an interest in the development of Prestel, together with in-house component suppliers and research laboratories:

1. *Philips*
   (a) Video Division
   (b) Business Equipment Division
   (c) Data Systems Division

2. *Pye*
   (a) Pye Video
   (b) Pye TMC
   (c) Pye Business Communications
   (d) Pye Labgear

As the implications of Viewdata for the Philips organisation unfolded, the Concern Centre at Eindhoven set up a small group to coordinate the international and interdivisional aspects of the new development. A similar coordinating function was suggested for all countries where Viewdata was expected to make a significant impact. In late 1978, a special UK Viewdata Product Manager had been appointed, reporting to the Managing Director of Philips Industries. He was given the task of coordinating the activities of the various divisions and interest groups and advising on future UK strategy. The role was seen to be largely "coordination and advisory" rather than directive. He was also asked to develop products which would be part of the

Viewdata armoury but which did not obviously fall within the jurisdiction of any particular division.

Personal computers were seen by the Viewdata Product Manager to be such an outside product and, by the middle of 1979, he had agreed on a Swedish prototype to be developed in the UK. Not only would this computer be fully compatible with an extended Prestel network, but it would also be a marketable product in its own right giving Philips a belated entry into the growing personal computer market. This market had grown from being the plaything of computer enthusiasts on the West Coast of the USA to a multi-million-dollar industry. Small companies such as COMMODORE and TANDY had developed and marketed personal computers and accompanying software. Larger organisations including Texas Instruments and ITT were setting up manufacturing facilities. It seemed an obvious product for the large Dutch multinational. Smaller businesses and professional people were the perceived target and were expected to spend £35m on the product in 1980. Questions about the supply of software and appropriate marketing channels had yet to be answered, as did the crucial issue of which arm of Philips in the UK would manufacture and market the product.

Viewdata as a Video Division Product

Philips Video Division's activity lay predominantly in the manufacture and sale of colour television sets. Pye Ltd had a similar activity so that in the market-place the two brands ostensibly competed with each other. Against the obvious cost disadvantages, this arrangement had the benefit of giving consumers an extended choice of Philips products. Increasing standardisation of components used by the two organisations was envisaged and the managers were in touch on a day-to-day basis. The Video Division and Pye were not, however, the sole suppliers of television sets for the Philips group as sets of screen sizes of 5" and below were considered to be the responsibility of the Audio Division.

The market for television sets in the UK had undergone a sharp change in the last six years. During the early seventies, consumer demand for colour sets had stretched the UK suppliers. Capacities had been expanded and imports had multiplied. All this had changed by early 1974 and the domestic manufacturers faced falling demand and growing imports. The industry, through its trade association, had demanded a curtailment of Japanese imports and, as a result, restrictions on the import of the larger screen sizes of 20" and above had been agreed. Currently, the Japanese were replacing imports by setting up joint ventures with manufacturers in the UK, often taking up production capacity abandoned by the UK partner. There were various interpretations of the strategy behind such moves and most of them had an ominous ring.

In common with the rest of the domestic set manufacturers, the Video Division was operating well below capacity in 1979. Analysts believed that industry capacity utilisation lay somewhere between 50% and 60%. About 30% of total domestic sales were being imported and such imports represented an even more significant proportion of the market for small sets. Demand for colour sets was forecast to be fairly static for the next few years at around the two-million-a-year mark (split 15:85 between small and large sets) and the Video Division could foresee only marginal gains in its share of 20% of the market. It was also forecast that the expiry of some German manufacturing patents in the early eighties would result in a substantial increase in imports.

Over the past few years, two factors had been conspiring to reduce demand. The number of households without a set was now low and set reliability had been improving. Increased reliability had brought with it an increase in the percentage of sets purchased. For monochrome sets, a vast majority of customers did not even bother to maintain service contracts. For colour television, the UK was still one of the world's largest rental markets with 80% of its colour sets rented, but a move towards direct ownership was also evident for colour. Nevertheless, the UK manufacturers supplying retail outlets also supplied the high street rental companies. The Japanese did not. They had bypassed the rental market and merchandised their sets with a strong reliability pitch.

The attitudes of users and rental companies were crucial to the market position of UK manufacturers. With technology improving every day, the user did not want to be stuck with an antiquated product. This consideration and a wish for a prompt, satisfactory service without a cost risk, were the main reasons for the growth of rental companies. The rental companies had coped splendidly with the service problems that were common when television was first introduced. Lately, however, some felt that rental companies had come to see themselves as providing the established product rather than a service to overcome user risk. Some rental companies were just as hesitant as individuals to buy Teletext and Prestel sets which ran the risk of being replaced with newer models. In fact, some high street rental outlets were even reluctant to demonstrate Prestel sets, as demonstration tied up their only telephone line. Nor had the rental companies expanded into the non-domestic market or shown any marked enthusiasm for either video cassette recorders or personal computers. There was also conflict between the reliability standards sought by rental companies and by direct owners. Owners wanted sets of a quality that removed the fear of major service costs but rental firms, though welcoming a level of reliability that cut down service needs, had discouraged manufacturers from offering and advertising unfailing performance.

Viewdata could provide a much needed impetus to Video Division sales as consumers replaced sets before they were technically obsolete and paid extra for the Prestel "chippery". Video Division analysts felt that the right retail price increment onto the price of a large screen set with remote control would be £50 for Teletext and a further £50 for Prestel. The percentage price increase for a Prestel facility would be quite noticeable even to customers already willing to purchase the more expensive, larger screen sizes. There were already indications of some unwillingness to pay for extra features. For the large 26-inch sets, sales with a remote control facility had grown from 60% to 90% over the past few years. But remote control was still far behind the penetration reached in the German market. Some argued that, since a remote control facility was a prerequisite to the sale of Prestel sets, Germany was a more promising market. Others were of the opinion that the British consumer would have more incentive to change upmarket to remote control and Prestel in one go. Since a dominant percentage of British colour sets was rented, there was a smaller commitment to existing hardware.

For the price to be attractive, a sufficient volume of sets must be produced. For Teletext to be priced at £50 over the basic set, Philips would have to achieve volume sales to the order of 50,000 per year just to break even. With 20% of the market this implied total sales by all manufacturers of 250,000 sets — well above the few thousand currently being sold. The numbers for Prestel pointed the same way. If, however, total purchase of Prestel sets could be made to reach, say, half a million, then not only would costs per unit fall dramatically but it would be possible to enlist the help of new manufacturing techniques to bring down costs still further. In 1979, with the service still in its infancy, little could be said about the future. A thousand Prestel sets were operational and another 15,000—20,000 were budgeted for production by all manufacturers combined over the next year. The PO's estimate of demand was considered wildly optimistic, especially in view of the fact that Prestel was being marketed at a time when many products like Philips' own video cassette recorders and video long playing systems would be competing for the discretionary income of the consumer. Some companies appeared to be moving forward into volume production faster than others. ITT was one of them, with about 100 sets a week being produced at its factory at Hastings, against the planned 30 a week by Philips. There were rumours, however, that the Hastings factory was to be closed under ITT's rationalisation programme.

Business users could also produce a significant demand. Businessmen would be more inclined to pay the current price of £1,200 for a set, but their requirements would be different. They might not need colour sets and some might actually prefer monochrome. The keypad would be better received if it was an integral part of the VDU and television reception could well prove a distraction in some offices. One indication of the potential demand was that there were about 1.7 million telephone connections which were classified as business, of which 1.5 million had one line and about 16,000 more than 10 lines. Estimates of demand potential varied between 150,000 and 700,000 sets depending on the penetration assumed, but any such calculation was extremely sensitive to assumptions about small businesses.

The Video Division management was fully aware that, though it had the outlets and expertise to sell to the domestic market, the business market would require significantly different capabilities. New business rental companies and new marketing aids, like leasing, would be needed. Users would be more demanding and, in addition to Prestel hardware, business software would be expected. Outside consultants would be needed to advise the larger clients on the way in which a Prestel service should be managed and to integrate the facility with existing computer and office services. The Video Division had already engaged one consultant to conduct seminars on Prestel, offer editing and data maintenance service to the IPs and advise potential customers on system hardware and software. With this step, Video was moving into territory which fringed on the domain of Philips Data Systems.

Data Systems and Business Equipment Division (BED)

The UK arms of both the Data Systems and Business Equipment Divisions were small in comparison with the overall activities of Philips Industries. In the UK, both were selling divisions only, with manufacturing carried out by overseas units. Data Systems imported computers which were sold to clients through a sales force of about 150 specialists who designed and adapted software to customer needs. BED sold a variety of Philips dictating machines through specialised office equipment dealers and word processors through agents who placed orders on BED and were given a commission on sales. The BED sales force of 12—14 salesmen was charged with ensuring that dealers and agents were promoting the sales of Philips equipment and were adequately supplied with goods.

Not only were Data Systems and BED small in themselves, they also had a small share of their respective markets. BED supplied only 6% of all word processors sold in the UK. On the other hand, it did lead in the dictation machine market with over 50% market share — currently under active attack from Sony. It was more difficult to define what constituted the relevant market for Data Systems and to be precise about share. The field was dominated by IBM, ICL, Honeywell, Burroughs and Digital, while newer companies like PET and TANDY were exploiting the personal computer end of the market. While some of the giants were moving down, the little boys were moving up and the changing technology kept the market in a state of turbulence.

Data Systems had, over the past several years, concentrated on two segments of the computer business — office systems and complete systems for banks. The latter were by Data Systems' standards big jobs, with each project in the £1—£10 million range. Office computer systems could range from electronic accounting systems costing from £5,000 to business systems priced at £50,000—£60,000. Data Systems had positioned itself towards the top of this range providing a complete service to small businesses which required more than a purely accounting system. With a continual drop in the price of hardware, however, this segment of the market was coming under increased pressure both from the mainframe manufacturers moving downwards and from personal and minicomputer firms moving upwards.

Prestel was seen by Data Systems' management as the opportunity that would enable it to "assume an important position at the lower end of the office equipment market". In early 1979 a start had been made in this direction with Data Systems moving into the private Viewdata market to provide companies with a service that would enable both company and Prestel information to be displayed. The addition of a word processor supplied by BED would provide an up-to-date editing facility. Though this service would be in competition with a similar GEC system, it was a major step forward within Philips as it brought together a minicomputer, editing terminal and a VDU made by the Video Division in a manner never attempted before.

Senior management at Data Systems felt that the combination of a TV set, a telephone line and a data processing ability could revolutionise the office equipment industry. All this equipment would in time be supplemented by other Philips products like the newly developed video discs that were capable of storing the entire Encyclopaedia Britannica on one side. Markets would also be created for VCRs to store graphic data and for audio cassettes to store digitally coded data. Such stored data could then be played on any suitably adapted television set. What was required to complete the system in the view of Data Systems' management, were components like copiers, typewriters and printers which would permit a complete office equipment service to be offered. How such products would be procured was something that needed to be decided in the long run; for the moment, a successful launch into the private viewdata market was the prime objective. Data Systems had, as part of its promotion campaign, arranged a series of workshops where prospective clients could spend a day to see how a private system would help solve their individual problem. These workshops had stimulated a great number of enquiries.

Data Systems faced both allies and competitors within the Philips organisation. The Business Equipment Division was a natural partner — private Viewdata systems would mean a new market for products of both divisions. The products themselves were becoming so similar that coordination between the two organisations had been set in motion at Eindhoven level. The outlets of the two divisions would complement each other so that word processors would profit by being sold through a specialised system sales force, and BED dealers would eventually provide an outlet for data processing equipment where the software component was minimal. Both saw in Viewdata an opportunity to increase their low market share and to develop a segment that was not dominated by the bigger competitors yet showed all the signs of rapid growth. The segment could almost be described as business customers who could be "sold" a consumer durable. It was in this activity that the seeds of eventual conflict lay between Data Systems and BED on the one hand and the Video Division and the developers of personal computers on the other.

Pye TMC Pye TMC saw Prestel in an entirely different light. Pye TMC was one of the four suppliers to the British Post Office of telephone handsets and accessories. It viewed Prestel not as an adapted television set but as an extension of the public telephone network and, therefore, within its product area. The company had suffered reverses as a supplier of transmission equipment and had been excluded from development work in the new-generation all-electronic exchange called "System X". Nevertheless, TMC had, over the years, developed the technical capability to "purpose design" advanced electronic circuits for push button and speciality telephones giving it a significant competitive advantage, and it continued to manufacture Private Automatic Branch Exchanges (PABXs). Over the past few years, TMC had recorded a dramatic volume comeback in its sales of telephone handsets to the Post Office. There was a very close relationship with the PO which was, in effect, the dominant customer. In fact, Pye TMC had never really developed a sales force to sell either to the consumer or to business markets. Prestel offered not only a technological challenge but also an opportunity to develop selling strengths that would better equip TMC to meet the future.

The Post Office had maintained a monopoly in communications and effectively determined the equipment its subscribers could obtain. In the declared interests of network safety, the PO leased to subscribers handsets manufactured to its own specifications by selected subcontractors. All "add-ons" to telephone handsets and anything that incorporated a modem were vetted by the PO and installed under the supervision of its engineers. Answering machines and large PABXs of over 100 lines were exceptions. These were supplied independently by PO-approved contractors although the PO still supplied and installed the terminals to connect these systems to the public network. In the case of Prestel, manufacturers had been permitted to sell equipment with an incorporated modem for the very first time. The PO, however, had plans to use its contacts and marketing skills to sell Prestel sets in competition with other sellers of adapted television sets. The PO would acquire what it wanted to market from its subcontractors, of whom Pye TMC was one.

In permitting other competitors to enter the field of selling "add-on" equipment directly to telephone subscribers, the PO had already made a significant departure from tradition. This could be a watershed in the way business was transacted in the telecommunications field. If the present Government went ahead with its plans to split the PO into Postal and

Telecommunication services and liberalised the manner in which "add-on" equipment could be installed, the repercussions for subcontractors like Pye TMC would be very significant indeed. Business for telephone ancillary equipment would require user marketing skills, though it would be some time before UK subscribers could buy handsets from "phone shops" to plug in themselves, as was common in the US.

Pye TMC had developed a Prestel television set called "Visa". Some parts had been procured from the Video Division, others had been developed in-house. Visa was aimed specifically at the business market — it was monochrome, had an integral keyboard and was a desk-top model with the ability to interface with copy printers and software on tape. TMC felt that it was the business sector that would provide the initial demand for Prestel services and the future programme for the development of Visa terminals was aimed at this segment. Visa 2 would permit an "order entry" facility. Visa 3 would permit transmission of both speech and data and Visa 4 would have an electronic mail capability. At the end of this development programme, Visa 4 would be intelligent enough to be linked directly through the public switching network to offer point-to-point communication and a private Viewdata service would no longer require an intermediate computer. If everything went according to plan, Visa development would contribute a turnover of £3—£5 million per year in three years' time.

As the development of Visa continued, there had been efforts to identify which subgroups in the business sector would provide the most appropriate target for Visa products. Though it was still no more than a plan, the 1.7 million business users of telephones had been classified by perceived enthusiasm for Prestel. The most likely to adopt Prestel, in TMC's view, were the users of extensive telecommunications systems and those employing more than 2,000 employees. The second group included those with a thousand or so employees. In the third category were small businesses and the professions. In terms of numbers, there were about 2,000 prime businesses, about 200,000 in the second category and the rest were classified as small businesses. It was only when the third category had been sufficiently penetrated that anything like a mass business market could be said to exist.

The Post Office, with its own marketing and servicing facilities, was an obvious outlet for Visa terminals and talks were under way for a mutually satisfactory arrangement. General promotion in the form of brochure and press advertisements had already been undertaken. The aim was to position Visa as a Prestel facility that would be part of an integrated office system for larger firms. Pye TMC was of the view that a comprehensive Prestel service must be capable of integrating with the internationally standardised telex networks so that printed messages could be sent from any Visa terminal. This would require that interfaces be developed to integrate the 40-character Prestel system to the 65-character telex network. This approach differed from Philips Data Systems which did not see this integration as crucial, though both managements agreed that interfaces would be necessary initially to enable in-house computers to communicate with any Prestel network.

TMC was aware that its existing channels into the market-place would need to be supplemented. It proposed initially to enlist the help of other companies in the Pye group. Possibly BED's office equipment dealers would provide an outlet. In the longer run, an in-house sales force would be developed and appropriate dealers and distributors identified. They believed that this was the only way that an adequate competitive position could be achieved against other Post Office telephone suppliers like GEC and ITT who were developing Prestel systems of their own. While there were products under development at Pye TMC such as "New Generation Keyphones" that would perhaps provide greater return on investment, none of them offered the impetus that would enable the company to reshape itself for a rapidly changing market and reduce its dependence on the PO. That was the biggest attraction of Prestel.

Pye Business Communications (PBC)

Pye Business Communications was seen by TMC as one of the companies which would be able to assist in marketing Visa terminals. PBC was already a customer. It sold PABXs and handsets manufactured by TMC to clients requiring branch exchanges or private telephone systems; but PBC sold more than hardware, it supplied complete systems tailor-made to solve a communication problem. System selling best described PBC's £13—£14 million turnover. Beside telephony, PBC sold complete systems for closed circuit television networks and for the sound and audio requirements of customers. This latter category included facilities like intercoms, conference audio and public address networks. PBC brought in all components and hardware for these requirements, and designed the systems to meet very specific requirements. A closed circuit TV network, for example, would differ markedly for a museum, a factory or a traffic control agency. The first would need a system that emphasised security; the second, one that optimised process control; while the third would require surveillance. In each case, it might be necessary to integrate the new offering with other networks already in operation. Nevertheless, 70% of PBC's supplies came from Philips factories somewhere. As these supplies were largely in the fields of Electro-Acoustics and Telecommunications, PBC reported to the two concerned Philips Divisions in Eindhoven.

The company employed a team of 60 Commercial Project Engineers who were trained to evaluate the hardware needs of a client and their integration into the existing system. Further design backup was provided by Technical Project Engineers who were well versed in the requirements of various categories of clients and if still further "customising" was necessary, this was done by a group of specialists in fields like digital control and various aspects of electronics. Between them, these three groups were able to offer a tailormade article that would provide the most cost-effective way of solving a particular communication problem. Another team of 120 Service Engineers then installed, commissioned and often maintained the system on a casual or contractual basis depending on whether an outright sale had been made or whether leasing or rental facilities had been extended.

In 1979, about 50% of PBC's business was in the supply of telephone systems. The Post Office had approved the newer generation of electronic exchanges marketed by Philips and TMC. This equipment not only made it possible to connect branch exchanges of up to 8,000 lines each, but also to offer telephone handsets that could be programmed to transfer and dial calls and remember important telephone numbers — facilities that were available only after cumbersome handwiring on electromechanical exchanges.

It was this interest in telephony and communication systems that had brought PBC into contact with Viewdata. As more and more electronic exchanges were installed and handsets acquired a measure of intelligence, it was evident that not only speech but text transmission would be possible over the public switched network. Viewdata terminals could play a large part in the development of the office of the future in enabling subscribers to communicate speech and text directly to each other without using the Prestel information network or going through an in-house computer. This scenario was in keeping with TMC product development plans regarding "Visa" terminals. The intelligence would lie ultimately not in a central computing facility but in the personal terminal on the executive's desk which would be able to receive messages and store them in "soft" electronic memories. The intelligent terminal would permit the executive to store files locally and do calculations and data manipulations as required. The terminal would be a cross between a telephone and a personal computer with a display unit. Such a terminal could have a local hard printer but there was no reason why any printing, if required, should not be done in a central graphics facility using non-impact machines. The installation of such terminals would have an impact on corporate telex and printing services which would no longer be required in their present form. As executives ceased to be intimidated by desk-top computers, the benefits and privacy of data on personalised and transportable floppy discs would be realised.

Any linkup that permitted subscribers to communicate speech and text directly need have little to do with the information provided by Prestel. PBC argued that, if companies had wanted a Prestel-like data service, the capability had existed for some time to set it up. Since this had not happened, it was obviously not needed. Prestel was now a product looking for a market — possibly hopelessly. Moreover, the cumbersome access and branching procedures required did nothing to promote adoption of Prestel. Prestel, though, would not be completely wasted as it would survive as a peripheral facility available to those who had acquired intelligent terminals.

Though PBC and Data Systems had much in common in the way they saw the progress of Viewdata services, there were some differences. Both identified the business sector as a starting point and both felt that Viewdata, in its generic form, would be the starting point of the office of the future and Prestel only a peripheral facility. Where they differed was in their view of the terminals required and the importance of the Prestel network as distinct from its information services. Data Systems saw a computer as a central feature supported by inhouse terminals which were relatively dumb but used the Prestel network to communicate. PBC visualised intelligent terminals based on a personal computer which could also operate as word processors using the ordinary public telephone link for communication.

If such futuristic development came about, it was likely that PBC, with its experience of telephony and system selling, was a serious contender for a central position in any project undertaken to bring Philips closer to the office of the future.

Pye Labgear Pye Labgear was the smallest of the Philips units interested in Viewdata. With a turnover of about £2 million, 200 employees and a commercial sales force of five, it manufactured and sold "interface" equipment to wholesalers, the larger chain stores and rental companies. It offered devices such as amplifiers that improved transmission and reception of TV signals and also manufactured electronic equipment on a contractual basis for the Post Office, Ministry of Defence and other organisations.

When Teletext had become a commercial service in the mid seventies,

Labgear had started the manufacture of external adaptors which enabled ordinary monochrome and colour sets to receive the new service. Though an external adaptor performed adequately and was a viable alternative to the acquisition of a set with incorporated chippery, the quality of the picture was inferior and this was more noticeable on the larger screens. The sale of Teletext adaptors had risen to about 2,500 per year when a strike and the consequent postponement of the ITV Teletext service had resulted in a significant setback. An improved version of the Teletext adaptor was scheduled to be launched in 1979 and expected to retail at around £250.

For Prestel, the company had produced a small batch of similar adaptors called "Viewdapta" which did not receive Teletext. Viewdaptas could be used for both domestic and non-domestic markets and, though final pricing was still uncertain, it was unlikely that the domestic customer would obtain this device for less than £400. Labgear hoped to sell Viewdaptas both to its traditional customers like specialist wholesalers, retail chains and rental companies as well as anyone who required to adapt a set. The latter category included all the Philips companies which might wish to adapt a TV set as part of their own marketing programme.

The Issues   The appointment of a Viewdata coordinator at the Philips Industries UK headquarters was seen to be useful in keeping management of different divisions informed of each others' activities — but little else. In fact, divisional executives were sceptical about the usefulness of a function that had been designed with "no real responsibility and little power". To some it epitomised a typical Philips syndrome where "coordination was a substitute for action". Many felt it crucial that somebody should identify which markets should be aimed for, with what products, and by whom. Though some work had been done in mapping the various divisional interests, the channels and possible markets, this was no more than a basis for further discussion. There was concern that products like Prestel adaptors and personal computers were being developed on an *ad hoc* basis. Did the company really wish to put its weight behind an unbrandable device like adaptors, and how would this affect its policy on Prestel sets? In a similar vein, though the value of personal computers to the Philips repertoire was obvious, it was still unclear as to who would market it and provide the all-important software.

Though disagreement continued over the nature of coordination, there was agreement that this was essential. The Viewdata concept was obviously interdisciplinary and would, in the long run, be sold to both domestic and non-domestic customers and as an innovation for many different uses. It differed substantially from most new products which were easier to assign for both manufacturing and marketing to one company division. Three alternatives to single division allocation each raised problems:

(i)   Multiple divisional marketing — multiple divisional manufacture.
(ii)   One divisional manufacture — multiple marketing.
(iii)   A new grouping of divisions.

Multiple manufacturing could lose economies of scale and possibly had already happened with Video and TMC making their own Prestel sets. Single divisional manufacture would require inter-divisional coordination and raise problems of accountability. Finally, a new grouping of companies would, in addition, raise questions of how the traditional products would be looked after. As further products like personal computers were added, the decisions would become even more involved. It was becoming clear that the traditional structure needed to be questioned but yet there were fears that if too much discussion focused on divisional responsibilities, the concern for Viewdata could degenerate into a demarcation dispute at the expense of action in the market.

Even though there was a consensus of opinion that the market should be attacked, there was no clear idea of what its dimensions were or what the animal looked like. Far into the future, complete domestic and office systems would emerge, but how should Philips get there, and with what intermediate products? Differences in the type of products and systems required for domestic and business markets needed to be catered for. The dimensions and specifications of sets and the future of Viewdata needed to be decided. It was still uncertain whether the domestic customer, if he bought Prestel and could afford to use it, would alter his viewing habits so as to use the Prestel capability, or whether he would require a second VDU and second telephone line. There was no market research to answer these queries.

If the behaviour of the interested divisions reflected their assessment of the situation, it seemed that the business market was the most likely to take off. But each division argued that the hardware that enabled such take-off would be different. Not surprisingly, the one most favoured was usually part of their present repertoire. Some divisions accused others of asking themselves not how to promote Viewdata but how continuing involvement in this technology would give them a more viable business position. Blinkered by considerations of hardware and territoriality, it was said they couldn't possibly hope to see the market, let alone attack it. As divisions with traditionally domestic orientation edged into industrial markets and industrial salesmen began selling upgraded consumer durables, it seemed possible that the various subunits were on a collision course. The organisational benefits of independent development had to be weighed against the costs of duplication of effort and any suggested solution brought the firm back into the tangled issues of responsibility and accountability at Concern level.

Only when the basic strategy issues had been resolved could a whole host of secondary decisions be made. These included: what influence should be brought to bear on the PO and other governmental bodies? What opportunities existed for Philips as an information provider? What part should it play in the international standardisation of Viewdata?

To some managers it appeared that minor tuning of Philips' strategy and structure would be able to accommodate Viewdata. Others, who saw in Viewdata the first of a new class of products that would cross traditional divisional boundaries, fundamentally disagreed. Even if Prestel failed, Viewdata had arrived to stay and the issues that it raised for Philips must be given an unequivocal answer.

APPENDIX
The Philips
Organisation

N.V. Philips Gloeilampenfabrieken was founded in 1891 in Holland by Gerard Philips to produce filament lamps. From this humble beginning, the company had evolved to become one of Europe's largest multinationals with operating units in 125 countries and production units in 65.

In 1979, Philips had 14 product divisions, all but four headquartered in Eindhoven (see p. 263). Product divisions were responsible for Philips' performance in defined product/market fields and were organised into commercial, technical and financial functions. The commercial side was responsible for worldwide market strategy, product policy and intercompany supplies, the technical side for international coordination of product development and production.

Jointly responsible for performance within individual countries were Philips' National Organisations (NOs). National Organisations were headed by a board, or Comité Central de Direction, composed of commercial, technical and financial directors under the leadership of the Commercial Director. Commercial and technical responsibilities at their lower management levels were often dedicated to a particular range of products and, therefore, associated with a particular Product Division. The local commercial departments held dominant responsibility for local selling activity and worked closely with product divisions to ensure that goods supplied met local requirements. The technical side of the National Organisation was concerned primarily with the design, development and manufacture of products to standard prices agreed with the commercial department. The extent of the local commercial department's influence depended on the proportion of the plant output for local consumption.

Manufacturing centres were divided into two broad categories: International Product Centres (IPCs) and National Product Centres (NPCs). In IPCs, the technical side of the Product Division was responsible for factory loading, finished stock and distribution to the warehouses of the receiving National Organisations, while the NO itself was responsible for manning, procurement, factory stock levels and plant efficiency. In NPCs, the National Organisation was responsible for all activities of planning and executing deliveries of finished goods internally and to other NOs. Product divisions retained only what was officially termed "normal guidance". A majority of UK factories was by 1979 operating as IPCs.

The basic relations between the Philips Concern and a National Organisation could best be represented as a matrix (Figure 1). Within this matrix, any given NO could be working with any combination of the 14 product divisions in selling or

Figure 1

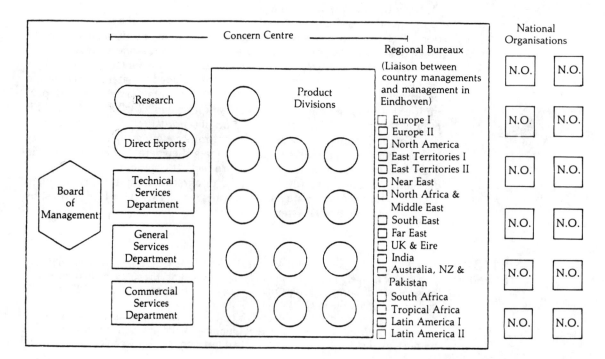

manufacturing, depending on the local market and the extent of local manufacturing facilities.

At the head of the matrix organisation was the Philips N.V. Board of Management (BOM). The Board was the ultimate arbiter on all strategic and policy questions. It formulated strategic policy and made appointments to the most senior positions within the Concern Centre and the National Organisations. As the final executive authority within the Concern, the Board monitored the performance of both NOs and product divisions. Discussions on performance, investment programmes, research and other issues were carried on between the BOM and the corresponding executive board of the more important National Organisations.

The Concern Centre also housed specialised functional departments which provided services to the main technical and commercial activities in the product divisions and to the Board of Management. These departments had links with similar services in National Organisations and provided an important integrating mechanism between the Concern Centre and NOs. Another linking mechanism was the regional bureaux system. The 12 regional bureaux, staffed with representatives from a group of NOs, had the task of promoting the interests of their constituent National Organisations at the Concern Centre.

The planning cycle was the primary coordination mechanism between Concern and National Organisations. Firstly, a broad 8–10-year strategic plan was outlined by the Philips top management. Next, a rolling four-year plan was constructed to "create capacity" to meet the strategic objectives. The process of compiling this four-year plan was dominated by the Product Division which enlisted the help of the concerned NOs so that they would evolve complementary plans and programme activities. Next, the four-year plans were translated at National Organisation level into "one-year activity plans" for the year ahead. Finally, these plans were broken down into three four-month planning periods.

The accounts department at Eindhoven received summarised accounts from the NOs and IPCs eleven times a year. At the end of the year, the group results were presented internally in a manner that took cognisance of the matrix structure and the concept of joint responsibility — the figures were aggregated across countries to give an assessment of a product division's performance and across product divisions to give a comparable index for a particular National Organisation.

It was recognised that the organisational structure was less than perfect. The stress on multiple links emphasised a style of decision making that looked more at long-term gains than short-term profitability. The layer on layer of staff responsible for a particular decision reduced agility and the split between marketing strategy and selling was, at best, artificial and unsuitable for some products. Some believed that the bureaucratic organisation nurtured risk aversion. The emphasis was on group consensus and, though protagonists pointed to the Japanese miracle based on a similar management philosophy, the critics cited many instances where delay had resulted in significant competitive disadvantage.

The Divisions of Philips N.V.

The 14 Product Divisions and the major postwar additions to their product ranges were:

1. Lighting

- Gas discharge lamps, flashbulbs, high quality fluorescent tubes.
- Increased emphasis on development of related products (e.g. light fittings) and systems (e.g. lighting for motorways, airports, etc.).

2. Elcoma

- Wide range of electronic components, e.g. semi-conductors, integrated circuits, solid state and MOS devices, microprocessors.

	• Picture tubes, electronic subassemblies, X-ray image intensifier tubes.
3. Audio	• Portable radios, car radios. • Record players, hi-fi stereo systems, cassette players.
4. Video	• Large screen monochrome and colour TV. • Portable monochrome TV.
5. Major Domestic Appliances	• Washing machines, driers, cookers, refrigerators, freezers.
6. Small Domestic Appliances	• Irons, coffee makers, electric blankets, toasters, mixers, sunlamps, "Philishaves", beauty-care equipment, hair dryers, digital clocks.
7. Telecommunications & Defence Systems	• (a) *Radio & Radar (RR)* Broadcast transmitters, mobile radio transmitters, radio-link transmitters and receivers, military and civil radar, airline seat reservation systems, navigational beacons (VHF), road traffic control systems. • (b) *Telephony & Telegraphy (TT)* Telephones, automatic public and private exchanges (STD) equipment, telegraph equipment, police radio —telephone links.
8. Medical Systems	• Increased automation of equipment and procedures for greater efficiency, e.g.: 　radio diagnostic equipment for heart disease 　irradiation therapy equipment
9. Science & Industry	• Measuring, analytical and control equipment for laboratory and industrial applications, e.g.: 　X-ray spectrometers 　highly automated electron microscopes 　pollution measurement equipment 　automatic control instrumentation for wide-range systems
10. Electro Acoustics	• Development and manufacture of audio-visual communication and information systems, e.g.: 　sound systems for conference centres 　sound control desks for theatre use 　video recording and VCR equipment 　dictation equipment, intercom systems (e.g. outside broadcasting vans)

educational products and systems
(e.g. language labs, projectors,
special tape recorders, CCTV
equipment)
word processors

11. Pharmaceutical—Chemical
(Philips—Duphar)

- (a) *Health Division*
  Human health products (medicines
  and vaccines), animal health products (veterinary vaccines and
  other specialities), biochemicals
  (e.g. vitamins A and D), isotopes
  (e.g. cyclotron "Cartrix" — pre-
  filled disposable syringes).
- (b) *Crop Protection Division*
  Insecticides, fertilizers, herbicides
  and fungicides.

12. Applied Industries

- Production and sale of intermediate
  and basic materials to other product
  groups and third parties, e.g.:
  corrugated cardboard and other
  packaging, philtite and plastic
  products, wire and wire products,
  diamond dies

13. Glass

- Production of about 150 different types
  of glass, mainly for light products and
  TV screens

14. Data Systems

- Office and small business computers,
  data equipment, terminal systems,
  minicomputers, information network
  systems

POLYGRAM

(Philips' music activities were part
of a joint enterprise with Siemens A.G.,
Munich in which the two partners each
held a 50% interest.)

- Records under the Philips, Pye, Polydor
  Deutsche Gramophone Heliodor labels,
  musicassettes and other pre-recorded
  tapes, music publication (Chappel and
  Intersong), TV film production.